All That We Share

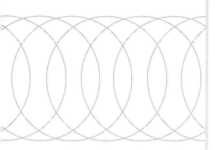
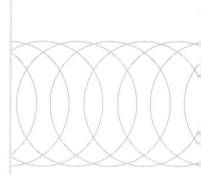

*How to
Save the Economy,
the Environment,
the Internet,
Democracy,
Our Communities,
and Everything Else
That Belongs to
All of Us*

All That We Share

A Field Guide to the Commons

Jay Walljasper
and On the Commons

With an introduction by
Bill McKibben

THE NEW PRESS

NEW YORK
LONDON

Pages 257–59 constitute an extension of this copyright page.

Requests for permission to reproduce selections from this book should be mailed to:
Permissions Department, The New Press, 38 Greene Street, New York, NY 10013.

Published in the United States by The New Press, New York, 2010
Distributed by Perseus Distribution

LIBRARY OF CONGRESS CATALOGING-IN-PUBLICATION DATA
Walljasper, Jay.
All that we share : how to save the economy, the environment, the
Internet, democracy, our communities, and everything else that belongs to
all of us / Jay Walljasper and On The Commons ; with an introduction by Bill
McKibben.
p. cm.
"A Field Guide to the Commons."
Includes index.
ISBN 978-1-59558-499-1 (pbk. : alk. paper) 1. Commons. 2. Community
development. I. On the Commons (Organization) II. Title.
HD1286.W35 2010
333.2—dc22
2010026947

The New Press was established in 1990 as a not-for-profit alternative to the large,
commercial publishing houses currently dominating the book publishing industry.
The New Press operates in the public interest rather than for private gain, and is committed
to publishing, in innovative ways, works of educational, cultural, and community value
that are often deemed insufficiently profitable.

www.thenewpress.com

Book design and composition by Lovedog Studio
This book was set in Monotype Sabon

Printed in the United States of America

2 4 6 8 10 9 7 5 3

To Commoners around the world
working to create a brighter future for all

Contents

Chapter 3: Tales of the Commons Today

Chapter 4: All That Endures

Chapter 5: A New World of Economics

Chapter 9: Liberating Information and Culture

Chapter 10: What You Can Do to Restore the Commons

Epilogue: What Would a Commons-Based Society Look Like?

Appendix A: The Commons Canon

Appendix B: A Commons Dictionary

Appendix C: Resource Guide

Commons Sense

My Journey to the Commons

FOR A LONG TIME, I HAD ONLY THE dimmest idea about the commons. It had something to do with English grazing land, a park in downtown Boston, and student lounges inside many university buildings. And, oh yes, there was a strip mall a couple miles from my house called Calhoun Commons.

Then several years ago, reading an article in *YES!* magazine (see Jonathan Rowe's "From Asian Villages to Main Street USA" in chapter 2), I discovered that "the commons" means something far bigger. From national parks and public libraries to the World Wide Web and scientific knowledge, we enjoy the benefits of many things that are jointly rather than privately owned.

I was editor of *Utne Reader* magazine at the time and resolved to dig deep into the subject for an upcoming issue. The commons struck me as one of those "aha!" revelations, which can transform the way people view the world. It might do for the struggling causes of social justice and ecology what "the market" did for capitalism in the 1970s—shine new light on familiar ideas in such a way that folks take them seriously again.

The commons also grabbed me on a personal level. Throughout my career as a writer I had covered everything from international politics and urban planning to arts and travel. I relished the sheer variety of new topics to pursue, but worried that I was suffering from a hopeless case of journalistic ADD. I simply could not concentrate on any particular field. The minute I vowed to learn all I could about the destruction of the Amazon, I suddenly was seized with a raging curiosity about *forró* music in northeastern Brazil.

Here at last was a unifying theme. The commons was my beat. From community groups revitalizing city neighborhoods to adventurous cooks reintroducing local cuisines, I realized all the stories that excited me flowed from the same source: a deep conviction that people and places thrive when we honor what belongs to everyone.

Even my off-hour pleasures involved the commons—telling fairy tales to my son, strolling city sidewalks with my wife, exploring new styles of beer with the neighbors on Friday nights. These are no one's personal possessions—not "Stone Soup," not Selby Avenue in St. Paul, not India Pale Ale. They are cultural endowments for us to share.

Soon I was spotting examples of the commons everywhere I looked. Knock-knock jokes my son brought home from school. The English language, which I played with all day long. The city park outside the *Utne Reader* office in downtown Minneapolis. The Mississippi River, which provides our drinking water. Police and fire protection. Local, national, and international citizens' organizations making the world a better place to live.

For me, the commons opened up new ways of thinking about what's important in life. I felt grateful to the nameless heroes who struggled to establish public schools, wildlife preserves, blood banks, labor unions, youth ski programs, medical research institutes, art museums, social welfare legislation, blues festivals, bike trails, and .orgs—and to all those who keep them going today. I began to ponder what I could do to ensure that the commons remains healthy for future generations. While my own actions fall short of sainthood, I'm proud to report that now I pick up other people's litter, attend more public meetings, buy less bottled water, and collaborate with neighbors on various projects.

The commons also opened up a new path in my work. My own research into the com-

> **Common sense may be rediscovered in a sense of the commons.**
>
> —Peter Linebaugh, historian

mons activated a keen interest in the fate of public spaces. I started writing about how parks, streets, squares, sidewalks, downtowns, farmers' markets, neighborhoods, local businesses, and other gathering spots are essential to society. They're the crux of our social lives—the places where we connect as friends, neighbors, and citizens. Soon I was in regular contact with the staff of Project for Public Spaces (PPS), a New York–based group that's helped people improve their communities since 1975. Later, after I left *Utne Reader* to write for the Netherlands-based magazine *Ode*, I also joined the PPS staff as a senior fellow and continue to work with them from my home in Minneapolis.

In 2007 came an opportunity to plunge headlong into the commons. I became a fellow at On the Commons, a citizens network that highlights the importance of the commons in modern society. My happy task is spreading the word about commons-based solutions to current problems and co-editing OnTheCommons.org with David Bollier, author of two definitive books in the field: *Silent Theft* and *Viral Spiral*. Bringing things full circle, Jonathan Rowe was one of the founders of the organization with Harriet Barlow and Peter Barnes. I am thankful to On the Commons for supporting me in creating this book.

Working with a knowledgeable, dedicated team—led by co-directors Julie

Ristau and Ana Micka—showered me with new evidence of how everyday people put these ideas into action. And I am deeply appreciative for inspiration from the authors and activists who allowed me to republish their insights here. The biggest lesson I've learned through this journey is that the commons is not merely an assortment of things—natural resources, cultural treasures, public places—but also a way of sharing and working with others to create a better and future.

I'm convinced that, as more people become aware of it, the commons will spark countless initiatives that make a difference for the future of our communities and the planet.

I AM KEENLY GRATEFUL to my colleagues at On the Commons, without whom this book would not be possible: Harriet Barlow, who envisioned the need for this book and made it possible in a variety of ways; Peter Barnes, who inspired the title and a host of great ideas; David Bollier, who generously shared his expansive knowledge of the commons and offered indispensable counsel; Julie Ristau, who helped every inch of the way with her insight and limitless capabilities; Ana Micka, who offered a steady hand and quick mind throughout the process; Alexa Bradley, Dave Mann, Brad Lichtenstein, Kathryn Milun, Jonathan Rowe, and others who continually expanded the frontiers of commons thinking. I also thank Vadim Lavrusik for his thorough photo research; Marsha Micek for her critical art consulting; Marc Favreau for his editorial insights; and all the contributors who allowed us to publish their insights and ideas. The responsibility for any shortcomings, however, rests squarely on my shoulders.

—*Jay Walljasper*
Minneapolis, Minnesota
June 2010

The Commons Offers a New Story for the Future

IT WAS TWO YEARS BEFORE THE FIRST Earth Day in 1970 when Garrett Hardin penned the famous essay "The Tragedy of the Commons," and it fit a certain bleak and despairing mood of the time. Paul Ehrlich had just published *The Population Bomb*, a Malthusian account of a world overwhelmed by sheer numbers of people. Against the backdrop of that gloom, Hardin's theory came as another dose of bad news, "proving" that we also had no hope of controlling our appetite for natural resources. Because no one owned the oceans or the atmosphere, we would inevitably fish and pollute them into oblivion. Hardin offered a few suggestions, but his title summed it up: we were witnessing a tragedy whose script could not be revised.

Oddly, a decade later, his argument fit just as easily the exuberant, privatizing mood of the Reagan years. No one owns the sky or the sea? Well, then, let's sell them! The race was on to privatize everything, from fishing rights to kids' playgrounds, on the theory that this was the only way to manage them well. Society was the problem, the individual was the solution.

The only thing that Hardin's argument *didn't* fit was the facts, at least not all of them. For eons communities had managed to protect all kinds of resources without private ownership. In America and in England, it's true, a couple of centuries of enclosure and corporatization made this harder to recall. But around the world, most of the pasture lands, forests, and streams had long been controlled by communities, drawing on deep traditions of custom and collective wisdom. Even in the United States, we had classic examples—the acequia irrigation systems of New Mexico, which may be the only sustainable water systems in the American West, or the lobster fishery of Maine, protected from overfishing less by law than by long custom.

And in the years since "The Tragedy of the Commons" appeared, even a cursory glance around the landscape reveals that Hardin's gloom has been disproven a thousand times. For example, I'm willing to bet that many of the people reading this book turned on their local public radio station this morning. Here's how public radio works: give away your product for free with no advertising, and then twice a year wheedle people to make a donation to pay for it. Turn that in as your business plan at some bank and they'll laugh you out the door, but public radio has been the fastest-growing sector of the broadcast industry for years. And now we have low-power FM and community radio, not to mention the explosion of free content on the Internet.

I've spent most of my life as a writer—and one of the sweetest parts of that job is knowing that whatever I produce ends up in a library, an institution dedicated to the idea that we can share things easily. There are innumerable other examples—and they are the parts of our lives that we usually care most about. They don't show up on balance sheets because they're not producing profit, but they *are* producing satisfaction.

These things we share are called commons, which simply means they belong to all of us. Commons can be gifts of nature—such as fresh water, wilderness, and the airwaves—or the products of social ingenuity, like the Internet, parks, artistic traditions, or the public health service. But today much of our common wealth is under threat from those hungry to ruin it or take it over for selfish, private purposes.

> **The commons is a crucial part of the human story that must be recovered if we are to deal with the problems now crowding in on us.**
>
> —Bill McKibben

The most crucial commons, perhaps, is the one now under greatest siege, and it poses a test of whether we can pull together to solve our deepest problems or succumb to disaster. Our atmosphere has been de facto privatized for a long time now—we've allowed coal, oil, and gas interests to own the sky, filling it with the carbon that is the inevitable by-product of their business. For a couple of centuries, this seemed mostly harmless—CO_2 didn't seem to be causing much trouble. But two decades ago, we started to understand the effects of global warming, and now each month the big scientific journals bring us new proof of just how vast the damage is: the Arctic is melting, Australia is on fire, the pH of the ocean is dropping fast.

If we are to somehow ward off the coming catastrophes, we have to reclaim this atmospheric commons. We have to figure out how to cooperatively own and protect the single most important feature of the planet we inhabit—the thin envelope of atmosphere that makes our lives possible. Wrestling this key prize away from Exxon Mobil and other corporations is the great political issue of our time, and some of the solutions proposed have been ingenious—most notably the idea put forth by commons theorist

Peter Barnes and others that we should own the sky jointly and share in the profits realized by leasing its storage space to the fossil fuel industry. For that to work, of course, we would have to reduce that storage space quickly and dramatically. Barnes's cap-and-dividend plan (see "A Commons Solution to Climate Change" in chapter 8) offers one way to make that economically and politically feasible.

But for this and other necessary projects to succeed, we need first to break the intellectual spell under which we live. The last few decades have been dominated by the premise that privatizing all economic resources will produce endless riches. Which was kind of true, except that the riches went to only a few people. And in the process they melted the Arctic, as well as dramatically increasing inequality around the world. Jay Walljasper performs the greatest of services with this book. It is—choose your metaphor—a bracing slap across the face or the kiss that breaks an enchantment. In either case, after reading it, you will be much more alive to the world as it actually is, not as it exists in the sweaty dreams of ideologues and economics professors. The commons is a crucial part of the human story that must be recovered if we are to deal with the problems now crowding in on us. This story is equal parts enlightening and encouraging, and it is entirely necessary for us to hear it.

—*Bill McKibben*

Chapter 1

What Is the Commons?

What, Really, Is the Commons?

What we own together, and how we cooperate to make things happen

WELCOME TO THE COMMONS.

The term may be unfamiliar, but the idea has been around for centuries. The commons is a new use of an old word, meaning "what we share"—and it offers fresh hope for a saner, safer, more enjoyable future.

The commons refers to a wealth of valuable assets that belong to everyone. These range from clean air to wildlife preserves; from the judicial system to the Internet. Some are bestowed to us by nature; others are the product of cooperative human creativity. Certain elements of the commons are entirely new—think of Wikipedia. Others are centuries old—like colorful words and phrases from all the world's languages.

Anyone can use the commons, so long as there is enough left for everyone else. This is why finite commons, such as natural resources, must be sustainably and equitably managed. But many other forms of the commons can be freely tapped. Today's hip-hop and rock stars, for instance, "appropriate" the work of soul singers, jazz swingers, blues wailers, gospel shouters, hillbilly pickers, and balladeers going back a long time—and we are all richer for it. That's the greatest strength of the commons. It's an inheritance shared by all humans, which increases in value as people draw upon its riches.

At least that's how the commons has worked throughout history, fostering democratic, cultural, technological, medical, economic, and humanitarian advances. But this natural cycle of sharing is now under assault. As the market economy becomes the yardstick for measuring the worth of everything, more people are grabbing portions of the commons as their private property. Many essential elements of society—from ecosystems to scientific knowledge to public services—are slipping through our hands and into the pockets of the rich and powerful.

The Wealth We Lost

One example of what we're losing comes right out of today's headlines about spiraling health care costs. The creation of many widely prescribed drugs, which millions of people depend upon, was funded in large part by government grants. But the exclusive right to sell pharmaceuticals developed with public money was handed over to drug companies with almost nothing asked in return. That means we pay exorbitant prices for medicine developed with our tax dollars, and many poor people are denied access to treatments that might save their lives.

Another even more absurd example concerns a subject that you would think stirs no controversy—yoga. Through centuries of evolution as a spiritual practice, any new yoga poses or techniques were automatically incorporated into the tradition for everyone to use. But beginning in 1978 an Indian named Bikram Choudhury, now based in Beverly Hills, copyrighted certain long-used hatha yoga poses and sequences as his own invention, Bikram Yoga, and he now threatens other yoga studios teaching these techniques with lawsuits.

The good news is that people all around us are beginning to take back the commons. Neighbors rising up to keep their library open, improve their park, or find new funding for public schools. Greens fighting the draining of wetlands and the dumping of toxic waste in inner-city neighborhoods. Digital activists providing access to the Internet in poor communities and challenging corporate plans to limit our right to information. Indigenous people instilling their children with a sense of tradition and hope. Young social entrepreneurs and software engineers seeking new mechanisms for people to share ideas.

Not all of these people think of themselves as commons activists. Some may not even be familiar with the term. Vel Wiley, the longtime director of Milwaukee's public access TV channels, stood up at a commons event and declared, "When I was asked to be a part of this conference, I thought the commons was for people like Greenpeace, an environmental cause. But I understand now that I have been advocating for the commons

The sky, the earth, parklands, scientific knowledge, and even the Internet belong to all of us.

over the last twenty years. I realize we're not just a small group advocating that the people have a voice in the broadcasting media. We're all a part of something so much bigger, and that helps me to keep going."

It's not necessary that everyone adopt the word *commons*. What matters is that people understand that what we share together (and how we share it) is as important as what we possess individually.

Parallels to the Origins of Environmentalism

Growing interest in the commons today resembles the origins of the environmental movement in the 1960s. At that time, there was little talk about ecology or the greening of anything. There was, however, a lot of concern about air pollution, pesticides, litter, the loss of wilderness, declining wildlife populations, the death of Lake Erie, toxic substances oozing into rivers, oil spills fouling the oceans, lead paint poisoning inner-city kids, suburbia swallowing up the countryside, mountains of trash piling up in landfills, and unsustainable farming practices ravaging the land. Yet the word *environmentalism* did not become a household word until the first Earth Day—April 22, 1970. Bringing an assortment of issues together under the banner of environmentalism highlighted the connections between what until then had been seen as separate causes and fueled the unexpected growth of the environmental movement over the next few years.

The commons offers the same promise of uniting people concerned about the common good in many forms into a new kind of movement that reshapes how people think about the nature of ownership and the importance of collaboration in modern society.

A New Way of Thinking and Living

More than just a philosophical and political framework for understanding what's gone wrong, the commons furnishes us a toolkit for fixing problems. Local activists eager to revitalize their community and protect open space are setting up land trusts—a form of community ownership distinct from both private property and government management. Savvy Web users use the cooperative properties of the Internet to challenge corporations who want to undermine this shared resource by fencing it off for private gain. Villagers and city dwellers around the world assert that water is a commons, which cannot be sold, depleted, or controlled by anyone.

These kinds of efforts extend the meaning of the commons beyond something you own to a bigger idea: how we live together. Peter Linebaugh, a preeminent historian of the commons, has coined the word "commoning" to describe the growing efforts he sees to protect and strengthen the things we share. "I want to stress the point that the commons is an activity rather than just a material resource," he says. "That

What Is a Commons-Based Society?

*A way of life that values what we share
as much as what we own*

A commons-based society refers to a shift in policies and values away from the market-based system that has dominated modern society for the past two hundred years, with a particular vengeance in the past thirty. A commons-based society would place as much emphasis on social justice, democratic participation, and environmental protection as on economic competitiveness and private property. Market-based solutions would be valuable tools in a commons-based society, as long as they do not undermine the workings of the commons itself.

—Jay Walljasper

brings in the essential social element of the commons."

David Bollier, one of the leading theorists of the commons on the international stage, has defined the term as a social dynamic. "A commons arises whenever a given community decides it wishes to manage a resource in a collective manner, with special regard for equitable access, use and sustainability. It is a social form that has long lived in the shadows of our market culture, and now is on the rise," he wrote in the British political journal *Renewal*.

Julie Ristau and Alexa Bradley, community organizers with extensive experience, find that many people have internalized the competitive ethos of the market mentality so fully that they believe any cooperative action is doomed to fail. They're losing the ability to even think of working together. Yet at the same time, Ristau and Bradley detect in others "a broad yearning for hope, connection, and restoration. We see a remarkable array of efforts to reconstitute community, to relocalize food, to move toward cooperative economics, to better harmonize our lives with the health of our planet. These efforts spring from a deep human need and desire for different ways of interacting and organizing resources that will help us reconstitute our capacity for shared ownership, collaboration, and stewardship."

Growing numbers of people are taking steps that move us, gradually, in the direction of a commons-based society—a world in which the fundamental focus on competition that characterizes life today would be balanced with new attitudes and social structures that foster cooperation. This vision is emerging at precisely the point we need it most. Deeply held myths of the last thirty years about the magic of the market have been shattered by the implosion of the global financial bubble, creating both an opening and an acute need for different ways of living.

To deliver us from current economic and ecological calamities will require more than administering a few tweaks to the operating system that runs our society. A complete retooling is needed—a paradigm shift that revises the core principles that guide our culture top to bottom. At this historical moment, the commons vision of a society where "we" matters as much as "me" shines as a beacon of hope for a better world.

—*Jay Walljasper*

Why Should We Care About the Commons Today?

Yes, it's history—but also our best hope for the future

Both the idea and the reality of the commons have been declining since at least the eighteenth century. Why now, at the beginning of the twenty-first century, should we struggle to revive them?

The simple answer is that we have to.

Despite the many benefits it brings us, the economic market operates like a runaway truck. It has no internal mechanism telling it when to stop—to stop depleting the commons that sustain it. To put it another way, we've been living off a fat commons bank account for centuries, and now it's running low. We must start making some deposits so we'll have something for tomorrow.

If our old Manifest Destiny was to carve up the commons, our new task is to rebuild it. We must do this to protect the planet, enhance our quality of life, reduce inequality, and leave a better world for our children.

—*Peter Barnes*

Where to Find the Commons

From open source to dance steps, it's all around

 Air & water

 The Internet

 Parks, libraries, streets & sidewalks

 Our DNA

 Blood banks, soup kitchens, twelve-step groups, museums, nonprofit organizations

 Dance steps & fashion trends

Social Security, the National Weather Service, police protection & other essential services

Fishing & hunting

The airwaves (radio, television, cell phone)

 Christmas, Halloween, Passover, Ramadan, Mardi Gras & all holiday traditions

◎ Poker, hopscotch & soccer

◎ Biodiversity

◎ Taxpayer-funded medical & scientific research

◎ Wikipedia

◎ Robin Hood, Athena & the Little Mermaid

◎ Sushi, pizza, tamales & family recipes

◎ The jump shot, kimonos, bookkeeping systems
& the Heimlich maneuver

◎ Public education, public transportation & other
public services

◎ Open-source software

◎ Jokes, fairy tales, slang & anecdotes

◎ The oceans, Antarctica & outer space

—*On the Commons*

A Day at the Museum

Two starkly different views of the future

Day at the Museum: Scenario 1

You stroll down the sidewalk and come to the corner right across from the museum. The light turns red. Cars zip past. You push the pedestrian button on the light pole, and soon the light changes so you can get across.

As you walk, you take a deep breath of the crisp fall air. You know downtown suffers air pollution problems, but today it seems clear and beautiful. The museum has free admission on Tuesday, and you are happy that you could rearrange your work schedule this week to take advantage of it. You climb the stairs and enter through the turnstile, but before heading off into the museum you decide to use the bathroom. It is neat and clean, with environmentally friendly low-flow flush toilets. Coming out of the stall, you wash your hands at the sink with the soap and paper towels provided. Outside the restroom, you stop at the drinking fountain and then, refreshed, eagerly stroll in the direction of the exhibits.

. . .

Day at the Museum: Scenario 2

You step onto the sidewalk leading to the museum through a turnstile, flashing your FASTRAK card at a machine operated by a corporation that subcontracts with the city to maintain sidewalks in this part of town. A GPS monitor on your belt deducts $1 for every twenty blocks that you walk. (This monitor has the advantage of "keeping you safe," according to the new marketing campaign, because if you fall or are the victim of a crime, you can press a button so that police or an ambulance can easily find you.) In well-traveled zip districts, like downtown, you pay a $2 surcharge to use the sidewalks. ("Prevents overcrowding," say the FASTRAK ads.)

You arrive at the corner right across from the museum and put a quarter in the meter, which activates the walk light. You have ten seconds to make it across the street before the roaring traffic resumes (25 cents more would get you twenty seconds). A few teenagers and a homeless woman cross without paying, alert for the private security guards that may throw them off the sidewalk. Not everyone can afford the monthly FASTRAK card, so they sneak onto the sidewalk between turnstiles or walk in the road alongside speeding cars. Pedestrian fatalities have quadrupled since the city auctioned sidewalk rights to corporations two years ago.

People passing you wear oxygen masks with various brand names emblazoned in bright colors. So far, you have chosen not to buy "fresh air" in lightweight tanks that can be easily worn when you go outside. You are not convinced the free air is that dangerous. In fact, today it seems crisp and clear. The museum entry is half price on Tuesday, only $14 with special coupons you get when making a purchase at the Gap. But you have to put up with Gap advertising throughout the exhibit. There are fewer advertisements on the days when you pay full price.

Once inside the museum, you pay $3 to use the bathroom and another $1 for washing your hands with automatically premeasured units of water, soap, and paper towel. Had you planned ahead, you would have used the Porta-Potty on the street, which costs only $1.75 but with no sink, only a Handi-wipe dispenser costing another buck. You look for a drinking fountain, until realizing how futile that is. Bottled water sells for $6 from a vendor who also runs the bathroom concession. You've spent enough already, you decide, and, still thirsty, trudge off in the direction of the exhibits.

—*Kim Klein*

> **The commons means simply: places we share, systems we share, ideas we share, culture we share.**
>
> —*Peter Barnes, entrepreneur*

Is This a New Version of Communism?

No, *it's a tradition of cooperation with deep roots in American life*

MANY AMERICANS HAVE TROUBLE TALK-ing about the commons because we lack a proper vocabulary for discussing collectiv-ist endeavors. Any talk of sharing, coopera-tion, or collectively managed resources can conjure the ghosts of Marx, Lenin, Mao, and Stalin.

The first thing to understand about the commons is that it is generally distinct from government. Government can provide useful assistance—laws, information, fa-cilitation—but the commons is more about people doing things for themselves, taking responsibility for their own resources di-rectly as a community.

This practice has a long tradition in American life. Yet on many occasions it is also true that "we the people" ask our government to be stewards of all sorts of commons, such as national parks, Social Security, land-grant colleges, the National Weather Service, the U.S. Public Health Service, and much more.

The contemporary commons movement is *not* an attempt to rehabilitate commu-nism. Communism is an archaic, impracti-cal system that favors the state and capital over the commons (as evidenced, for exam-

Today's commoners follow Groucho more than Karl.

Big League Action

See the commons at work in the NFL, NBA, and Major League Baseball

Do the ideas associated with the commons, especially regarding wealth and economics, sound exotic or unworkable to you? Well, consider that some of America's beloved national institutions are run along similar lines: the National Football League, the National Basketball Association, and Major League Baseball.

Each league shifts money from the richest teams to the poorest in order to keep the game fair and interesting to fans. And the draft process used in all three sports gives losing teams an advantage at signing the best young players.

Even George Will, the Republican columnist and devoted baseball fan, sees the logic in this. "The aim is not to guarantee teams equal revenues, but revenues sufficient to give each team periodic chances of winning if each uses its revenues intelligently."

Welcome to the commons. Now let's play ball.

—*Jonathan Rowe*

ple, by the former Soviet Union's decades-long environmental degradations). This system is also indifferent to the importance of subsidiarity in governance (control at the lowest possible levels) and to the actual diversity of humanity in its local contexts. Communism and even socialism today are not truly commons based, because they rely upon centralized, hierarchical bureaucracies to achieve state-directed economic goals.

Archetypal commons, by contrast, tend to function at scales that enable decentralized participation and decision making. They are generally structured to protect transparency, social equity, and other extramarket values and generally do not vest authority in centralized bureaucracies and credentialed expertise that may or may not be responsive. Archetypal commons generally disperse governance as broadly as possible as a means to leverage participants' local knowledge, personal commitment, and the ability to enforce community norms in protecting the shared resource.

New Language for a New Era

If we look beyond the past thirty years of extreme capitalism and its ethic of out-of-control individualism, we can begin to see that there is a long and successful history of managing the commons without squelching freedom. Indeed, evolutionary scientists make it clear that the human species has survived and evolved only because it has had great capacities to cooperate and collaborate and to build stable communities based on trust and reciprocity.

The newly emerging commons movement is recovering this past. The goal is not to romanticize it but to apply the cooperative instinct that is perhaps literally in our genes to the realities of contemporary society. We need to rediscover and reinvent the commons—an idea that is quite distinct from communism and other large-scale bureaucratic and authoritarian failures of the twentieth century.

—David Bollier

Do I Need Livestock to Join This Movement?

Questions about the word commons

Not everyone likes the word *commons* to describe the emerging political interest in things we all share. Here are some of the objections I've heard about the term:

- "Not to be totally punny, but the word is too common. You don't want such an ordinary word describing something as important as the commons."

- "It is too British. I live in New York City—we don't do too much grazing here."

- "It is so old-fashioned. When I hear it, I think I am going to have to endure a reenactment of Ben Franklin or someone like that."

- "It is too rural. I feel like I have to go somewhere carrying a small sheep."

—*Kim Klein,*
kimkleinandthecommons.blogspot.com

Sheep are optional for today's commoners.

Chapter 2

Why the Commons Matters Now

From Asian Villages to Main Street USA

Caring for the common good enriches us all

MY WIFE GREW UP IN WHAT WESTERN experts call a "developing" country, and the social life of her village revolved largely around a mango tree. People gathered there in the evening to visit and tell stories. Some of my wife's warmest childhood memories are of playing hide-and-seek late into the evening while the parents chatted and exchanged *tismis*, or gossip.

The tree was more than a gathering place. It was an *economic* asset in the root—and neglected—sense of that word. It produced a bonding of neighbors, an information network, an activity center for kids, and a bridge between generations. Older people could be part of the flow of daily life, and children got to experience something that has become scarce in the United States today—an unstructured and noncompetitive setting for play with their parents still close at hand.

In "developed" countries, we spend hundreds of billions of dollars on everything from community centers to kids' movies in trying to provide such an experience, usually with much less positive effect. Yet typical economists studying this community would deem it to be in a pathetic state of underdevelopment. They would urge "modernization," which means making people pay money to buy substitutes for what the tree provided for free.

That's the story of the commons, which means the part of life that lies outside both the market and the state as typically conceived. The commons is the hidden economy, everywhere present but rarely noticed. It provides the basic support systems of life—both ecological and social.

The commons is basic to our lives. One can imagine life without a Commerce Department or an Amazon.com, but not without a shared language and clean water. This implies a large responsibility. "We are temporary possessors," wrote English philosopher Edmund Burke, and we "should not think it amongst [our] rights to cut off the entail, or commit waste on the inheritance."

Yet because there is no accepted language with which to talk about the commons nor a legal framework to protect it, it is subject to constant invasion, expropriation, and abuse. The result is a statistical illusion of progress—an increase in monetary transactions that hides the reality of decline in the larger calculus of well-being. Shade trees give way to air conditioners, quiet to pharmaceutical calming agents—we all grow poorer even as the official indicators show "the economy" going up. And the poor themselves are impoverished the most, because more of life is pushed into the realm that requires money. Those with the least money end up even farther behind.

Four Characteristics of a Commons

Commons are run by informal rules and structures. People don't need a contract in order to take a walk, a lease to sail in the ocean, an insurance policy to call a neighbor for help. They don't pay royalties to use an apt expression or get a license to tell fairy tales to their kids. But it often takes new laws and lawyers to protect some commons.

Commons are generally free of price tags and advertising. The market economy is always pushing its "goods" and "services" in our faces. A commons, by contrast, is just there waiting to be used. Often it is discovered rather than invented or created. If a swimming hole exists, people will find it. Social commons arise spontaneously—the sidewalk that becomes a jump-rope arena or vending bazaar, the old sofa in the vacant lot that becomes an inner-city equivalent of the village tree.

Commons are a source of serendipity. Commons are not like the market economy, which is obsessed with a narrow spectrum of human concern—the making of money—and tends to ignore anything that doesn't appear on a corporate balance sheet. A commons, by contrast, engages people in a broader way and produces multiple layers of positive effect. Open-source software creates an informal network of collaborators who give their time and talents freely. A neighborhood park gives rise to communities of dog walkers, chess players, basketball players, and parents with kids.

Commons foster thriving culture. Culture thrives in a commons. Compare the menu in a Chinese restaurant—which draws freely from the culinary commons—with the one in a McDonald's with its trademarked items. Languages are one of the ultimate commons, and they grow richer by the day as people, without recognition or compensation, add words and expressions.

How the Commons Fits with the Government and the Market

The point here is not to romanticize the commons or suggest it should be everything. Markets do some things very well, as do governments. The point rather is that we need boundaries to prevent the market—and the government, too—from drowning out the commons and its essential role in our lives.

Larry Gonick

The commons is not the same as the public sector. In fact, the state can destroy the commons as effectively as the market can, as seen in the experience of former Communist countries. As Czech playwright and president Václav Havel has eloquently explained, the sense of community withered as the state sought to occupy every inch of social space.

By the same token, market arrangements, on the right scale, can actually enhance the commons. The neighborhood coffee shop and stores on Main Street, for example, are crucial to the fabric of a community.

First Steps to Reclaiming the Commons

The commons can overlap both the public and the private. It is a different *dimension* of property, and it needs legal protection, just as private property has. This is a crucial point. A market is not an act of nature; it does not arise spontaneously, nor is it divinely ordained. Take away the legal and institutional structure created by government—the money system, banking and securities laws, copyrights and patents, military protection of foreign oil production, and so forth—and the modern market economy could not exist.

If the market requires such an elaborate array of props, it is not surprising that the commons needs some as well. More space on the public airwaves for community and nonprofit stations. Boundaries against the commercial huckstering that fill the aural and visual environments. Reform of antiquated zoning laws and subsidies for sprawl that undermine the social commons of traditional Main Streets.

The list goes on. Such steps would not mean more government intrusion. To the contrary, they would mean less corporate intrusion, and more economic and social space in which community could flourish and people could follow their own lights. Nor would such steps violate property rights, as market fundamentalists assert. These steps would protect property rights—*common* property rights.

Fresh Thinking About Property Rights

Property rights are the thread that connects many of the disparate battles in which people of conscience are engaged. Pollution is not just a health threat. It is a violation of common-property rights. Sprawl is not just an inefficient use of land and energy. It depletes the social commons, which rarely thrives in a landscape of freeways and malls. The commercial invasion of childhood is not just a matter of obesity and hyperactivity. It involves larger questions about the cultural commons—the stories that young people are told, and to what end.

For decades the libertarian right has been fighting what it calls "takings" of private property by government. Now it's time to fight the taking of what belongs to us all.

—Jonathan Rowe

An Islamic Tradition

Conservationists revive a version of common ownership established by Muhammad

A glance at history turns up the names of many heroes—from Robin Hood to Chief Joseph to Gandhi—who stood up to protect the commons on behalf of future generations. One name from history not likely to be associated with the commons is Muhammad. Yet the holy prophet of the Islamic world sought to preserve special landscapes for everyone. Today, Muslim environmentalists are trying to reinvigorate this tradition.

There was an ancient Middle Eastern tradition of setting aside certain lands, called *hima* ("protected place" in Arabic), for the enjoyment of local chieftains. Muhammad "transformed the *hima* from a private enclave into a public asset in which all community members had a share and a stake, in accordance with their duty as stewards (*khalifa*) of God's natural world," according to Tom Verde, a student of Islamic studies and Christian-Muslim relations at the Hartford Seminary.

In the seventh century, Muhammad declared the region of Al-Madinah, now the holy city of Medina, "to be a sanctuary; its trees shall not be cut and its game shall not be hunted." Many of the *hima* lasted well into the twentieth century, when the tradition fell victim to modern beliefs about land ownership.

Now Middle Eastern environmentalists are invoking the idea of *hima* to protect the region's threatened woodlands, grasslands, wetlands, and rangelands. In 2004 the Society for the Protection of Nature in Lebanon helped local residents establish two of the first new *hima* in the hilltop town of Ebel es-Saqi. "The *hima* has had a very positive effect in the community," said Kasim Shoker, mayor of a nearby town. "Not only has it helped improve the economy [through ecotourism], but it has made the local people recognize the value of the land and have greater respect for its biodiversity."

—*Jay Walljasper*

The Commons Is Not a Tragedy

Elinor Ostrom's 2009 Nobel Prize debunks theories saying cooperative ownership leads to environmental ruin

THE BIGGEST ROADBLOCK STANDING in the way of wider acceptance of the commons came tumbling down in 2009 when Indiana University professor Elinor Ostrom shared the Nobel Prize for economics.

Through the decades Ostrom, seventy-seven, has documented how communities around the world equitably and sustainably manage common resources such as grazing lands, forests, irrigation waters, and fisheries over the long term. The Nobel Committee's recognition of her work effectively answers popular theories about the "tragedy of the commons," which hold that private property is the only effective method to prevent finite resources from being ruined or depleted.

Elinor Ostrom, the first woman to win the Nobel Prize for Economics, highlights successful examples of the commons in Kenya, Nepal, Switzerland, Turkey, and Los Angeles.

This idea was popularized by wildlife biologist Garrett Hardin in a 1968 essay in *Science* magazine, in which he declared that people who share land in commons will inevitably degrade it. But Hardin later quali-

Eight Principles for Managing a Commons

Elinor Ostrom's guide to protecting shared resources

1. Define clear group boundaries.

2. Match rules governing use of common goods to local needs and conditions.

3. Ensure that those affected by the rules can participate in modifying the rules.

4. Make sure the rule-making rights of community members are respected by outside authorities.

5. Develop a system, carried out by community members, for monitoring members' behavior.

6. Use graduated sanctions for rule violators.

7. Provide accessible, low-cost means for dispute resolution.

8. Build responsibility for governing the common resource in nested tiers from the lowest level up to the entire interconnected system.

—*Elinor Ostrom*

fied his views, saying that he was referring to a situation in which there is no community involvement and no rules in governing in managing the land—which, of course, means it is not a commons.

Awarding the world's most prestigious economics prize to a scholar who champions cooperative behavior greatly boosts the legitimacy of the commons as a framework for solving our social and environmental problems. Ostrom's work also challenges the current economic orthodoxy that there are few, if any, alternatives to privatization and markets in generating wealth and human well-being.

"When local users of a forest have a long-term perspective, they are more likely to monitor each other's use of the land, developing rules for behavior," she cites as an example. "It is an area that standard market theory does not touch."

. . .

There's More to Life Than Property Rights

Columbia University economist Joseph Stiglitz, also winner of a Nobel Prize, comments, "Conservatives used the tragedy of the commons to argue for property rights, and [that economic] efficiency was achieved as people were thrown off the commons. . . . What Ostrom has demonstrated is the existence of social control mechanisms that regulate the use of the commons without having to resort to property rights."

The Nobel Committee's choice of Ostrom is significant, considering that many winners of the prize since it was initiated in 1968 have been zealous advocates of unrestricted markets, such as Milton Friedman, whose selection in 1976 helped fuel the rise of market theory as the be-all and end-all of economics during the 1980s.

While right-wing thinkers scoff at the possibility of resources being shared in a way that maintains the common good, arguing that private property is the only practical strategy to prevent destruction, Ostrom's scholarship shows otherwise.

"What we have ignored is what citizens can do and the importance of real involvement of the people involved," she explains.

A classic example of this was her field research in a Swiss village where farmers tend private plots for crops but share a communal meadow to graze their cows. While this would appear a perfect model to prove the tragedy-of-the-commons theory, Ostrom discovered that in reality there were no problems with overgrazing. That is because of a common agreement among villagers that no one is allowed to graze more cows on the meadow than they can care for over the winter—a rule that dates back to 1517. Ostrom has documented similar effective examples of "governing the commons" in her research in Kenya, Guatemala, Nepal, Turkey, and Los Angeles.

Ostrom is the first woman to be awarded the economics prize, which some observers say helps explain her emphasis on the role of people's relationships in our economic arrangements rather than the focus on individualized market choices expounded by many male winners of the Nobel.

Equally noteworthy is the fact that Ostrom was not trained as an economist but as a political scientist—a factor that may be even more useful in explaining her outside-the-box approach to economics.

Yale economist Robert Shiller welcomed her selection for the prize as an opportunity to merge thinking in the two fields. "Economics has become too isolated and stuck on the view that markets are efficient and self-regulating. It has derailed our thinking."

Elinor Ostrom has always been explicit in recognizing the importance of the commons. She helped found the International Association for the Study of the Commons, also based at Indiana University, and her selection as a Nobel laureate marks a milestone in the emergence of a commons-based society.

—*Jay Walljasper*

The View from Africa

Elinor Ostrom's research reaffirms the value of cooperative cultures

Much time has already been spent in justifying or dismissing President Obama's selection for the 2009 Nobel Peace Prize. In contrast, little attention has been paid to another Nobel awardee, Elinor Ostrom. I argue that the choice of Ostrom for this important award is perhaps more significant for Africa's poor than the recognition bestowed upon President Obama, the collective pride we as Africans feel for Obama's international respect notwithstanding.

Since the 1960s, the predominant policy prescription for ensuring the sustainable use of land resources in Africa has been the individualization of commonly held land. This move was largely driven by neoclassical economists, following the theory of the tragedy of the commons.

Evidence now suggests that this individualization of common property has yielded neither the economic nor the environmental benefits envisaged. According to Marcel Rutten, a Dutch scholar who undertook extensive research work in Kajiado—one of the three Maasai districts in Kenya where the individualization of land was heavily promoted through the establishment of ranches—the amount of land suitable for grazing declined by over 40 percent between 1982 and 1990, leading to increased poverty in the district, not to mention wanton environmental degradation.

Ostrom's research suggests that, far from

Kenyan economist Korir Sing'Oei says Ostrom's Nobel Prize may be more significant for Africa than Obama's.

being a tragedy, the commons can be managed from the bottom up for a shared prosperity, given the right institutions. The utilization of her economic theory will unlock the potential of common-property management, which, if better deployed, could serve to ensure a more people-centered development in Africa. Such a shift will protect vulnerable communities and individuals from the unchecked market and environmental shocks that currently imperil their existence and threaten global food security.

—*Korir Sing'Oei*

We Need a New Language of Collaboration

The commons is everywhere yet remains invisible because we lack the words to talk about it

LANGUAGE IS A SILENT COMMISSAR IN our political and economic life. What we can say—what we can even think—depends largely on the words that are available for us to use. William James, the psychologist and philosopher, once said, "It is hard to focus the attention upon the nameless." That's one reason that there is so little discussion of the commons in our public life and why there is so little awareness of it.

There is a business section in many newspapers and on many news Web sites but no commons section; a *Marketplace* show on public radio but no show called *Commonplace*; stock market reports but no corresponding daily feedback on the condition of the commons.

The vocabulary of the market economy is everywhere. Such basic terms as value, benefit, wealth, interest, good, and market itself (which in the original sense of the word, a marketplace, is actually a commons) are suffused with market connotations.

Compare the words available to us for discussing, say, the ownership of a business with that for discussing everyone's stake in the sky or the ocean or a park. There is no

lexicon of the commons for much the same reason there is little history of it: the victors tell the stories. Native Americans, say, or European peasants would have given us a different version of the world, with a vocabulary encoded a different way.

What we cannot grasp through language, we cease even to notice. Offer new words, however, and we get new insight.

—*Jonathan Rowe*

An Emerging Vocabulary of Hope

Here are some examples of the new language of the commons, drawn from the dictionary at the end of this book. No longer simply a noun, it is becoming an adjective, too, in the form of "commons-based solutions" or "commons-based society," and even a verb.

Commons: What we share. Creations of both nature and society that belong to all of us equally and should be maintained for future generations.

Commons-based society: A society whose economy, political culture, and community life revolve around promoting a diverse variety of commons.

Commons-based solutions: Distinctive innovations and policies that remedy problems by helping people manage resources cooperatively and sustainably.

Commoners: In modern use, the people who use a particular commons, especially those dedicated to reclaiming and restoring the commons.

Commoning: A verb to denote the social practices used by commoners in the course of managing shared resources and reclaiming the commons; popularized by historian Peter Linebaugh.

—Jay Walljasper

A Global Call to Reclaim the Commons

A manifesto from the World Social Forum

The 2009 World Social Forum in Belém, Brazil, which drew 133,000 participants from around the globe, drafted a manifesto calling upon "all citizens of the world to deepen the notion of the commons." The following is an excerpt. You can read the full text and become a signatory at bienscommuns.org/signature/appel/index .php?a=appel.

Humankind is suffering from an unprecedented campaign of privatization and commodification of the most basic elements of life: nature, culture, human work, and knowledge itself. In countless arenas, businesses are claiming our shared inheritance.

The dismal consequences of market enclosures can be seen in our declining ecosystems: the erosion of soil and biodiversity, global climate change, reduction of food sovereignty. As more citizens discover this reality, a new vision of society is arising—one that honors human rights, democratic participation, inclusion, and cooperation.

The signers of this manifesto, launched at the World Social Forum of 2009, call upon all citizens and organizations to commit themselves to recovering the Earth and humanity's shared inheritance and future creations. Let us demonstrate how commons-based management—participatory, collaborative, and transparent—offers the best hope for building a world that is sustainable, fair, and lifegiving.

This manifesto calls upon all citizens of the world to deepen the notion of the commons and to share the diverse approaches and experiences that it honors. In our many different ways, let us mobilize to reclaim the commons.

Caring for Those Who Care

Although we pay little or nothing for it, caregiving is priceless to modern society

YOU ARE LIKELY ONE OF THE UNSUNG heroes of modern life—part of a massive commons-based mobilization of people who keep our society and economy running. I am talking about parents raising kids, friends and family helping out parents, people caring for their aged relatives and neighbors, volunteers doing what needs to be done in the community, and anyone looking out for someone else.

"In our economic system, to go uncounted is to be undervalued," notes University of Massachusetts economics professor Nancy Folbre. "We have inherited an accounting system that measures the productivity of work by its rate of market pay. This accounting system ignores the value of unpaid work and understates the value of paid work that is partly motivated by affection or obligation."

Putting a monetary value on all this caregiving work is impossible, she says, but even orthodox economists know that without this work things would fall apart almost immediately.

. . .

The Most Important Sector of Our Economy

"Instead of chattering on about the *new economy* or the *high-tech sector*," Folbre says, "we should address problems in the *care sector* of our economy. This sector includes the unpaid labor provided within families and communities as well as the underpaid work of child care, elder care, nursing, and teaching."

This work is disproportionately provided by women, which partly explains why it is undervalued. Even paid work requiring skills in nurturing and caring for people— arguably the most important jobs in our society—offers significantly lower wages than comparable positions that involve the same level of education, work experience, and personal characteristics.

That's why employee turnover rates at child care centers and elder care programs are 40 percent each year. Why many dedicated teachers leave the classroom after a few years to seek better paying, less demanding work. Why there is growing concern that a generation of nurses is about to

Caregiving, work traditionally done by women, is shockingly low-paid today.

retire with fewer young people following them into a profession that has become increasingly stressful.

Caregiving—like other aspects of the commons—can be used up, depleted, exhausted. And we have assumed that our resources for caregiving are limitless because we pay little or nothing for them. But there is a price. As Folbre notes: "If we don't figure out how to reward care better—and to share it more equally—we are likely to see its bounty decline."

—*Jay Walljasper*

What's the Commons Worth?

In the United States alone, more than all private wealth

Natural Assets

In 2002, economists Robert Costanza and Paul Sutton estimated the contribution from natural ecosystems to the U.S. economy at $2 trillion. Their calculation of "ecosystem services" represents the benefits humans derive from natural ecosystems, including food from wild plants and animals, climate regulation, waste assimilation, fresh water replenishment, soil formation, nutrient cycling, flood control, pollination, raw materials, and more.

If $2 trillion represents the yearly contribution of nature to the U.S. economy, what's the underlying value of America's natural assets? One way to answer this is to treat yearly ecosystem services as "earnings" produced by the "stocks" of natural assets. These earnings can then be multiplied by the average price/earnings ratio of publicly traded stocks over the last fifty years (approximately 17:1) to arrive at an estimated natural asset value of $34 trillion.

This figure is, if anything, an underestimate, because it ignores a singular aspect of nature: its irreplaceability. If Corporation X goes out of business, its useful assets will be picked up by another corporation. If a natural ecosystem disappears, however, it can't be easily replaced. Thus, an *irreplaceability premium* of indeterminate magnitude should be added to the $34 trillion.

Social Assets

The value of community and cultural assets has been studied less than that of natural assets. However, we can get a sense of its immense price tag by considering a few examples.

The Internet, which is not owned by anyone, has contributed significantly to the U.S. economy since the early 1990s. It has spawned a host of huge new companies (Google, Amazon, eBay, to name a few); boosted the sales and efficiency of existing companies; and stimulated educational, cultural, and informational exchange. How much is all that worth?

A study by Cisco Systems and the University of Texas found that the Internet generated $830 billion in revenue in 2000. Assuming the asset value of the Internet is 17 times the yearly revenue it generates, we arrive at an estimated value of $14 trillion— a figure that has no doubt risen considerably since 2000.

Another valuable social asset is the complex system of stock exchanges, laws, and communications media that makes it possible for Americans to sell stock easily. Assuming that this socially created "liquidity premium" accounts for 30 percent of stock market capitalization, its value in 2006 was roughly $5 trillion. (If that much equity were put in a mutual fund whose shares belonged to all Americans, the average household would be $45,000 richer.)

Not-for-profit cultural activities, which operate outside the for-profit economy and thus are part of the commons, also pump billions of dollars into the U.S. economy. A 2002 study by Americans for the Arts found that nonprofit art and cultural activities generate $134 billion in economic value every year, including $89 billion in household income and $24 billion in tax revenues. Using the multiplier 17 suggests that America's cultural assets are worth in excess of $2 trillion.

These three examples alone add up to about $20 trillion. The long list of other social assets—including scientific and technical knowledge, our legal and political systems, our universities, libraries, accounting procedures, and transportation infrastructure—suggests that the total value of our social assets is comparable in magnitude to that of our natural assets.

Tallying $34 trillion each for natural and social assets provided by the commons in the United States adds up to *more than all private wealth* (stocks, bonds, real estate, etc.), which in 2007 equaled $58 trillion, according to the U.S. Census Bureau. That said, there are two important differences between our common and private wealth:

+ Our private wealth is superbly organized (property rights, corporations, lobbyists, etc.) to expand at the expense of common wealth. By contrast, our common wealth is poorly organized and extremely vulnerable to private takings.

+ Our private wealth, owned mostly by a small minority, pays cash dividends to its owners. Our common wealth, owned by everyone, does not.

—*Peter Barnes*

> If you steal $10 from a man's wallet,
> you're likely to get into a fight. But if you steal billions
> from the commons, co-owned by him and his descendants, he may not even notice.
>
> —*Walter Hickel,*
> *former Alaska governor*

We Power

Out of people's yearnings come possibilities for a shift from "me" to "we"

THROUGH OUR EXPERIENCE WITH NUmerous community projects, we've come to see how deeply contemporary society is immersed in the market mentality. So long as market fundamentalism remains the lens through which most Americans see the world, it will be very difficult for people to envision a commons-based society, let alone work to revive actual commons that are under threat in their communities. This realization led us to examine how people's social, political, and even personal consciousness is conditioned by their belief in the market as the only efficient system to organize society, and to look for points of entry for introducing commons-based ideas. Below are a few key elements we've uncovered in a series of commons workshops we convened with members of citizens groups and community organizers in the Upper Midwest.

We cannot protect something that we do not first recognize. Things that are unseen and unnamed can be depleted or appropriated with little opposition. Identifying and naming these things as commons give them a new sense of significance, value, and legitimacy.

In workshops, we note that the loss of many commons has gone almost unnoticed, then raise questions such as: What enables people to see the commons? What language do we need for expressing our relationship and stake in the commons? This sparks discussion about how the market paradigm has been sold to us as the pinnacle of human ingenuity—which leads to explorations about how to offer people an alternative view of the world.

Claiming the Commons

Everyone has a relationship to the commons and a stake in its well-being. We lay claim to a commons first by declaring that there are things belonging to all of us and then by seeing ourselves as protectors, sustainers, even co-creators of the various commons all around us. This includes environmental resources, community institutions, online initiatives, and social accomplishments.

At the heart of the commons dwells the spirit of *we*—a force we all recognize deep within us that we want to reclaim. But we feel separated from this we. Our everyday world runs by a different set of operating instructions: I, me, mine—*my* success, *my* health, *my* survival. We feel cut off from the potential of our collaborative imagination. We share a collective unconscious that yearns to rediscover the *we*—the commons.

Paradigm Found

It is jarring to realize just how far modern culture has drifted from the commons existence that for ages was central to human society. Our sense of *we* has been assaulted, chipped away at, forgotten. Of course, we can't retreat back to the past. But it's important to look at what we have lost and how that affects us today.

Thomas Kuhn, the historian of science who popularized the phrase "paradigm shift," defines a paradigm as "an entire constellation of beliefs, values, techniques, and so on, shared by the members of a given community . . . [as] a set of unassailable, unconsciously accepted truths." He goes on to describe the dramatic revolution of thought needed to make a shift—to break out of the deeply held beliefs of an old paradigm that no longer serves us.

What happens when we apply this thinking to our market-based society and the re-emerging idea of the commons?

In one of our workshops, participants hit upon the idea of colonization as a way to describe how we became separated from the commons. Our culture is saturated in the market paradigm. The concepts of consumer, ownership, private, worth, and profit define how we think about ourselves, our relationship to each other, and everything we encounter. It displaces all other ways of making connections and finding meaning.

Colonization denotes total economic, social, and cultural domination of one people by another. It instills a belief system—a paradigm—that legitimizes large-scale theft and repression, making them seem entirely natural.

The market paradigm justifies damage that is done to people's lives as inevitable and dismisses the possibility of another way of life as naive and romantic. The commons continually erodes under the force of the market paradigm and eventually disappears from our view. In accepting the complete dominance of the market paradigm, people unconsciously relinquish a part of themselves that is sustained by the commons.

Imagination = Hope

Envision what would happen if the commons paradigm became a fundamental framework for modern life, gradually outstripping the market paradigm. That's not easy to do. It requires a leap from our usual thinking. It involves cracking open the constraints on our imaginations that prevent us from seeking a true transformation of society.

Yet we have found that people identify and value commons experiences in their own life as well as in the stories of their families, communities, and country. The commons is an imaginable (even if largely forgotten)

Community gardens epitomize the rewards that arise when people work together.

reality, not just a theoretical concept. A re-awakening of our ability to embrace a commons perspective seems possible.

To explore the potential of a commons paradigm means not just formulating policies and programs, but excavating our feelings and recollections. Remembering is the first step in locating missing information that we can use to discover a new story about how we can live and thrive. As is often said, we cannot return to the past, but we can appropriate it, recover it, and use it to shape a new direction for the future.

Challenging the Old Story

Before any new commons paradigm can emerge, we must understand what the old market paradigm tells us about what's possible and what's not. Even though we don't often think about this old story that runs through our heads, it keeps a remarkably firm grip on our overall thinking in the following ways.

+ Our value is determined by economic status. Hope for the future is tied to making more money to buy more goods and services.
+ It's natural that there are big winners and sorry losers in society. The winners have earned their wealth, fair and square. If you have not lived up to your expectations, the fault is largely yours.
+ We are all on our own. Competition is the only efficient, rational way to run a society, so don't expect much help in getting ahead. You can make it if you try.
+ Lower-income people have mostly themselves to blame. Watch out for them; they want what you have but aren't willing to work for it.
+ Government intervention in the econ-

omy tends to reward the undeserving, thereby weakening the entire society.

+ Infinite economic growth is the measure of a strong economy.
+ Economic health is more important than environmental health.
+ Frugality and conservation are old-fashioned virtues that are not really important to our future.
+ Don't talk about your salary or economic standing with anyone else—it is inappropriate under any circumstances.

This old story keeps us isolated, ashamed, fearful, and most important silent. We don't connect with others to discover common solutions to our problems. We feel powerless, unable to challenge the way things are or join with others to make change.

Discovering the New Story

Slowly but persistently a whole constellation of ideas associated with the commons is taking root among small groups around the world. Out of all this we see the birth of a new story to guide us into the future, which can be partly summarized in the following points:

+ We are better people, more caring and sharing, than how the old market paradigm defines us.
+ In most ways, the market-based society failed to deliver on its promises. Even those "winners" who amassed wealth did not generally experience a sense of happiness or fulfillment. They continued to need more and more stuff. And the rest of us were left feeling anxious, exhausted, insecure, and disconnected from each other.

+ The old economic story is not the natural order of the universe. We can work together to create an economy that looks out for everyone, bringing us together rather than driving us apart. We can feel secure without working long hours, doing meaningless work, and seeing poorer people as a threat.
+ Both government and the market can make positive contributions to our lives, if they operate in ways that boost rather than deplete the commons.
+ Nearly everyone can play a valuable role in society, and no one should be cast out from the economy or forced to live in poverty.
+ The measures necessary to restore our natural environment and save the planet will actually strengthen our communities and enhance our lives rather than diminish them.
+ There is enough to go around. Sufficiency, not wealth, is the opposite of poverty.
+ There are many valuable assets that belong to us all, and they should be used in a sustainable way to create an equitable world.

• • •

Tapping into People's Deep Yearnings

A brighter commons future, however, is in no way ensured. The radical acceleration of privatization has diminished the number and quality of commons experiences in people's lives. And as their real-life connections to the commons decline, so does the ability even to think in terms of the commons and to believe that it amounts to anything relevant in the twenty-first century.

Still, as the commons erodes in the world today, it continues to rise up within us as a yearning—an unmet need for deeper connection with the people and natural world that sustain us, a persistent call from the deep recesses of our consciousness saying that life means more than buying and selling.

Rabbi Irwin Kula describes this as a universal human trait. "Our yearnings generate life. Desire animates. We are urged to go for it, to seek answers to our deepest questions. When we uncover our deepest longings, life yields illumination and happiness. Far from being a burden, our yearnings become a path to blessing."

—Julie Ristau & Alexa Bradley

Let's Tap the Power of Social Customs

Informal sanctions work better than laws in creating a happy society

Social custom is a powerful force in our lives, often more effective in changing our behavior than laws. Most people think little of exceeding the speed limit in their cars (which is clearly illegal) but would hate to be thought of as cheapskates who undertip waitresses (which is perfectly legal).

Jonathan Rowe suggests making use of this form of commons to achieve important social goals. "Instead of tax breaks for people who trade in their old cars for new ones with slightly better gas mileage, what if the government offered a refund to *everyone* if gasoline consumption declined by a certain amount? We'd look at our neighbors' gas-guzzling SUVs in a different way, and eventually so would they.

"This commons-based approach, unlike the current individual incentives, would reinforce an awareness that we are all in this together—and it would work better to boot."

—Jay Walljasper

Silke Helfrich

Connecting commoners across continents

If there is one thing that Silke Helfrich has learned in her world travels, it is the cross-cultural appeal of the commons. As the director of the German-based Heinrich Böll Foundation's office in Mexico City from 1999 to 2007, Helfrich and her team hosted one of the first major international conferences on the commons, in 2006, bringing together commoners from throughout Latin America, North America, and Europe.

Working in Latin America and Europe, Helfrich stresses the strategic value of the common good.

The event was a rare gathering in which rural farmers, free-culture advocates, water activists, and opponents of genetically modified crops could begin to forge a shared vision of the commons. Many of them had suffered personally from destructive neoliberal trade policies, the privatization of public services, and deregulation of government protections. Their communities had suffered from enclosures of land and crops that decimated people's livelihoods and local ecosystems. In such circumstances, a language of the commons—or *bienes comunes* in Spanish—makes a lot of sense.

"Five companies control 90 percent of the copyrights in the music industry," notes Helfrich. "Whatever area we look at, we are confronted with concentration—of control, money, and power. These processes of concentration have an immediate impact on the rights of use of everyone and on the vitality and diversity of the commons."

Now living in her native Germany, Helfrich engages with activists, academics, business-people, and politicians to explain the strategic value of talking about the commons. She travels throughout Europe meeting with leading theorists of the commons and frontline activists. She publishes the latest news about commons developments on her German-language blog at www.commonsblog.de, and she edited the 2008 book *Who Owns the World? The Rediscovery of the Commons.*

The commons makes sense to Helfrich because it gets beyond the classic division of haves and have-nots, of owners and non-owners, and of public and private. "The commons," according to Helfrich, "is about the missing *third* element—people as active participants, co-owners, and citizens in their communities, people with relationships of responsibility toward each other and the resources that we all share together."

—David Bollier

Chapter 3

Tales of the Commons Today

Fifth of July

A Declaration of Interdependence

WALK INTO A RESTAURANT, AND THE waiter will bring you a glass of water right away. This act acknowledges water as a life-giving resource that we all share in common. Simple decency demands that we're offered a drink to slake our thirst.

I was reminded of this tradition of interdependence over Independence Day weekend. My family was celebrating the holiday on my wife's family farm, which sits two miles north of the Iowa-Minnesota border. Very early on the fifth of July, I took off on my bike for a short spin around the block—which is a brisk four-mile ride as blocks are measured in the rural Midwest. It was a beautiful morning, with the sun casting golden light on the cornfields and butterflies flitting through tall grasses along the gravel road. I kept on riding, using the towering grain elevators I saw in the east as my guiding star.

When I finally made it to Rake, a small Iowa town of about two hundred where the grain elevators stood, I realized that I cycled much farther than I imagined on a day much hotter than I expected and forgot to bring a water bottle. I was parched. My tongue felt like an old rag left out in the summer sun.

I cruised Main Street looking for a gas station or diner or ice cream stand, anywhere I could get a drink of water. But no place was open this early on a holiday weekend. Finally at an old gas station transformed into some kind of office, I spotted a pop machine. Ah, deliverance!

Now, I am quite familiar with all the environmental and social justice arguments against bottled water, and I unequivocally agree. It is a potent symbol of privatization of the commons. But at this point, my throat felt dangerously dry. I ran up to the machine like a wanderer in the desert coming upon an oasis, opened my wallet, and gratefully fed it a buck. But the machine rejected my first bill. Then it rejected my second, even though it was crisp and new. My third was spat out almost immediately. So was my fourth, which was also my last.

What was I to do? My first instinct was to knock over the machine, use the handlebars of my bike to bust it open, and then distribute free bottles of water to everyone in town as a swashbuckling act of resistance against

the forces of corporate greed. But I quickly realized my bike would probably suffer more from this noble plan than the pop machine. It would be a long, hot walk back to my in-laws' farm pushing a mangled bike.

Civic Virtue in a Glass of Water

It's then I remembered the admirable American ethic of free water. No one, not even a sweaty out-of-towner, could be refused a refreshing drink of H_2O. The generous people of Rake would be proud to provide me a glass of water as a sign of their civic virtue. They would probably even add ice, I fantasized, and maybe a twist of lemon.

The only problem was that the streets were completely deserted this early on a lazy Saturday morning. And I wasn't ready to test my commons theory to the extent of knocking on strangers' doors, especially when there was a good chance folks would still be in their pajamas.

Pedaling around town for a few minutes, I finally spotted a man loading his car for a trip. But he was back inside before I had the chance to catch his attention. I circled the block four times in hopes that he would return with another suitcase to deposit in the still-open trunk. But he was otherwise occupied. An intimate good-bye, I guessed.

My body was beginning to feel weak. It was time for a shift in strategy. Parks, I reasoned, always have water fountains. So finding one became my new quest, which was accomplished in about thirty seconds. (Rake is a very small town.) The park sat near the railroad tracks with a nice playground and well-kept picnic shelter, making it look like a Hawkeye version of a Norman Rockwell illustration—except without cute, slightly mischievous kids.

But no fountain was to be seen. Wait a minute—I noticed two doors on the side of the picnic shelter. Could they be . . . yes! Restrooms. I let my bike fall to the ground and sprinted over, worried that like a lot of public places today Rake's bathrooms would be locked or be out-of-order—a tragedy of the commons for our times. I urgently tried the door, and it opened. I saw a sink . . . good. The room smelled of fresh paint . . . good. And the water faucet worked . . . hallelujah! I greedily gulped about a dozen handfuls of water straight from the tap.

Stepping back into the bright sunshine, I noticed an old weathered metal plaque on the side of the picnic shelter. It honored the U.S. Department of Interior's Heritage Conservation and Recreation Service along with the State Conservation Commission for help in restoring the picnic shelter.

Where Does Government Fit into the Commons?

The role of government in sustaining and supporting the commons is a lively topic

> Discovering the commons is like the invention of the microscope. Suddenly we can see what was there all along.
>
> —Jay Walljasper, commons commentator

whenever people interested in creating a commons-based society come together. Some in this emerging movement view state-supported efforts to manage shared assets with a note of skepticism, placing more hope in looser civic organizations. Others see government oversight of the commons as a more practical strategy in many instances than depending on groups of citizens. No one advocates either complete government control of the commons or none at all. The debate is simply about where the line between government and community responsibility is best drawn.

But let me tell you that, in this case, I am profoundly glad these government agencies were there to help Rake maintain its picnic shelter—and help me, many years later, quench my thirst. It's possible that the people of Rake on their own might have held bake sales and sold raffle tickets to fund repairs to the park. But no one knows for sure. I have seen plenty of places where that didn't happen, and now water fountains are dry and restroom doors permanently locked.

Hopping on my bike for the ride back to Minnesota, I began to wonder if the Heritage Conservation and Recreation Service still existed. I never heard of it. Was it able to survive years of zealous privatization and federal budget cuts to continue helping communities across the country? Back at the farm, after pouring down three tumblers of water, I looked up the Heritage and Conservation Service on the Internet and found my suspicions confirmed—Ronald Reagan dismantled it in the early 1980s. But twenty-five years later, the Web is full of tributes from people remembering its accomplishments.

I find it sadly ironic that a politician like Reagan, who proudly called himself a conservative, would go after a program devoted to "conservation and heritage." Those values are an important part of the traditional American spirit that we celebrate each year at the Fourth of July.

Yet the picnic shelter in Rake is still in good shape today, with a fresh coat of paint and running water. Through some form of government, volunteer, or joint action, this small outpost of the commons is being maintained. We may have the State Conservation Commission (also honored on the sign) or Rake's local government or 4-H kids or hardworking private citizens to thank.

But to whomever credit is due, I want to raise a glass of cool water and propose a toast: *Thank you, and long live the commons!*

—*Jay Walljasper*

Wash Day in the Philippines

Villagers spurn "development" that weakens community life

My brother-in-law, who does rural development work in the Philippines, told me about the surprise he discovered working on a new water system in a mountain village. The project was built in two steps, with water first being pumped to a common containment pool and then later piped to individual houses.

The system was built under the assumption that people would appreciate the convenience of doing their wash at home, the way Americans and Europeans do. Yet even after stage two was completed, women in the village continued to use the common pool to wash clothes. For these women the washing was not just domestic work. It was a social occasion.

These village women did not want the convivial dimension of their work stripped away. Modern convenience in this case also means loneliness.

—*Jonathan Rowe*

A Garden Grows in North Philadelphia

How artist Lily Yeh helped neighbors transform a hard-hit community

LILY YEH HELPED BRING A NEW SPIRIT to North Philadelphia—an inner-city ghetto hit hard by Reaganomics and the crack epidemic—when she began work there in 1989.

In many ways, Yeh was an extremely unlikely figure to make a difference in a struggling African American neighborhood. She is not a social worker, urban planner, or economic development expert, not a wealthy philanthropist, political power broker, or business executive. She is an artist who grew up part of a socially prominent family in Taiwan and came to the United States to attend the University of Pennsylvania, eventually becoming an art professor at the Philadelphia School of Fine Arts. The tough streets of North Philly must have felt as unfamiliar as the far side of the moon to someone from her background—Asia, Ivy League, art school.

In visiting a friend's dance studio in the neighborhood one day, Yeh was shocked at the state of things—deteriorating buildings and rubble-strewn lots reminiscent of photographs of bombed-out cities at the end of World War II. She didn't know where to start.

But she felt something had to be done, so she began to spontaneously pick up trash. This immediately drew the attention of local kids who wanted to know, she recalls, what "this crazy Chinese lady" was up to. Before long their parents were watching too, and Yeh realized she had collaborators for what was to be the most important art project of her life. As she kept returning to the area, growing numbers of neighborhood people joined in her evolving plans to clean up vacant lots, paint murals, and create an art park.

Village of Arts and Humanities

Twenty years later, this area is still poor, but a source of hope for the future can be found at the Village of Arts and Humanities. That's what the small art park has grown into—a tangible symbol of renewal encompassing more than 120 formerly abandoned lots that now host murals, sculpture gardens, mosaics, flowers, community gardens, playgrounds, performance spaces, basketball courts, art studios, even a tree farm.

"The entire community seems to take part in the use of the spaces," writes Kathleen McCarthy, who nominated the Village for the Project for Public Space's list of the world's Great Public Spaces. "As we walked down the street, trying to find one of the parks, a man walking beside us directed us to the Park, and told us the history of it. . . . He spoke with pride that this was a part of his community. We sat on the benches made of smashed tile and mirrors. . . . Across from us, women sat and smiled, waved. Children ran over and asked us to hide them during a game of hide-and-seek.

. . . I've never felt more welcomed in an unfamiliar place."

Six neighborhood buildings have been rehabbed into workspaces for the Village's arts projects. A day-care center has been established and abandoned houses refurbished. A new Village initiative, Shared Prosperity, aims to boost economic opportunities in North Philadelphia.

Residents now look forward each year to their annual neighborhood theater festival, featuring plays written by local young people—including several that were later performed as far away as Atlanta, New Hampshire, Mexico, and Iceland. Fall brings the Kujenga Pamoja festival (Swahili

Yeh poses in front of a mosaic at the Village of Arts and Humanities, a neighborhood project bringing new hope to the inner city.

for "together we build"), which culminates in an elaborate coming-of-age ritual for kids who have spent the summer working in job-training programs.

"One of the most powerful things I learned," Yeh told *YES!* magazine, "is that when you . . . transform your immediate environment, your life begins to change."

Yeh's observation was seconded by James "Big Man" Maxton, who gave up running drugs in favor of making mosaics for Village projects. He went on to teach hundreds of neighborhood kids both basic masonry skills and the creative discipline of making mosaics. "I was a lost soul in the community, disconnected from my family, looking for a way back to reality on the tail end of a twenty-two-year drug addiction," he remembered shortly before his death in 2005, crediting Yeh with "teaching me to believe in myself."

The Village of Art and Humanities has changed how residents of North Philadelphia think about their home. As the neighborhood has blossomed with safe common spaces where people can gather, its spirit and sense of itself has grown. And that changes how others view the neighborhood today. Philip Horn, director of the Pennsylvania Council for the Arts, notes that it "changed the perception of the [wider] community from 'there's something wrong with these people' to 'there's nothing wrong with these people.'"

The Art of Building Community

Leaving the project in the hands of neighborhood people, Lily Yeh has now founded Barefoot Artists, Inc., which draws on the experience of the Village of Art and Humanities to help struggling communities in the Congo, Kenya, the Republic of Georgia, China, Ecuador, Taiwan, Italy, and the Ivory Coast. She has spent a lot of time in Rwanda as a founder of the Rwanda Healing Project, which works with children to restore peace and beauty in communities ripped apart by the genocidal civil war.

Looking back on her work in North Philadelphia, Yeh reflects, "When I see brokenness, poverty, and crime in inner cities, I also see the enormous potential and readiness for transformation and rebirth. We are creating an art form that comes from the heart and reflects the pain and sorrow of people's lives. It also expresses joy, beauty, and love. This process lays the foundation of building a genuine community in which people are reconnected with their families, sustained by meaningful work, nurtured by the care of each other, and will together raise and educate their children. Then we witness social change in action."

—*Jay Walljasper*

Does Black Power Fit with Green Power?

Economist Marcellus Andrews on money, power, race, and the commons

I AM A PERIPATETIC ECONOMIST, SCHOLAR, and teacher whose career has included long stretches at Wellesley, Barnard, and the City University of New York. Somewhere along the way, I became a bit green in my views on economic life and policy, although my greenness has a distinctly black undertone.

I have become fascinated with the economics of sustainability by way of my concerns with economic justice—first by reading Amartya Sen, Partha Dasgupta, and many other brilliant theorists whose work is inspired by the drama of economic change in India. And then by the sheer complexity and scale of the issues involved in valuing natural capital and using it in ways that provide an ethical as well as efficient balance between current and future generations.

Opportunity and Danger in a Racially Divided Society

Economics is, among other things, the study of the distribution of well-being. Market systems work by restricting access to commodities, resources, and power to those who can pay. The idea of the commons is,

Andrews, a Barnard College professor, explores the tension between equality and sustainability.

I think, full of opportunity and danger, especially in a racially divided society with a fraying consensus on how to distribute access to opportunity and safety across color lines.

Hurricane Katrina showed the world what black Americans learn at our parents' knee: there is no "commons" in society, because the fact of common resources or shared space is nothing compared to the structure of social power. The common risks of climate change driven by the disequilibrium between our economic system and nature's rhythm are all too likely to become the profoundly *unequal* risks to life and livelihood between those who count in markets and politics and those who don't. New Orleans was expendable because it was poor, powerless, and carried the dark stain of its African heritage.

Likewise, my view of so many other proposals for managing our planet's resources in efficient and sensible ways is haunted by a deep sense that outcast peoples—vulnerable, marginal, disposable—have no bargaining power in negotiations over the pricing and management of collective environmental risks. In theory, everyone benefits from reductions in greenhouse gas emissions. But the vulnerable forever stand apart and below the powerful—even progressive green power. They remain objects of charity or even redistributive justice, but objects nonetheless. Charity becomes thin, stingy, evincing slight degrees of sadism, when the vulnerable are the wrong color.

•   •   •

The Greening of American Power

Green power, like all power in divided societies, will balance the needs of rulers and ruled. But green power—the use of public and private power informed by scientific, particularly ecological, and economic reason—is far more likely to be humane than other forms of power precisely because it is imbued with a sense of limits and balance. Indeed, green power, at its best, constructs better ways of pricing and managing collective risks, thereby mitigating the destruction of natural capital.

But our individual, family, and communal access to resources and the resulting unequal control of development are shaped by the political facts of society: we are born into families and communities of color, class, region, religion, and language, inheriting access to resources and levers of power or to the abyss of powerlessness.

As you can see, I am struggling with the uneasy relationship between sustainability and equality in a market- and technology-driven global economy, where economic and social innovation must now redesign capitalism to make it cleaner and ecologically viable, yet where the mechanisms of social/racial inheritance threaten to reinforce political and social power in unacceptable ways. Hardened as I am by my American blackness, I think about the economics of the commons in light of the fact that green power is unlikely to be shared fairly across American color lines.

—*Marcellus Andrews*

Why I Call Myself a Commoner

A day in the life

EACH DAY I WALK OUT OF MY MINNE-apolis house into an atmosphere protected from pollution by the Clean Air Act. As I step onto a sidewalk that was built with tax dollars for everyone, my spirits are lifted by the beauty of my neighbors' boulevard gardens. Trees planted by people who would never sit under them shade my walk. I listen to public radio, a non-profit service broadcast over airwaves belonging to us all, as I stroll around a lake in the park, which was protected from shore-line development by civic-minded citizens in the nineteenth century. The park, like everything else I have mentioned so far, is a commons for which each of us is responsible.

Frequently I visit the public library, where the intellectual, cultural, scientific, and informational storehouse of the world is opened to me for free—and to anyone who walks through the door. My work requires me to constantly keep up with new knowl-edge. My best tool is the Internet. The library and Internet, too, are commons.

Returning home I stop at the farmers' market, a public institution created by local producers who want to share their fare. The same spirit prevails at our local food co-op, of which I am the owner (along with thousands of others), and at community-run theaters and civic events. These commons-based institutions provide us with essential services, the most important of which is fun. Living in the commons isn't only about cultural and economic wealth; it's also about joy.

Candido Grzybowski, the Brazilian sociologist who co-founded the World Social Forum, advises, "If we want to work for justice, we should work for the commons." Protecting and restoring precious gifts from nature and from our foreparents for future generations is one the greatest privileges of a being a commoner.

—*Harriet Barlow*

> **The commons isn't only about cultural and economic wealth; it's also about joy.**
>
> —*Harriet Barlow,*
> *commons advocate*

Hometown Champions

How folks in one California town are pulling together to improve the community

IF YOU PASS BY TOBY'S FEED BARN IN Point Reyes Station, California—a small town bordering the Point Reyes National Seashore—there's a good chance you'll encounter Jonathan Rowe. Rowe spends a lot of time at Toby's coffee bar, a spot that he calls his commons office. Amid the hay bales and sacks of chicken feed, he writes on his laptop and surfs the Web while welcoming friendly interruptions from anyone in town.

Toby's is a good spot for taking the pulse of the Point Reyes community. Ranchers arrive in pickups to buy animal feed and hay. Other locals stop to chat after they get their mail at the post office next door. Parents grab a cup of coffee while doing errands with their kids. Tourists sit and bask in the small town scene.

Yet Rowe is no romantic rustic—he has logged plenty of time in high-powered settings. In the 1980s, he was a staff writer at influential publications such as the *Christian Science Monitor* and the *Washington Monthly*. He worked in Congress as a staff member for Representative (and then Senator) Byron Dorgan of North Dakota. Rowe also spent many years working with Ralph Nader on tax reform and other issues.

After a long stint in national politics and policy making, Rowe is now concentrating on one of the most important yet neglected sources of social renewal—neighbors. Working together with another local resident, Elizabeth Barnet, Rowe is exploring new ways to resurrect a hometown commons.

A Different Kind of Social Change

Through his years in Washington, Rowe witnessed how the political right had been revived by fresh ideas—or at least fresh packaging for old ideas. The commons intrigued him as a worldview that could advance a different kind of social change. "Through the Reagan years, I saw the appeal of market fundamentalism," he explains. "It talks about freedom and mobilizing creative energies, and doing it directly, without bureaucracy. Even if it's mainly polemic, it's effective. People working on the left had nothing like that."

Rowe has been studying the workings and excesses of market culture for more than thirty years; much of his thinking is summarized in a still timely 1995 cover story he co-authored for *The Atlantic* on the obtuse metrics of mainstream economics, particularly the gross domestic product, or GDP. The article, "If the GDP Is Up, Why Is America Down?," probed the way that economists equate economic growth with progress and happiness. He asked disarmingly simple questions, such as: Why is the proliferation of fast food and video games automatically deemed an advance over homemade meals and socializing with friends?

This line of thinking eventually led Rowe to view the commons as an antidote to conventional economics—a way to construct a positive, alternative vision for modern society. Through years of work in both journalism and activism, Rowe had come to appreciate how law and economics generally fail to take account of what lies outside the narrow precincts of monetized exchange. For him, the commons offered a new framework for talking about *human* economy, needs that a corporate market cannot meet. With his journalistic talents and political savvy, Rowe was one of the most prominent early voices drawing attention to the existence and importance of the commons.

• • •

Building the Commons in One Community

Three years ago, Barnet approached Rowe with the idea of exploring how Point Reyes Station and neighboring towns could develop a generative commons culture. Barnet is a longtime local resident whose husband, Rufus Blunk, built their home on a wooded hilltop in the nearby town of Inverness. Together they raise chickens, maintain a large garden and fruit trees, and home-school their three kids, while Elizabeth teaches yoga and engages in a wide array of local causes—as well as being the engine of the commons project.

To start, Barnet and Rowe organized a series of gatherings in living rooms and other venues to discuss the commons concept and how it might apply to Point Reyes Station. (The town is surrounded by a celebrated landscape, but partly for that reason, the need for common social spaces within the town itself has gotten short shrift.) Soon, with other community members, they organized an all-day workshop to walk around town and assess the possibilities for social space.

"The walk inspired people to look at their community as if they were actors instead of just the acted upon," Barnet recalls. The enthusiasm that day propelled the creation of West Marin Commons (WMC), named for the still-rural edge of Marin County where Point Reyes and neighboring towns are located. The group seeks, according to its mission statement, to "establish, preserve, and enhance both common spaces and the

life that occurs in them; and to create social infrastructure for resource sharing, conservation, and learning." Not surprisingly, these goals lead naturally to ways to address daunting global problems, such as poverty and climate change, on a local scale.

Springing into Action

Soon volunteers were at work on a number of projects in Point Reyes Station. On the lawn of the old Livery Building, behind Tomales Bay Foods, an organic food emporium, they created a garden that features native California plants. The garden provides an opportunity to teach about the natural history of the area, which is much of what visitors and residents seek in the surrounding national and state parks. The garden also includes a fence, arbor, and signage, built by a local artist out of recycled wood and driftwood from Tomales Bay. Along Mesa Road, behind Main Street, they worked with the local chamber of commerce and the county to reclaim a public right-of-way that had been covered with debris and brush. They added landscaping with native plants, and now parents can push strollers safely to the new toddler playground across the road. Before they had to use the street.

Now West Marin Commons is trying to acquire an empty lot in town in order to create a small park or *zocalo*, which is a central gathering place in most towns in Mexico. (Latinos are a significant presence in West Marin.) But this effort in Point Reyes Station shows that property does not have to be owned publicly or by a community organization in order to function as a commons. "Some of Point Reyes' best commons are privately owned," Rowe says, and cites the benches outside the Bovine Bakery on Main Street and the coffee bar at Toby's, where patrons sit on lawn furniture for sale.

The owner of the feed barn, Chris Giacomini, makes the place available for fundraisers and community functions. "Chris is a patron saint of the commons here," Rowe notes. "Common-ness is a spirit that pervades property. It's not always a matter of public versus private."

Reinventing the Do-It-Yourself Ethic

For those who see the commons as just another name for government or the public sector, it's important to note that the West Marin Commons has worked in part because of the minimal government presence in Point Reyes Station. The town is in the unincorporated portion of the county; government essentially consists of an elected representative to the Marin County board of supervisors, whose district covers a wide swath on both sides of the hill. A village association reviews local development proposals, but beyond that a do-it-yourself community ethos largely prevails. In a town with few official vehicles for civic deliberation, West Marin Commons is striving to build spaces, places, and social infrastructure through which community can grow. Its quarterly barn dances at Toby's are becoming part of the metronome of local life. While reviving community, it doesn't hurt to have some fun.

—*David Bollier*

Best Little Movie House in the Adirondacks

A *vacant theater becomes a favorite hangout*

IT IS SATURDAY NIGHT AT THE INDIAN Lake Theater in upstate New York. The previews of coming attractions are playing when suddenly the sound slows down to gibberish and the screen goes black. I am the projectionist, so I rush upstairs and find a tangled pile of film unraveling onto the floor. I run back downstairs to face the puzzled crowd, telling them I'm going to do my best to fix the problem. To my nervous surprise, everyone cheers.

The theater—on Main Street in Indian Lake, a small town of two thousand in the Adirondack Mountains—was closed for two years, so moviegoers are grateful to have the place back, and they're willing to cut me some slack.

When the theater shut its doors in 2006, local residents missed not only seeing the latest movie hits, but also having a congenial spot to see one another. In addition, the town's economy and culture suffered when the theater closed. Many local merchants reported that the loss of the theater adversely affected their businesses—from the ice cream shop and the hotel to local restaurants and antique stores. People came to town for a movie but stuck around to eat, shop, or see friends.

A Living Room for the Community

A group of citizens from towns throughout the region came together in fall of 2007 to devise a plan for purchasing and reopening the theater as a nonprofit community stage and screen. When word of the project spread across the Adirondacks, many folks sent donations to support it. A community board of directors, whose mission is strengthening the sense of community as well as watching the bottom line, now manages the operation.

The theater has a paid director, and young people make good wages selling tickets and popcorn. A corps of volunteers handles other tasks that make it possible for the Indian Lake Theater to host other events, such as school music and theater productions, public meetings, and even a Magic

The Indian Lake Theater recently threw a well-attended Titanic party to raise money for nonprofit groups in the Adirondacks.

Lantern performance to celebrate the town's sesquicentennial. The theater is now more of a local commons than ever.

Harriet Barlow, who helped organize efforts to save the theater, notes, "The theater provides a sort of living room for the community, a rare opportunity for cooperation and collaboration. Most of all, it makes people happy!"

—D. Megan Healey

Chapter 4

All
That Endures

A Brief History of Commons Destruction

*And how people, from Thomas Paine to Bob Dole,
have stood up for what's ours*

IN THE BEGINNING, ALMOST EVERY-thing was the commons. Humans roamed through it, hunting and gathering to meet their needs. Like other species, we had territories, but these were communal to the tribe, not private to the person.

Agriculture arose about ten thousand years ago, and along with it came permanent settlements and private property. Rulers granted ownership of land to loyal families. Often, military leaders distributed conquered land to their soldiers.

Despite the growth of private property, much land remained part of the commons. In Roman times, bodies of water, shorelines, wildlife, and air were explicitly classified as *res communes*, resources available to all. During the Middle Ages, kings and feudal lords often claimed title to rivers, forests, and wild animals, only to have such claims periodically rebuked.

In the seventeenth century, English philosopher John Locke sought to find a balance between the commons and private property. He believed that God gave the earth to "mankind in common," but that some private property is justified because it spurs humans to work. The trick was to get the right balance. People should be able to acquire private property, but only up to a limit. That limit is set by two considerations: first, it should be no more than they can make productive through their labor, and second, it has to leave "enough and as good in common" for others. This was consistent with English common law at the time, which held, for example, that landowners could draw water from a stream or river for their own use but couldn't diminish the supply available to others.

Despite Locke's quest for balance, the great majority of the English commons was later enclosed, which is to say privatized. Local gentry, backed by Parliament, fenced off village lands and converted them to private holdings. Impoverished peasants then drifted to cities and became industrial workers.

One observer of this transformation was Thomas Paine, the pamphleteer who spoke so eloquently for American independence. Seeing how enclosure of the commons benefited a few and disinherited many others,

Paine proposed a remedy—not a reversal—for enclosure, which he considered necessary for economic progress: compensation for loss of the commons.

Like Locke, Paine believed nature was a gift of God to all. "There are two kinds of property," he wrote. "Firstly, natural property, or that which comes to us from the Creator of the universe—such as the earth, air, water. Secondly, artificial or acquired property—the invention of men." In the latter, he reasoned, equality is impossible, but in the former, "all individuals have legitimate birthrights." Since these birthrights were being diminished by enclosure, there ought to be a compensation for that loss. Paine proposed a "national fund" that would do two things:

> [Pay] to every person, when arrived at the age of twenty-one years, the sum of fifteen pounds sterling, as a compensation in part, for the loss of his or her natural inheritance, by the introduction of the system of landed property: And also, the sum of ten pounds per annum, during life, to every person now living, of the age of fifty years, and to all others as they shall arrive at that age.

A century and a half later, the United States created a national fund to do part of what Paine recommended. We call it Social Security. We've yet to adopt the other part, but its basic principle—that enclosure of a commons requires compensation—is as sound in our time as it was in Paine's.

The Fate of the Commons in America

In the years since European settlement, America developed its own relationship with the commons, which in our case included the vast lands we took from native people and Mexico. Some Americans, exemplified by Thomas Jefferson, saw our commons as the soil from which we could build a nation of prosperous small farmers and proprietors. This philosophy led to passage of laws such as the Land Ordinance of 1785, the Homestead Act, the Morrill Land Grant College Act, and the Reclamation Act, which allocated family-size plots to settlers and financed schools to educate them. Many Americans, exemplified by Teddy Roosevelt, also cherished these lands for their wilderness and beauty, which led to the establishment of national parks, wildlife preserves, and wilderness areas.

At the same time, others in America viewed our common wealth as the means to their personal fortune and lobbied or bribed government officials to give away priceless lands to railroads, mining and timber interests, and speculators.

If an accounting could be made of all the private appropriations of commons through the years—not just land but other valuable resources—it would total trillions of dollars. The plot is almost always the same: when a certain commons acquires commercial value, someone tries to grab it. In the old days, that meant politically connected individuals; nowadays, it means politically powerful corporations.

RKB PRESENTS: THE RUSTY MUFFLER ORACLE

① BEFORE THE MODERN ERA, HUMANS EARNED THEIR LIVELIHOODS FROM THE "COMMONS."

...NO INDIVIDUAL OWNED THE COMMONS. BUT, ALL WERE FREE TO TAKE WHAT THEY NEEDED...

...THE OCEANS, LAKES, RIVERS AND STREAMS WERE FULL OF **FISH**, FREE FOR THE TAKING...

...THE FORESTS WERE A **SELF-REPLENISHING** STOREHOUSE OF FOOD, BUILDING MATERIALS AND CRAFT SUPPLIES...

...THE GRASSLANDS AND PASTURES SUPPORTED HERDS OF **RUMINANTS** THAT PROVIDED MILK, **FIBER**, HIDES AND MEAT...

...AS LONG AS HUMANS RESISTED THE **URGE** TO TAKE MORE THAN THEY NEEDED, THE COMMONS PROVIDED EVERYTHING FOR HUMAN SUBSISTENCE BEFORE THE INDUSTRIAL ERA.

Avidor AND Bewick 1/21/03

Ken Avidor

In 1995, for example, Congress decided it was time for Americans to shift from analog to digital television. This required a new set of broadcast frequencies, and Congress obligingly gave them—free of charge—to the same media companies to which it had previously given analog frequencies free of charge, despite the fact that the airwaves belong to all of us. Republican Senate leader Bob Dole opposed the giveaway. "It makes no sense," he said, "that Congress would create a giant corporate welfare program. . . . The bottom line is that the [broadcasting] spectrum is just as much a national resource as our national forests. That means it belongs to every American equally." But, just as before, the media companies got their free airwaves anyway.

What's astonishing about these takings isn't that they occur, but how unaware of them the average citizen is. As former secretary of the interior Walter Hickel said, "If you steal $10 from a man's wallet, you're likely to get into a fight, but if you steal billions from the commons, co-owned by him and his descendants, he may not even notice."

Enclosure, in which property rights are taken or given away by government, is half the reason our commons is in such a steep decline today; the other half is a form of trespass called *externalizing*—that is, corporations shifting their costs onto the commons. Pollution is the classic example of this.

With one hand, corporations take valuable stuff *from* the commons and privatize it. With the other hand, they dump bad stuff *into* the commons and pay nothing. The result is profits for corporations but a steady loss for everyone else, to whom the commons belong.

Capitalism Enters the Fray

Humans were ravaging nature long before capitalism was a gleam in Adam Smith's eye. Modern capitalism, however, has exponentially enlarged the scale of that ravaging.

A century ago, land, resources, and places to dump wastes were abundant; capital itself was the limiting factor. That's why rules and practices were developed that prioritized capital above all else.

In the twenty-first century, however, this is no longer the case. As economist Joshua Farley has noted, "If we want more timber, the scarce factor isn't sawmills, it's trees."

The world today is awash with capital, most of it devoted to speculation. By contrast, healthy ecosystems are increasingly scarce. If anything deserves priority today, it's nature's capital, yet capitalism rolls on, driven by the profit-maximizing demands of financial capital.

As a businessman and investor, I believe we can evolve to a new stage of capitalism, envisioned centuries ago by Locke and Paine, in which corporations and the commons work in balance. But we have no time to waste.

—*Peter Barnes*

A Brief History of Commons Endurance

A *sampling of commons wisdom through the ages*

By the law of nature these things are common to mankind—the air, running water, the sea, and consequently the shore of the sea.

—*Institutes of Justinian, 535 A.D.*

Anyone who reads this book, if he can write well, may add and change it if he likes. Since this is a book of "Good Love," lend it out gladly: do not make a mockery of its name by keeping it in reserve; nor exchange it for money by selling or renting it.

—*Juan Ruiz, archpriest of Hita, fourteenth century*

Society is indeed a contract; between those who are living, those who are dead, and those who are to be born.

—*Edmund Burke, English statesman, 1792*

A society grows great when old people plant trees whose shade they know they shall never sit in.

—*Greek proverb*

Nature's gifts are the common property of the human race.

—Thomas Paine

As we enjoy great advantages from the inventions of others, we should be glad to serve others by any invention of ours.

—Ben Franklin, who never sought a patent
for his popular Franklin stove

What made Theodore Roosevelt a conservation hero was his conviction that pelicans, two-thousand-year-old redwood trees, and ancient rock formations belonged to future generations of Americans.

—Jonathan Rosen, nature writer

A hundred times every day I tell myself that my inner and outer life are based on the labors of other men, living and dead, and that I must exert myself in order to give in the same measure as I have received.

—Albert Einstein

EDWARD R. MURROW: Who owns the patent on this vaccine?

JONAS SALK: Well, the people, I would say. There is no patent. Could you patent the sun?

—from a 1955 television interview with
the inventor of the polio vaccine

Pennsylvania's public natural resources are the common property of all the people, including generations yet to come.

—*Article 1, section 27, of the Pennsylvania state constitution, 1968*

Aloha is the essence of relationships in which each person is important to every other person for collective existence.

—*Hawaiian state law, 1986*

The right to private property, acquired or received in a just way, does not do away with the original gift of the earth to the whole of mankind.

—*official catechism of the Roman Catholic Church, no. 2403, 1992*

A public philosophy for the twenty-first century will have to give more weight to the community than to the right of private decision. . . . It will have to limit the scope of the market and the power of corporations without replacing them with a centralized state bureaucracy.

—*Christopher Lasch, social critic, 1994*

We all do better when we all do better.

—*Senator Paul Wellstone*

Let us demonstrate how commons-based management—participatory, collaborative, and transparent—offers the best hope for building a world that is sustainable, fair, and life-giving.

—*a manifesto from the 2009 World Social Forum*

The commons is primarily about constructing community—people as active participants, co-owners, and citizens in their communities, people with relationships of responsibility toward each other and the resources that we all share together.

—*Silke Helfrich, German commons activist*

The commons is a framework for reconstruction. Until now we have spent more time on resistance than on reconstruction.

—*Alberto Villarreal, Uruguayan environmental activist*

I am not a rich man but I am rich in favors, and I am rich in cooperation with others.

—*an elder of the Weyewan people, Indonesia*

The idea of the commons is beginning to have an impact on how people see themselves, how they think about the future, and how they work together to shape a better world.

—*Julie Ristau, commons animateur*

Is the Commons Un-American?

Thomas Jefferson and other founders would say no

ONE OF THE THINGS THAT BAFFLES ME about current political debate in America is how the word "independence" is so narrowly defined.

People's economic well-being can be held hostage by huge banks, oil companies, pharmaceutical giants, insurance companies, HMOs, and other powerful corporations, yet in political discussions, independence generally means one thing: the absence of government regulation, or any kind of cooperative effort.

Jefferson substituted the word "happiness" for "possessions" in the Declaration of Independence.

I was reminded of this by a headline in the *New York Times* crediting the "independent streak" of Houston residents for the city's miserably low recycling rate: 2.6 percent, worst in the country, four times less than others at the bottom of the list, like Dallas and Detroit.

"We have an independent streak that rebels against mandates or anything that seems trendy or hyped up," declared former mayor Bill White, even though he favored expanded recycling in the city. (Actually there's no law in Houston or most other places in the United States forcing people to recycle.)

This is surely not what Thomas Jefferson had in mind when he penned the word *independence* in his immortal Declaration. Embodying a true independent streak, Jefferson worked collectively with other American dissidents to free the thirteen colonies from the British crown. Jefferson and his compatriots would be shocked to see that what passes for independence today is a peevish resistance against "trendy and hyped up" chores that might result in a tiny bit more work on trash day.

Although influenced by John Locke and other philosophers stressing the pursuit of individual rights, they understood the commons as part of the social dynamic that allows societies to thrive. That's why Jefferson substituted the word *happiness* for the word *possessions* in declaring the need for "life, liberty and the pursuit of happiness," echoing Locke's famous phrase "life, health, liberty or possessions."

No one of that era, including capitalism's most fervent champion, Adam Smith, could conceive of a world where the market drove all economic, political, and ethical decision making. Social bonds created outside the marketplace by people working to solve common problems is what kept communities together then (and now). To refuse to join a cooperative effort, such as recycling in Houston, would not have been seen as "independent" by America's founders. It would have been seen as foolish and lazy.

—Jay Walljasper

A Revolution of the Rich Against the Poor

The loss of medieval commons still affects us today

MEDIEVAL EUROPEAN AGRICULTURE WAS communally organized. Peasants pooled their individual holdings into open fields that were jointly cultivated, and common pastures were used to graze their animals.

This system of village commons prospered for more than six hundred years at the base of the feudal pyramid, under the watchful but often nominal presence of the landlords, monarchs, and popes. Then, beginning in the 1500s, powerful new political and economic forces were unleashed, first in Tudor England and later on the continent, that ultimately destroyed villagers' communitarian way of life.

Through legal and political maneuvers, wealthy landowners enclosed (privatized) the commons for their own profits, impoverishing many villagers. "Enclosures have been appropriately called a revolution of the rich against the poor," noted the eminent historian Karl Polanyi.

* * *

The Opening Act of Colonialism

These acts paved the way for the industrial revolution. In the process, millions of peasants were dislodged from their ancestral homes and forced to migrate into the new industrial cities. If they were fortunate, they might secure subsistence employment in the new factories, whose owners eagerly took advantage of their desperate plight.

After the enclosure of the commons, land was no longer something that people belonged to, but rather a commodity that people possessed. Relationships were reorganized. Neighbors became employees or bosses. People began to view each other and everything around them in financial terms.

The European enclosure movement marked the beginning of a worldwide process of commodifying the land, ocean, and atmosphere of the earth, which is still being carried out today across the planet.

—*Jeremy Rifkin*

Origins of Our Economic Powerlessness

Ivan Illich traces poverty and consumer dependency back to the enclosure of the commons

COMMONS IS A MIDDLE ENGLISH WORD. People called commons that part of the environment which lay beyond their own thresholds and outside of their own possessions, to which, however, they had recognized claims of usage—not to produce commodities but to provide for the subsistence of their households. The law of the commons regulates the right of way, the right to fish and to hunt, and the right to collect wood or medicinal plants in the forest.

The enclosure of the commons inaugurates a new ecological order. Enclosure did not just physically transfer the control over grasslands from the peasants to the lord. It marked a radical change in the attitudes of society toward the environment. Before, most of the environment had been considered as commons from which most people could draw most of their sustenance without needing to take recourse to the market. After enclosure, the environment became primarily a resource at the service of "enterprises" which, by organizing wage labor, transformed nature into the goods and services on which the satisfaction of basic needs by consumers depend.

> The first sign of tyranny is government's complicity in privatizing the commons for private gain.
>
> —*Robert F. Kennedy Jr.*

Enclosure in the Streets of Mexico City

This change of attitudes can be better illustrated if we think about roads rather than about grasslands. What a difference there was between the new and the old parts of Mexico City. In the old parts of the city, the streets were true commons. Some people sat in the road to sell vegetables and charcoal. Others put their chairs on the road to drink coffee or tequila. Children played in the gutter, and people walking could still use the road to get from one place to another. Such roads were built for people. Like any true commons, the street itself was the result of people living there and making that space livable.

Ken Avidor

In the new sections of Mexico City, streets are now roadways for automobiles, for buses, for taxis, cars, and trucks. People are barely tolerated on the street. The road has been degraded from a commons to a simple resource for the circulation of vehicles. People can circulate no more on their own. Traffic has displaced their mobility.

Enclosure has denied the people the right to that kind of environment on which—throughout all of history—the moral economy of survival depends. Enclosure undermines the local autonomy of a community. People become economic individuals who depend for their survival on commodities that are produced for them.

—*Ivan Illich*

Liberty and Commons for All

The forgotten meaning of the Magna Carta

IN ONE OF HIS COMMUNIQUÉS FROM the Lancandon jungle of Chiapas, Subcomandante Marcos, the spokesman of the Zapatista indigenous people's revolt that burst upon the world in 1994, referred, of all things, to the Magna Carta. Why the Magna Carta, an eight-hundred-year-old document from medieval England?

Marcos went on to describe how the *ejido,* or traditional commons of Mexico enshrined in the national constitution, is being destroyed. He invoked the Magna Carta not only to assert the protections against state power that we associate with this famous English document, but to emphasize the right of people to claim common resources as well.

For eight centuries, the Magna Carta has been venerated for its establishment of political and legal rights. The Fifth and Fourteenth Amendments to the U.S. Constitution quote its language. Eleanor Roosevelt in her 1948 speech to the UN urging adoption of the Universal Declaration of Human Rights expressed the hope that it would take its place alongside the Magna Carta and the U.S. Bill of Rights. The Magna Carta has been deemed the foundation of Western democracy and invoked by many, including Winston Churchill, to glorify Anglo-American world dominance and empire building.

There is, I believe, a narrow conservative interpretation of the Magna Carta that stresses "freedom under law," and a more radical interpretation that establishes the commons and protects the rights of the poor to use it to earn their own livings.

Robin Hood, the Pope, and Commoners

In the middle of June 1215, on the Runnymede meadow along the Thames River, rebellious English barons unhappy with King John forced him to agree to the 63 chapters of the Magna Carta. It is well known that the charter establishes precedents for the rule of law, trial by jury, habeas corpus, and prohibition of torture. It also protected the interests of the Catholic Church, the feudal aristocracy, the merchants, and Jews, and it took an early step toward the emancipation

KING JOHN SIGNING THE GREAT CHARTER

erally belonged to the lord while grazing belonged to the commoners, and the trees to both. Grazing and hunting, gathering wood for fuel and construction, and picking berries and medicinal plants all sustained country people, especially the poor and widows, who had few other means of support. This is the forest many remember from the Robin Hood legends, based on the Yorkshire fugitive Robert Hod in 1226, who flourished at the moment of the Magna Carta.

The Norman Conquest disrupted these customs of the forest that had prevailed for centuries. The forest became the sole property of the king, although traditional patterns prevailed in many places. But in July 1203, King John instructed his chief forester, Hugh de Neville, to sell forest privileges "to make our profit by selling woods." This emboldened his opponents to demand that the forest once again become a commons open to all.

Upon leaving the barons at Runnymede, scarcely had the mud dried on his boots when King John resumed war upon his opponents and began to plot with the pope against them. Innocent III declared the Magna Carta null and void and prohibited the king from observing it. When King John died the next year, the fate of the charter—indeed its whereabouts—was uncertain.

In 1217, the new king, ten-year-old Henry

of women. But what is usually overlooked today is that the Magna Carta established a legal basis for the commons.

The charter opposed privatization of common resources by asserting universal rights to fish in waterways and draw livelihoods from the forests. These parts of the Magna Carta, if they are known at all, are often discarded as feudal relics or English peculiarities. To understand their importance, we need to know that the woods of that time were as important to people as oil is in ours.

Going back to the Anglo-Saxon era before the Norman Conquest of 1066, wooded commons were owned by individuals but used freely by the commoners. The soil gen-

III, was directed by his regents to grant a new charter of liberties, based on the 1215 charter, and "also a charter of the forest," drafted in 1217. But it was eighty years later when Edward I ordered that the charters become the common law of the land.

What the Commons Means Today

What value does the right of access to commons have for people living in modern societies today? Actually the rights laid out in this seminal document of Western law have their equivalents in modern social programs. Piscary, herbage, and pannage, the rights of commoners to fish and graze livestock on the lord's land, can be compared to food stamps and social security or welfare in the United States. Estover, firebotes, and turbary—the rights to harvest wood and peat from the commons forest—correspond to housing aid and energy assistance.

One aim in bringing this forgotten history of the Magna Carta back to the surface is to put the commons back into view as a fundamental right enshrined in one of the earliest documents of constitutional democracy. Another aim is to rouse today's commoners to think about protecting the commons through constitutional measures, as is already the case in Mexico, Venezuela, Ecuador, and Bolivia. The Magna Carta is a radical document at the root of our constitutional systems, and at the root of the Magna Carta is the commons.

—Peter Linebaugh

"Stealing the Common from the Goose"

A seventeenth-century rhyme still rings true

This seventeenth-century English folk poem is one of the pithiest critiques of the enclosure movement—the fencing of common land and turning it into private property.

—James Boyle

The law locks up the man or woman
Who steals the goose off the common
But leaves the greater villain loose
Who steals the common from the goose.

The law demands that we atone
When we take things we do not own
But leaves the lords and ladies fine
Who takes things that are yours and mine.

The law locks up the man or woman
Who steals the goose from off the common
And geese will still a common lack
Till they go and steal it back.

An Ancient Legal Principle Is More Important Than Ever

The public-trust doctrine remains a powerful tool for protecting the commons

THE PUBLIC-TRUST DOCTRINE IS A LEGAL principle stating that common resources such as water are to be held in trust by the state for the use and enjoyment of the general public rather than owned by private interests.

This idea of the public trust has a long and venerable history. It was codified back in the sixth century, when the Roman emperor Justinian decided to gather and condense all the unpublished rules and edicts handed down by his predecessors into a unified, coherent code of imperial law. Among them were the following: "By the law of nature these things are common to all mankind, the air, running water, the sea and consequently the shores of the sea."

Why It's Important Today

But the public-trust doctrine is more critical today than at any time in history because the commons is being enclosed in ways that were never before possible—from gene pools to the farthest reaches of outer space. The patenting of life-forms, the placement of weapons in space, the giveaway of the communications spectrum, the commercial invasion of childhood, and the temptation to privatize almost anything are just a few of the many new threats to the commons.

Over the course of its fifteen-hundred-year history, use of the public-trust doctrine has waxed and waned, depending on political climates and attitudes toward the commons. This edict has been used primarily to protect the public's interest in one very vital aspect of the commons: water and sometimes land covered by water, such as shorelines, beaches, and river bottoms. But by the eleventh century, a French law had decreed that "the public highways and byways, running water and springs, meadows and pastures, forests, heaths and rocks are not to be held by Lords; nor are they to be maintained in any other ways than that their people may always be able to use them."

The public-trust doctrine was eventually interpreted in England to mean that the king actually owned public lands, but held them in trust for the public. As new colonies were created in North America and Mesoamerica by English, French, and Spanish kings, the doctrine of the public trust, as it was then known, was adopted without argument as common law. The idea of the public trust was synonymous with America's promise of freedom, and several states eventually wrote some form of the ancient code directly into their constitutions.

Take for instance Article 1, section 27, of the Pennsylvania state constitution:

> The people have a right to clean air, pure water, and to the preservation of the natural, scenic, historic and aesthetic values of the environment. Pennsylvania's public natural resources are the common property of all the people, including generations yet to come. As trustee of these resources the Commonwealth shall conserve and maintain them for the benefit of all the people

The Commons Arises in U.S. Courts

During the early nineteenth century, the impoverished children of New Jersey began appearing at council meetings in towns and cities along the state's coast and waterways. After patiently awaiting their turn to speak, they testified that the livelihoods of their families were being threatened by wealthy oyster planters who had persuaded local courts to uphold the privatization of coastal and estuarial oyster beds from which the children's parents had freely gathered food. Their plight aroused the compassion of town councilmen, and led to America's first major test of the public-trust doctrine.

In the landmark case *Arnold v. Mundy*, the New Jersey Supreme Court upheld the ancient principle of public trust. Twenty-

Roman law declared—and court rulings through the years have upheld—the legal principle that no one owns rivers, lakes, the sea, or the air.

one years later, the U.S. Supreme Court affirmed the New Jersey court's interpretation of the public trust—a landmark case, because the public trust is not a federal doctrine.

Then in 1892 came an even more significant case upholding public trust. In *Illinois Central Railroad v. Illinois*, the U.S. Supreme Court held that a state legislature could not grant ownership of land under navigable waters to a private party, in this case the railroad, which had in effect been handed one thousand acres of Lake Michigan shoreline and underwater land—the entire waterfront of Chicago at the time. In this ruling, the court acknowledged a state's right to sell non-public-trust properties. But water and the ground beneath it "is a title held in trust for the people of the state, that they may enjoy the navigation of waters, carry on commerce over them and have liberty of fishing therein, freed from the obstruction or interference of private parties."

But in the early twentieth century, as private property achieved ascendancy over commons property, courts began to look the other way as state legislators handed over public properties to residential developers, landfill operators, and industrial parks. If considered at all, the public-trust doctrine was used only against what were considered obstacles to commerce and navigation.

In 1970 two things happened that placed the public-trust doctrine in a whole new light. Legal scholar Joseph Sax published a landmark article in the *Michigan Law Review* arguing the public-trust doctrine could be used for more than protection of navigation and commerce. The doctrine should, he wrote, be expanded far beyond navigable water to protect the soil, air, and other species—things "so particularly the gifts of nature's bounty that they ought to be preserved for the whole of the populace."

> The commons allows us to say some things are not for sale.
>
> —David Bollier, commons scholar/activist

And in April of that year, 20 million people came out to celebrate the first Earth Day. Even President Richard Nixon took notice that American voters were getting serious about the notion of having government protect the nation's land, air, and water from deadly pollutants.

The public-trust doctrine became firmly established as a tool to protect the environment in the legendary 1983 Mono Lake case—*Audubon Society v. the Los Angeles Department of Water and Power*—in which ecological preservation was ruled a justifiable reason for a potentially major change in private-property rights. The L.A. Department of Water and Power was drawing a substantial amount of water from the feeder streams supplying Mono Lake, causing the lake to recede at a rate that threatened the entire surrounding ecosystem.

The California Supreme Court, invoking the public-trust doctrine, ruled against

Los Angeles and for the lake. The decision asserted that common interest in some resources takes precedence over long-term private use and invoked the principle of *jus publicum*—that certain resources are of so common a nature that they defy private ownership. The Department of Water and Power appealed to the U.S. Supreme Court, which refused to hear the case.

Public Trust Today

It should be noted that the doctrine of public trust can potentially be used to ill effect. In the state of Washington in 1998, the jet-ski industry argued that a county ban on personalized watercraft on all ocean waters and one lake was in violation of the public-trust doctrine. The *Weeden v. San Juan County* case went all the way to the state supreme court, which upheld the ban.

Many steps have been taken over the past two hundred years to affirm and advance the public-trust doctrine as a tool for protecting pieces of our country where the public interest should prevail. But the long intervals between triumphant cases illuminate the glacial advance of any legal strategy that is up against the enormous forces of industrial expansion, urban sprawl, and the overwhelming judicial preference for private property.

Thankfully, there is a growing sentiment expressed in respectable law journals for enforcing a stricter doctrine and expanding the public trust to cover ecological resources in general, which in some cases has been affirmed in the courts. A district court on Long Island declared that "the entire ecological system supporting the waterways is an integral part of them and must necessarily be included within the purview of the [public] trust." A few courts have even accepted dry land, natural beauty, cultural artifacts, wildlife, a historic battlefield, and a downtown area as public trusts. Louisiana's constitution, like others, prohibits privatization of navigable riverbeds, but the state's interpretation of public trust also includes solar heat.

It's important to realize that public-trust litigation is unlikely to succeed in the absence of community activism and public education. After all, the nineteenth-century New Jersey oyster wars were not won, nor was the shoreline of Chicago saved and Mono Lake's ecosystem preserved, in the courtroom alone. They were all preceded by the public protest of "commoners" demanding that government exercise its public-trust mandate. As public-trust legal scholar Michael Warburton notes, "The doctrine is too valuable a public resource to leave with the legal profession."

—*Mark Dowie*

¡Viva la Acequia!

In New Mexico, common water rights have thrived for centuries

DRIVE DOWN ANY RURAL HIGHWAY IN northern New Mexico and you are sure to come across a valley with acequias—irrigation ditches that in some cases have existed for several centuries. You might not even notice them, but someone with a sensitized eye would immediately spot the green ribbons of farmland, pasture, cottonwood, and willow trees. Simple in their design, acequias move water from a common source of water—a spring or a stream—through a network of ditches to replenish fields that have been carefully tended for generations. These community-based irrigation systems are central to traditions of life on the land that have sustained families in New Mexico for generations and inspired many newcomers to embrace the acequia culture.

Acequias are one of the most enduring examples of human-made commons in North America. Their roots extend back thousands of years to people living in the arid lands of present-day India and the Middle East. The word *acequia* is of Arabic origin, meaning "bearer of water" or "that which quenches thirst." The acequias of the present-day Southwest combine Moor-ish traditions with Native American irrigation and agricultural techniques. They have shaped the landscape, culture, and communities of mestizos, *genizaros*, and *mexicanos* (collectively referred to as the Indo-Hispanic people).

In the United States, acequias are unique to New Mexico and southern Colorado, although remnants can be found in other areas of the Southwest. Their resilience in this area can be explained in part by the fact that acequias continue to be vital to the spiritual and material existence of communities in the region. Thousands of families continue to derive all or part of their livelihood from *ranchitos*, or small-scale farms and ranches. Even more important, acequias continue because of people's attachment to the place they live, to the miracles made possible with water, and to a cultural longing to continue ancestral practices and pass them on to future generations.

The deep cultural place that acequias (the word refers to both irrigation ditches and the community network that manages them) have in these communities can be explained to some extent by their communal

Acequias were a natural outgrowth of the commons worldview that water is a community resource—a belief that still underpins acequias today. The Indo-Hispanic villages faced tremendous challenges to survive in the arid environment of the Southwest. Bringing water to crops by constructing an acequia was one of the first priorities in establishing any community. Over time, these communities evolved intricate customs of distributing water based on the fundamental principle that water was essential to life and must be shared for the common good. Today, this practice, which is referred to as the *repartimiento* or *reparto*, is one of the central characteristics of the acequias. It is the day-to-day embodiment of the belief that water is life. It is also a living example of a community-based commons.

The Struggle to Protect Acequias

This commons view of land and water was challenged by the westward expansion of the United States, which culminated in the 1848 U.S. war against Mexico. Although the Treaty of Guadalupe Hidalgo, the agreement between the United States and Mexico that marked the end of the war, guaranteed the rights of the Mexicans who remained

roots. Generally, acequias were established as part of the community land grants under Spain and Mexico (although some were established on the same principles during the later period as a U.S. territory). Under that system, collective ownership of property was well established and fit well with the way of life of land-based people. Families owned their *suertes* (the lots that comprise today's small-scale farms and ranches), while the remaining lands, *vegas* (meadows/wetlands), and *montes* (mountains) were for the use of all the community. Before the advent of barbed-wire fence, families' livestock grazed throughout the mountains and valleys as a herd under the watchful eye of a shepherd.

in the ceded territories (including New Mexico), the vast majority of *mercedes*, or common lands, were expropriated through privatization or incorporation into federally managed U.S. lands. This loss remains vivid in the collective memory of the Indo-Hispanic people of the region.

But the acequias, also communally owned, remain largely intact. The Territorial Water Code of 1850 codified the basic principles of acequia governance, including the democratic election of the *mayordomo* (steward, or ditch manager) and the practice of sharing the water among acequias along the same stream system. However, later laws changed the nature of acequia water rights in fundamental ways.

Water law in the western United States is based on a doctrine that can be summarized as "first in time, first in right." For acequias, this was a mixed blessing. It seemed to conflict with the commons ethic of *repartimiento*, but it also implied a protected status for existing acequia water rights. Fortunately acequias' water-sharing customs are still recognized in state law.

According to acequia custom and tradition, water rights are attached to the land, not to the owner, and the right to use water depends upon maintaining good standing in the acequia by upholding responsibilities for cooperative maintenance. However, the water code and later laws explicitly defined acequia water rights as transferable. This left acequias vulnerable to absentee ownership by people with no stake in the community. This could lead to the piecemeal dismantling of communal practices needed to keep the water system working. In the broader sense, it created the danger that rural communities would lose their water rights in a market-based system that favors water flowing to regions with greater economic power.

After New Mexico joined the union in 1912, most of the traditional acequia practices continued uninterrupted until the 1960s when acequia *parciantes* (irrigators and water-right owners) started being named as defendants in water-rights lawsuits filed by the state. This caused understandable fear and divisiveness in the acequias, which eventually organized themselves into regional associations to unify for common defense. These associations stood up to defend acequia water-sharing customs and prevent the forfeiture of water rights by the state due to errors in mapping—essential work that continues to this day.

Shortly afterward, acequia associations became active on another front: protesting water transfers. Pressures to shift scarce supplies of water from agriculture to suburban development began to mount in the 1980s with unprecedented population

> Our dependency on one another is a point of strength rather than a problem.
>
> —*Julie Ristau,*
> *commons animateur*

growth and urbanization in the state. Acequia associations became actively engaged in fighting the transfer of their water rights, making the case that water was vital to the survival of their communities and integral to the cultural heritage of the state. Results were mixed, but it became clear to developers and others seeking to transfer acequia water rights that communities would be vocal in their defense of their water and their way of life.

Restoring Traditions Through State Law

In the 1990s the acequias came together to form the Congreso de las Acequias, a statewide federation that represents more than five hundred local acequia systems. In recent years, acequias restored recognition of traditional acequia governance in state law and challenged the idea that water is a commodity to be bought and sold.

Our ancestors might not have imagined the extent of work necessary today just to protect the acequias. Yet because of their dedication to the principles of collective stewardship and governance, our current generation has inherited a remarkable legacy unique to the present-day Southwest. Many thousands of acequia *parciantes* are able to continue this rich way of life by irrigating their crops and maintaining the cultural and spiritual traditions intertwined with the acequias. But not forgotten are those who for countless generations left an imprint on the land and communities of the Southwest with their hopes, energy, prayer, laughter, and work.

—*Paula Garcia*

Do Native People's Resources Belong to Everyone?

Potential friction between indigenous people and commons activists

The purest examples of commons-based societies today are found in indigenous cultures. By resisting the widespread privatization that rules the rest of the world, tribal peoples offer inspiration and practical teachings about how to instill a greater sense of the commons in our lives. This would seem to make indigenous people a natural ally for activists wanting to protect and promote the commons. But some indigenous people and their advocates are wary.

Waziyatawin, a Wahpetunwan Dakota Indian and professor of indigenous governance at Canada's University of Victoria, explains, "Whenever I hear someone say something belongs to all of us, I want to say, 'Yes, after it was stolen from us.' Not everyone should be able to own indigenous culture. It does not belong to 'all of us.'"

Waziyatawin asks the emerging commons movement, "How will your vision of the commons work toward justice for indigenous peoples, who are still routinely denied spaces within our homelands?"

Preston Hardison, a natural resources and treaty rights analyst for the Tulalip Tribes of Washington state, says that indigenous cultures around the world vary greatly in how open they are to sharing culture and resources. "Some knowledge is secret, sacred." He adds, "There

Waziyatawin, a professor of indigenous governance at Canada's University of Victoria, asks the commons movement to help secure justice for tribal communities.

are other questions that deserve attention. What claims does a global civil society have on the knowledge and cultural heritage of indigenous people?"

Hardison notes that "many indigenous peoples support efforts to build a global commons and willingly share some of their worldviews, arts, stories, music, and practices.

"But this should not be assumed," he cautions. "Nor should it be assumed that any knowledge that has 'leaked' out beyond indigenous communities should be considered part of the public domain."

—Jay Walljasper

Our Home on Earth

Winona LaDuke outlines lessons from indigenous cultures for restoring balance

GIIWEDINONG MEANS "GOING HOME" IN the Anishinaabeg language. It also means north, "the place from which we come." The word denotes something that is lacking in modern industrial society today. We cannot restore our relationship with the earth until we find our place in the world. This is our challenge today: where is home?

I returned to the White Earth Reservation in Minnesota about thirty years ago after being raised off-reservation, which is a common circumstance for our people. White Earth is my place in the universe. It's where the headwaters of the Mississippi and Red rivers are.

People of the Land

Anishinaabeg is our name for ourselves in our own language; it means "people." We are called Ojibwe, or Writers, derived from *ojibige* ("to write"), on our birch-bark scrolls. Our aboriginal territory and where we live today is in the northern parts of five U.S. states and the southern parts of four Canadian provinces. We are people of lakes, rivers, deep woods, and lush prairies.

Now, if you look at the United States, about 4 percent of the land is held by Indian people. But if you go to Canada, about 85 percent of the population north of the fiftieth parallel is native. If you look at the whole of North America, you'll find that the majority of the population is native in about a third of the continent. Within these areas, indigenous people maintain their own ways of living and their cultural practices.

There are a number of countries in the Western Hemisphere in which native peoples are the majority of the population: Guatemala, Ecuador, Peru, and Bolivia. In some South American countries, we control as much as 22 to 40 percent of the land. Overall, the Western Hemisphere is not predominantly white. Indigenous people continue their ways of living based on generations and generations of knowledge and practice on the land.

On a worldwide scale, there are about five thousand indigenous nations. Nations are groups of indigenous peoples who share common language, culture, history, territory, and government institutions. It is said that there are currently about five hundred million of us in the world today, depending on how you define the term *indigenous*. I define it as referring to peoples who have continued their way of living for thousands of years. In 2007 the United Nations finally passed the UN Declaration of the Rights of Indigenous Peoples, recognizing our unique status in the world. Four countries opposed this: the United States, Canada, New Zealand, and Australia. However, New Zealand recently signed the declaration.

Indigenous peoples believe fundamentally in a state of balance. We believe that all societies and cultural practices must exist in accordance with the laws of nature in order to be sustainable. We also believe that cultural diversity is as essential as biological diversity in maintaining sustainable societies. Indigenous people have lived on earth sustainably for thousands of years, and I suggest to you that indigenous ways of living are the only sustainable ways of living. Most indigenous ceremonies, if you look to their essence, are about the restoration of balance—they are a reaffirmation of our relationship to creation. That is our intent: to restore and then to retain balance and honor our part in creation.

Therefore, when I harvest wild rice on our reservation, I always offer *asemaa* (tobacco) because when you take something, you must always give thanks to its spirit for giving itself to you. We are very careful when we harvest. Anthropologists call this reciprocity. This means that when you take, you always give. We also say that you must take only what you need and leave the rest. Because if you take more than you need, you have brought about imbalance, you

have been selfish. To do this in our community is a very big disgrace. It is a violation of natural law, and it leaves you with no guarantee that you will be able to continue harvesting.

We have a word in our language that denotes the practice of living in harmony with natural law: *minocimaatisiiwin*. This word points to the way you behave as an individual in a relationship with other individuals and in relationship with the land and all things. We have tried to retain this way of living and this way of thinking in spite of all that has happened to us over the centuries. I believe we do retain most of these practices in our community, even if they are overshadowed at times by individualism.

How Indigenous and Industrial Cultures Clash

I would like to contrast indigenous thinking with what I call industrial thinking, which is characterized by five key ideas that run counter to what we native people believe.

♦ First, instead of believing that natural law is preeminent, industrial society believes that humans are entitled to full dominion over nature. It believes that man—and it is usually *man*, of course—has some God-given right to all that is around him. Industrial society puts its faith in man's laws, in the idea that pollution regulations, fishing and hunting regulations, et cetera, are sustainable.

- Second, industrial society strives to continually move in one direction defined by things like technology and economic growth. In indigenous societies, we notice that much in nature is cyclical: the movement of moons, the tides, the seasons, and our bodies. Time itself is cyclical. Instead of modeling itself on the cyclical structure of nature, industrial society is patterned on linear thinking.

- Third, industrial society holds a different attitude toward what is wild as opposed to what is cultivated or "tame." In our language, we have the word *indinawayuuganitoog* ("all our relations"). That is what we believe—that our relatives may have wings, fins, roots, or hooves. Industrial society believes wilderness must be tamed. This is also the idea behind colonialism, that some people have the right to civilize other people.

- Fourth, industrial society speaks in a language of inanimate nouns. Things of all kinds are not spoken of as being alive and having spirit; they are described as mere objects, commodities. When things are inanimate, "man" can take them, buy and sell them, or destroy them. Some scholars refer to this as the commodification of the sacred.

- A fifth aspect of industrial thinking is the idea of capitalism itself, which is always unpopular to question in America. The capitalist goal is to use the least labor, capital, and resources to make the most profit. The intent of capitalism is accumulation. So the capitalist's method is always to take more than is needed. With accumulation as its core, industrial society practices conspicuous

Indigenous people from around the world gathered in New York to protest the Belo Monte Dam in Brazil, which would destroy traditional communities living along the Xingu River.

consumption. Indigenous societies, on the other hand, practice what I would call conspicuous distribution. We focus on the potlatch—the act of giving away. In fact, the more you give away, the greater your honor.

Modern industrial societies must begin to see the interlocking interests between their own ability to survive and the survival of indigenous peoples' culture. Indigenous peoples have lived sustainably on the land for thousands of years. I am absolutely sure that our societies could live without yours, but I'm not so sure that your society can continue to live without ours.

Sustainability in Action

All across the continent, there are small groups of native peoples who are trying to regain control of and restore their communities.

I'll use my own people as an example. The White Earth Reservation is thirty-six by thirty-six miles square, which is about 837,000 acres. A treaty reserved it for our people in 1867 in return for relinquishing a much larger area of northern Minnesota. Out of all our territory, we chose this land for its richness and diversity. There are forty-seven lakes on the reservation. There's maple sugar, there are hardwoods, and there are all the different medicine plants my people use. We have wild rice, we have deer, we have beaver, we have fish—we have every food we need. On the eastern part of the reservation, there are stands of white pine; to the west is prairie land where the buffalo once roamed. Our word for prairie is *mashkode* ("place of burned medicine"), referring to native practices of burning as a form of nurturing the soil and plants.

Our traditional forms of land use and ownership are similar to those found in community land trusts being established today. The land is owned collectively, and each family has traditional areas where it fishes and hunts. We call our concept of land ownership *anishinaabeg akiing*, "the land of the people," which doesn't imply that we own our land but that we belong on it. Unfortunately, our definition doesn't stand up well in court, because this country's legal system upholds the concept of private property.

We have maintained our land by means of careful management. For example, we traditionally have "hunting bosses" and "rice chiefs," who make sure that resources are used sustainably in each region. Hunting bosses oversee rotation of trap lines, a system by which people trap in an area for two years and then move to a different area to let the land rest. Rice chiefs coordinate wild rice harvesting. The rice on each lake has its own unique taste and ripens at its own time. Traditionally, we have a "tallyman," who makes sure there are enough animals for each family in a given area. If a family can't sustain itself, the tallyman moves them to a new place where animals are more plentiful. These practices are essential to sustainability and to maintaining what some now call the commons.

An Indigenous Bill of Rights

The United States and Canada were among only four nations opposing the historic UN declaration

After twenty-two years of negotiations, the United Nations in 2007 voted 143–4 to endorse the Declaration of the Rights of Indigenous Peoples. While not a legally binding document, the declaration affirms two key rights for tribal peoples: ownership of their traditional lands and the opportunity to continue their traditional way of life.

The United States, Canada, Australia, and New Zealand stood alone in objecting to the declaration. (New Zealand has since endorsed the measure.) All four nations have substantial populations of native peoples who seek to reclaim some of their stolen lands. The groundbreaking document got virtually no attention in the U.S. media.

The document declares, "Indigenous peoples have the right to self-determination. By virtue of that right they freely determine their political status and freely pursue their economic, social and cultural development. Indigenous people, in exercising their right to self-determination, have the right to autonomy or self-government in matters relating to their internal affairs and local affairs."

The document continues, "Indigenous people have the right to maintain and strengthen their distinct political, legal, economic, social and cultural institutions, while retaining the right to participate fully, if they so choose, in the political, economic, social and cultural life of the state."

—*Jay Walljasper*

How We Plan to Get White Earth Back

Our reservation was reserved by treaty in 1867. In 1887 the Nelson Act and subsequently the General Allotment Act were passed to teach Indians the concept of private property, but also to facilitate the removal of more land from Indian nations. The federal government divided our reservation into eighty-acre parcels of land and allotted each parcel to an individual Indian, hoping that this would somehow force us to become farmers and adopt the notion of progress—in short, to be civilized.

The allotment system was alien to our traditional concepts of land. In our society a person harvested rice in one place, trapped in another place, gathered medicines in a third place, and picked berries in a fourth. These locations depended on the ecosystem; they were not necessarily contiguous. But the government said to each Indian, "Here are your eighty acres; this is where you'll live." Then, after each Indian had received an allotment, the rest of the land was declared "surplus" and given to white people to homestead or "develop." What happened to my reservation happened to reservations all across the country.

The state of Minnesota took our pine forests away and sold them to timber companies, and then taxed us for the land that was left. When the Indians couldn't pay the taxes, the state confiscated the land. But how could these people pay taxes? In 1910, they could not even read or write English.

I'll tell you a story about how my great-grandma was cheated by a loan shark. She lived on Many-Point Lake, where she was allotted land. She had run up a bill at the local store because she was waiting until fall when she could get some money from wild rice harvesting and a payment coming from a treaty annuity. So she went to a land speculator named Lucky Waller, and she said, "I need to pay this bill." She asked to borrow fifty bucks from him until the fall, and he said: "OK, you can do that. Just sign here and I'll loan you that fifty bucks." So she signed with a thumbprint and went back to her house on Many-Point Lake. About three months later she was ready to repay him the fifty bucks, and the loan shark said, "No,

you keep that money. I bought your land from you." He had purchased her eighty acres on Many-Point Lake for fifty bucks. Today that location is a Boy Scout camp.

The White Earth Reservation lost 250,000 acres to the state of Minnesota because of unpaid taxes. By 1920, at least 99 percent of the original White Earth Reservation land was in non-Indian hands. This was done to native peoples across the country.

We have exhausted all legal recourse for getting back our land. The Federal Circuit Court ruled that to regain their land, Indian people had to file a lawsuit within seven years of the original time of taking. Still, we believe that we must get our land back. We really do not have any other place to go. That's why we started the White Earth Land Recovery Project. Our project is like several other projects in Indian communities. We are not trying to displace people who have settled there. A third of our land is held by federal, state, and county governments. That land should just be returned to us. It certainly would not displace anyone. Some of the privately held land on our reservation is held by absentee landholders, many of whom have never seen that land; they do not even know where it is. It is a commodity to them, not home. We hope to persuade them to return it to us.

Our project also works to reacquire our

> Tribal elders in New Mexico call the commons "mine-ours."
>
> —*Paula Garcia, community activist*

Bernard Perley

The race to save an overlooked treasure

Half the languages now spoken on Earth are expected to become extinct in the near future. And with them disappears a large share of our cultural commons—priceless knowledge about subjects ranging from medicinal plants to ecological systems to human nature.

Most people see this enormous loss as a sad but inevitable by-product of modern progress. Yet Bernard Perley, an anthropologist at the University of Wisconsin–Milwaukee, resists the idea that there is nothing we can do. Drawing on his background as a scholar, artist, architect, and Indian, he is trying to fashion a revival of Maliseet—a tongue now spoken by approximately 1,800 native people along the St. John River in Maine, New Brunswick, and Quebec. It is predicted to become extinct in twenty years.

Maliseet is Perley's native tongue, and he didn't speak a word of English when he started grade school in the 1960s. But he almost forgot how to speak Maliseet during years of schooling in Maine public schools, the University of Texas, and Harvard. Perley's approach to saving Maliseet is simple: "reinstill the language with prestige. I try to link the language with things that are important and valuable, like the oral tradition and the natural landscape."

Perley's efforts have taken him into schools, where he helps students make art and other

Perley, an anthropologist, uses art projects to spark schoolkids' interest in the Maliseet language.

forms of creative expression to discover their language, showing how it is an integral part of the local landscape and their lives.

"The world's languages are one of the world's commons that need to be protected," he adds. "A language is a worldview, a part of our collective human heritage. When we lose a language, we lose a way to solve problems and a particular way of seeing the world. There is a wealth of knowledge, a wealth of riches in them."

—Jay Walljasper

land by purchase. We bought some land as a site for a roundhouse, a building that holds one of our ceremonial drums. We bought back our burial grounds, which were on private land, because we believe that we should hold the land where our ancestors rest. We purchased a former elementary school, which is now the home of our new radio station and a wind turbine. In 2009, which is the twentieth anniversary of our project, we acquired 1,400 acres. We use some of this land to grow and gather sustainable products that we sell: wild rice, maple syrup and candy, berry jams, and birch-bark crafts.

Sustainable Communities, Not Sustainable Development

In conclusion, I want to say there is no such thing as sustainable development. Community is the only thing in my experience that is sustainable. We all need to be involved in building communities, not focused solely on developing things. We can all do that in our own way, whether it is European American communities or indigenous communities, by restoring a way of life that is based on the land.

The only way you can manage a commons is if you share enough cultural experiences and values so that what you take out of nature doesn't upset the natural balance—*minobimaatisiiwin*, as we call it. The reason native cultures have remained sustainable for all these centuries is that we are cohesive communities. A common set of values is needed to live together on the land.

Finally, I believe industrial societies continue to consume too much of the world's resources. When you need that many resources, it means constant intervention in other peoples' land and other peoples' countries. It is meaningless to talk about human rights unless you talk about consumption. In order for native communities to live and teach the world about sustainability, the dominant society must change. If modern society continues in the direction it is going, indigenous people's way of life will continue to bear the consequences.

—*Winona LaDuke*

Chapter 5

A New World of Economics

Good News About Your Net Worth

We are all co-owners of some very valuable assets

LET ME OFFER SOME GOOD NEWS ABOUT the state of your wealth. Sure, the 401(k) tanked, the house lost a big chunk of value, and things are looking shaky at work. But what you possess individually accounts for only part of your true net worth. Each of us also owns a stake in some extremely valuable assets: clean air, fresh water, national forests, the Internet, public universities, blood banks, rich cultural traditions, and more.

Just like personal property, the things we share enhance our lives in countless ways—roads we travel, parks where we gather,

Parks, libraries, streets, the environment, and even break dancing routines are all part of the commons.

publicly funded medical and scientific breakthroughs we take advantage of, accumulated human knowledge we use for free many times each day. In fact, without these commonly held resources, our modern society and market economy would never have gotten off the ground.

When the economy appeared to be booming, many of us didn't care about the commons; it hardly seemed to matter that the local recreation center was in disrepair and Social Security was in trouble. Private health clubs and IRAs would meet those needs. But today, Americans are increasingly grateful for services and opportunities provided for us outside the for-profit economy.

Your Inheritance Is Threatened

But the news about our common wealth is not all good. It faces major threats. The financial downswing created new pressures to balance state and local government budgets by hacking away at critical services and programs, which we all depend on. Transit, public schools, libraries, medical assistance, social services, and parks have been on the chopping block in most communities. The cutbacks, of course, hit middle- and lower-income folks the hardest.

And the economic decline follows several decades when our common wealth was raided by corporate executives, a scandal that began with Ronald Reagan and reached a crescendo during the George W. Bush administration. Fortunately, this unprecedented looting of the commons sparked a new movement of "commoners" from all walks of life who are standing up to protect things that belong to us all. More than just an activist cause, the commons is becoming a model for thinking differently about how we make decisions, manage resources, and think about responsibilities.

—*Jay Walljasper*

The Economy Won't Prosper Until We Invest in the Commons

Robert Reich explains how we can evolve from consumerism to the common good

MANY PEOPLE ASSUME THAT AMERICAN consumers will eventually regain the purchasing power needed to keep the economy going full tilt. That seems doubtful. Median incomes dropped during the last recovery, adjusted for inflation, and even at the start weren't much higher than they were in the 1970s. Families went on a spending binge over the last thirty years despite this because women went to work outside the home, everyone started working longer hours, and then, when these tactics gave out, people went deeper and deeper into debt. This indebtedness, in turn, depended on rising home values, which generated hundreds of billions of dollars in home-equity loans and refinanced mortgages. But now that the housing bubble has burst, the binge has ended. Families cannot work more hours than they did before and won't be able to borrow as much, either.

It is also assumed that if Americans had the money to keep the spending binge going, they could do so forever. Yet only the most myopic adherent of free-market capitalism could believe this to be true. The social and environmental costs would soon overwhelm us. Even if climate change were not an imminent threat to the planet, the rest of the world would not allow American consumers to continue to use up a quarter of the planet's natural resources and generate an even larger share of its toxic wastes and pollutants.

This would be a problem if most of what we consumed during our binge years were bare necessities. Instead we binged on *stuff*. But surely there are limits to how many furnishings and appliances can be crammed into a home, how many hours can be filled manipulating digital devices, and how much happiness can be wrung out of commercial entertainment. The current recession is a nightmare for people who have lost their jobs, homes, and savings, and it is part of a continuing nightmare for the very poor. That's why we have to do all we can to get the economy back on track. But most other Americans are now discovering they can exist surprisingly well buying fewer of the things they never really needed to begin with.

What We're in Danger of Losing

What we most lack, or are in danger of losing, are the things we use in common—clean air, clean water, public parks, good schools, and public transportation, as well as social safety nets to catch those of us who fall. Common goods like these don't necessarily use up scarce resources; most often, they conserve and protect them. Yet they have been declining for many years. Some have been broken up and sold as more expensive private goods, especially for the well-to-do—bottled water, private schools, security guards, and health clubs are just a few examples. Others, like clean air, have fallen prey to deregulation. Others have been whacked by budget axes; the current recession is forcing states and locales to ax even more. Still others, such as universal health care and preschools, never fully emerged.

Where does this logic lead? Given the implausibility of consumers being able to return to binge spending, along with the undesirability of our doing so even if we could, and the growing scarcity of common goods, there would seem to be only one sensible way to restore and maintain aggregate demand. That would be through government expenditure on the commons. Rather than a temporary stimulus, government would permanently fill the gap left by consumers who cannot and should not be expected to resume their old spending ways. This wouldn't require permanent deficits as long as—once economic growth returns—revenues from a progressive income tax refill the coffers.

—*Robert B. Reich*

> **The gradual transition to a commons-based society would bring more opportunity and comfort to our lives.**
>
> —*Phillip Cryan, union organizer*

Who's Responsible for Google's Success?

The founders deserve credit, but they didn't do it alone

GOOGLE'S FOUNDERS, LARRY PAGE AND Sergey Brin, became billionaires when their company went public just nine years after meeting as Stanford University graduate students.

If anyone fits the bill as "self-made men," they do.

Or do they?

While we applaud their hard work and ingenuity—and that of their Google colleagues—we should remember this: Google is built on the Internet, which was created by U.S. public tax dollars and nurtured by a continuing partnership of government, universities, and industry.

What "Self-Made Men" Owe the Rest of Us

The world's greatest venture capitalist isn't one of the financial geniuses lionized in business magazines. It's Uncle Sam, whose taxpayer investments and innovations produced the Internet, the Human Genome Project, and much more. Nick Szabo, a re-tired executive of a semiconductor equipment manufacturer, calls Silicon Valley "a creation of the taxpayer."

Since 1958, an estimated 75 percent of all engineers and scientists engaged in scientific research have worked for federally subsidized ventures through both the public and private sectors. Google's founders and employees come from the nation's top schools. And the top schools—public and private—depend on federal research dollars funded by taxpayers.

The presidents of MIT and Harvard wrote recently that federal research funding "is the lifeblood of our institutions. The return on this federal investment is enormous. More than 50 percent of U.S. economic growth during the past 60 years has been due to technological innovation, much of it stemming from university research."

American taxpayers have helped Google in other ways. How many of the investors, employees, and customers of Google benefited from public education? How many contracts did Google make that are enforced by a publicly financed judicial system? How many patents protect Google from someone else using its intellectual property, thanks to our federally funded patent system?

How the Commons Creates a Good Business Climate

A regulated marketplace, with rules governing disclosure and accounting practices, gives investors the confidence they need to part with their money. The wealth possibilities are only as good as society's institutions that maintain the trust. In short, Google is a dramatic example of the way in which society's investment creates fertile ground for private wealth creation. And what are the obligations of recognizing society's investment?

One is to give back to society through charitable giving. Google's founders have already pledged a percentage of the company's stock to a foundation—an example we should all try to emulate.

The second obligation is to support the public investment and infrastructure that fosters the success of individual and enterprise in this country. Rather than clamoring for tax cuts and drilling the tax code for every possible loophole, it means paying back society so we can keep the ground fertile for the next Google to emerge.

Jim Sherblom, a venture capitalist and former chief financial officer of the biotech firm Genzyme Corp., says, "The opportunities to create wealth are all taking advantage of public goods—like roads, transportation, markets—and public investments. None of us can claim it was all personal initiative. A piece of it was built upon this infrastructure that all have this inherent moral obligation to keep intact."

In other words: the commons.

So let's balance our kudos for Google with a proper accounting of society's role in individual good fortune and a commitment to strengthen our public infrastructure for the future.

—*Chuck Collins*

> Show me a first-generation fortune and I'll show you a successful partnership between a talented individual and society's invisible venture capitalist, the commons.
>
> —*William H. Gates Sr.*

People's Republic of North Dakota

*How a state-owned bank stabilizes
the economy, supports worthy projects,
and saves taxpayers money*

The financial crisis of the past couple of years shows that when the chips are down, it's the government and taxpayers who do the bidding of the banks, not vice versa. Our common wealth is used to shore up private wealth because the "free market" is seen as the only realistic vehicle for advancing the common good.

But is it? Perhaps our biggest problem is a lack of imagination. For example, why not consider starting state banks? If the right wing is going to blast any government action, no matter how innocuous, as "socialism," why not make the most of it? Why not actually recoup some of the benefits of taxpayer money for taxpayers themselves?

A radical idea, you say? Well, that's what happens in North Dakota, a state that has been reliably Republican in every presidential election except one since 1936.

The Bank of North Dakota was started in 1919 by the state legislature to counteract out-of-state bankers and grain dealers who manipulated markets and credit to farmers in the state. Today, when the economy gets bogged down and commercial banks become skittish about making loans to even the most worthy projects, the Bank of North Dakota is a reliable alternative. The bank may help explain why North Dakota has weathered the Great Recession with fewer bumps than almost any other state. Unemployment was only 3.6 percent at the time we went to press (the lowest in the country), and there is a state budget surplus.

In the midst of the economic crash in 2009, the Bank of North Dakota had profits of $58.1 million (on a loan portfolio of $2.67 billion), which was the sixth consecutive year of record profits. Over the past decade, the bank has channeled about $300 million to the state treasury, where it supplements the budget of the state government and keeps taxes lower.

Because the Bank of North Dakota is not obliged to maximize returns for private investors but rather to serve the common good—within the bounds of responsible banking practices—it can spend time and energy trying to make deals work rather than summarily rejecting them as too risky or not lucrative enough.

—*David Bollier*

It's Time to Reconsider Public Ownership

A surprising economics lesson from Germany's most successful brewery

FOR THIRTY YEARS, THE MESSAGE DICtated by corporate executives, financial gurus, and political leaders around the world has been clear: government has no useful role to play in business. Deregulate everything in sight and then let the market work its magic—that was Ronald Reagan's and Margaret Thatcher's recipe for prosperity, which was eventually adopted around the world.

And it worked—in a few select places. Tony suburbs and upscale urban enclaves around the globe wallow in luxury not seen since the 1920s, if not the day of Louis XVI and Marie Antoinette. (Remember the annual December news reports of Wall Street traders buying $500 bottles of wine to celebrate the arrival of their annual bonuses?)

Meanwhile like most people around the world, the majority of Americans struggled to stay afloat as good jobs dwindled and wages declined in terms of buying power. Is it any wonder that people took out risky loans during a time when the housing boom

seemed the only way to get ahead financially?

Then, at a moment's notice, the old rules and certainties about the economy were tossed out the window when the financial sector took a nose dive. Government intervention in the economy was demanded—right now!—by the same high rollers who amassed fortunes thanks to business deregulation.

But let's stop a minute and think about this. If it's such a swell idea for the state to assume control of a failing company, with taxpayers covering the losses, then it must be an even better idea for government to run successful companies that make billions of dollars and provide the public with important services.

In this new era, when the old economic theories no longer apply, we owe it to ourselves to take a second look at public ownership of businesses—an idea scorned since the 1980s.

In recent years, billions of dollars of assets in publicly owned telephone, broad-

even industries that do not provide basic services might benefit the public if they were run by the state. (This assessment, of course, depends on whether you see beer as an essential public service.)

I learned about the remarkable success of the Rothaus Brewery, owned since 1806 by the German state of Baden-Württemberg, not on some wild-eyed nouveau-leftist Web site, but in the *New York Times*. What made Rothaus newsworthy to the *Times* was not its ownership structure but the fact that it had doubled its business since 1992 while beer sales throughout Germany (dominated by huge corporate breweries such as Lowenbrau and Beck's) have plunged 13 percent. Even more amazing, the small brewery accomplished this feat without any radio or TV advertising. Loyal beer drinkers, especially young ones, carry out the company's marketing strategy by telling their friends about Rothaus.

"Even the fact that it is wholly owned by the state of Baden-Württemberg lends it a sense of homeyness in a rootless era," the *Times* reports. "That, in turn, has given it credibility with the anti-corporate, anti-globalization crowd. In Germany, where capitalism is viewed with deep mistrust and populism is on the upswing, that is not such a small audience."

The beer is particularly popular in cosmopolitan Berlin. "I could never identify myself with a beer like Beck's," notes Basti Wisbar, a bartender at Waldohreule, a

casting, railroad, airline, health care, and key industrial companies around the world have been handed over to private investors in what amounts to the largest giveaway in human history. Once public property, which citizens could influence through their elected officials, these strategic businesses are now accountable to no one but their shareholders, who often don't even live in the country.

The time is ripe to experiment with government ownership in certain industries, not just to protect the economy but to restore the commons. This makes the most sense for essential services like transportation, housing, health care, and insurance.

The Little Brewery That Could

And judging by the success of a small government-owned brewery in Germany,

tavern in the countercultural neighborhood of Kreuzberg.

What makes matters even more interesting is that this state-owned brewery is managed by a former politician from the Christian Democrat party, which is Germany's dominant conservative force. The Christian Democrats have dominated Baden-Württemberg's politics since 1948, but the popular state-owned brewery has never been privatized.

In light of dramatic changes in the economy right now, people everywhere might be advised to follow the lead of Germany's radical beer drinkers and conservative politicians by experimenting with government ownership of businesses as way to promote a commons-based society— where a mix of ownership approaches can spread prosperity and create an economy that better withstands financial upheavals. Cheers!

—*Jay Walljasper*

Alaska and Texas Spread the Wealth

How oil revenues benefit every citizen

Under Alaska's constitution, the state's natural resources belong to its citizens. In the 1970s when oil began flowing from state-owned lands on the North Slope, Republican governor Jay Hammond pushed for the royalties to be shared among Alaska's citizens. Many battles later, the legislature agreed to a deal: 75 percent of the state's oil revenue would go to the government as a replacement for taxes. The remaining 25 percent would flow into the Alaska Permanent Fund, which would be invested on behalf of all Alaskans.

Since 1980, the Permanent Fund has grown to $30 billion and pays equal dividends to all Alaskans (including children) out of the income earned from its investments. Annual dividends have ranged from $800 to nearly $2,000 per person, depending on the performance of the stock market. In effect, the Permanent Fund is a giant mutual fund managed on behalf of all Alaskan citizens, present and future. Even after the oil runs dry, it will continue to benefit the people.

Texas does something similar with its Permanent School Fund, which since 1954 has returned proceeds from offshore oil and gas leases to the state's public schools, thus investing in a better future for all Texans.

—*Peter Barnes*

Capitalism 3.0

Piecemeal reforms are not enough—we need a new operating system for our economy

I'M A BUSINESSMAN. I BELIEVE SOCIETY should reward successful initiative with profit. At the same time, I know that profit-seeking activities have unhealthy side effects. They cause pollution, waste, inequality, anxiety, and no small amount of confusion about the purpose of life.

I'm also a liberal, in the sense that I'm not averse to a role for government in society. Yet history has convinced me that representative government can't adequately protect the interests of ordinary citizens. Even less can it protect the interests of future generations, ecosystems, and nonhuman species. The reason is that most—though not all—of the time, government puts the interests of private corporations first. This is a systemic problem of a capitalist democracy, not just a matter of electing new leaders.

If you identify with the preceding sentiments, then you might be confused and demoralized, as I have been. If capitalism as we know it is deeply flawed and government is no savior, where lies hope?

This strikes me as one of the great dilemmas of our time. For years the right has been saying—nay, shouting—that government is flawed and that only privatization, deregulation, and tax cuts can save us. For just as long, the left has been insisting that markets are flawed and that only government can save us. The trouble is that both sides are half right and half wrong. They're both right that markets and the state are flawed, and both are wrong that salvation lies in either sphere. But if that's the case, what are we to do? Is there, perhaps, a missing set of institutions or sector of society that can help us?

Tragedy of the Market, Tragedy of the Government

Pondering this dilemma a number of years ago, my initial thoughts focused on climate change caused by heat-trapping gases that humans dump into the atmosphere. I saw the problem instead as a pair of tragedies: first a tragedy of the market, which has no way of curbing its own excesses, and second a tragedy of government, which fails to protect the atmosphere because polluting corporations are powerful and future generations don't vote.

This way of viewing the situation led me to a hypothesis: if the commons is a victim of market and government failures, rather than the cause of its own destruction, the remedy might lie in strengthening the commons.

But how might that be done?

According to prevailing wisdom, commons are inherently difficult to manage because no one effectively owns them. If Waste Management Inc. owned the atmosphere, it would charge dumpers a fee, just as it does for landfills on earth. But since no one has title to the atmosphere, dumping proceeds without limit or cost.

There's a reason, of course, why no one has title to the atmosphere. For as long as anyone can remember, there's been more than enough air to go around and thus no point in owning any of it. But nowadays things are different. Our spacious skies aren't empty anymore. We've filled them with invisible gases that are altering the climate. In this new context, the atmosphere is a scarce resource, and having someone own it might not be a bad idea.

But who should own the sky?

That question served as the epicenter of my thinking about the commons, which led me to the idea of Capitalism 3.0.

Prosperity won't happen simply by tinkering with the gears of our economic system; we need a complete retooling.

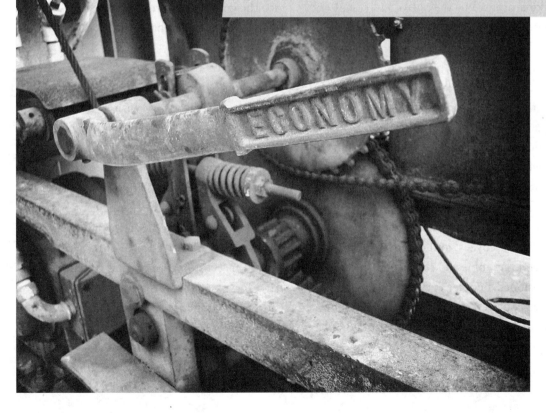

An Upgrade for Our Economy

In his 1973 book *Small Is Beautiful*, E.F. Schumacher argued that capitalism as it currently exists is dangerously out of sync with both nature and the human psyche. As an alternative, he envisioned an economy of small-scale enterprises, often employee owned, using clean technologies.

With Schumacher's vision in mind, I started, ran, and served on the boards of numerous "socially responsible" businesses. The unifying theme of all these ventures was that they sought to earn a profit and improve the world at the same time. Their managers were strongly committed to multiple bottom lines: they knew they had to make a profit, but they also had social and environmental goals.

In 1995 I retired from Working Assets, a credit card and phone company I co-founded in 1982 that donates 1 percent of its gross sales to nonprofit groups working for a better world. I began reflecting on the profit-making world I'd emerged from. I'd tested the system for twenty years, pushing it toward multiple bottom lines as far as I possibly could. I'd dealt with executives and investors who truly cared about nature, employees, and communities. Yet in the end, I'd come to see that all these well-intentioned people, even as their numbers grew, couldn't shake the larger economic system loose from its single-minded focus on profit.

In retrospect, I realized the question I'd been asking for many years was: Is capitalism a brilliant solution to the problem of scarcity, or is it itself society's central problem? The question has many layers, but explorations of each layer led me to the same verdict. Although capitalism started as a brilliant solution, it has become the central problem of our day. It was right for its time, but times have changed.

When capitalism started, nature was abundant and capital was scarce; thus it made sense to reward capital above all else. Today we're awash in capital and running out of nature. We're also depleting many social connections that bind us together as communities and enrich our lives in non-monetary ways. This doesn't mean capitalism is doomed or useless, but it does mean we have to modify it. We have to adapt it to the conditions of the twenty-first century rather than the eighteenth. And that can be done.

But how do you revise a system as vast and complex as capitalism? And how do you do it gracefully, with a minimum of pain and disruption? The answer is, you do what Bill Gates does: you upgrade the operating system.

Much as our Constitution sets forth the rules for government, so our economic operating system lays down the rules for commerce. I use the possessive *our* to emphasize that this economic operating system belongs to everyone. It's not immutable, and we have a right to upgrade it, just as we have a right to amend our Constitution.

With a new operating system—a version I call Capitalism 3.0—the key innovation is a new set of institutions I call the commons

A Trust Fund for Every Child

Making good on the promise of equal opportunity

Though America thinks of itself as a land of opportunity, not everyone enjoys the same chance to succeed. One out of five children is born into poverty, while a very select few inherit millions.

One way to even life's odds is to give every baby a trust fund. Senator Charles Schumer (D-NY) has sponsored legislation to create tax-free savings accounts for all newborns. The federal government would deposit $500 into each account ($1,000 for children in low-income households). When they turn eighteen, the children could use their savings for education, buying a home, or investments.

Yale professors Bruce Ackerman and Ann Alstott have gone further, proposing "stakeholder grants" of $80,000 to nearly all Ameri-

can children when they turn eighteen. Use of the money would be unrestricted, but there'd be two conditions for receiving it: a high school degree or equivalent and the absence of a criminal record. The grants would be financed by a small tax on existing wealth.

This is not a radical, untested idea. Every child born in Britain today has a trust fund. The government kicks in $440 to start the funds. It makes an additional gift at age seven. All interest earned by the funds is tax-free. Parents, family, and friends can add up to $2,000 a year. At age eighteen, the children can decide how to use their funds. (The new Conservative UK government is stopping the plan beginning in 2011.)

—*Peter Barnes*

sector. Instead of having only one engine—that is, the corporate-dominated private sector—our improved economic system would run on two: one geared to maximizing private profit, the other to preserving and enhancing everyone's common wealth. These twin engines—call them the corporate and commons sectors—would feed and constrain each other. One would cater to our "me" side, the other to our "we" side. When properly balanced—and achieving that balance would be the government's big job—these twin engines would make us

more prosperous, secure, and content than our present single engine does or can. And it would do that without destroying the planet.

A New Kind of Capitalism Looks Like This

Capitalism 3.0 would introduce a number of key changes in how the economy operates: new property rights, birthrights, and institutions that would enlarge the commons sector in a variety of ways. Among these are:

+ A series of ecosystem trusts that protect air, water, forests, and habitat;
+ A mutual fund that pays dividends to all Americans—one person, one share;
+ A trust fund that provides start-up capital to every child as he or she reaches adulthood;
+ A risk-sharing pool for health care that covers everyone;
+ A national fund based on copyright fees that supports local arts; and
+ A limit on the amount of advertising.

Getting from here to there is, of course, the big challenge. We've been stymied up to now by the fact that our government tilts heavily toward private corporations. But with the economic upheaval of the past few years, it's possible that a window of opportunity has arrived. It's possible to imagine that we could fortify the commons. The government—acting on behalf of commoners—could assign new property rights to commons trusts, build commons infrastructure, and spawn a new class of genuine co-owners. Then, when corporations regain political dominance (as they inevitably will) they won't be able to dismantle the new system. New commons-sector institutions will have safeguards and stakeholders; they will be in place for the long haul. And in time, corporations will accept the commons as their business partner. They'll find they can still make profits, plan farther ahead, and become more competitive.

The important thing is to build the new system bit by bit, as opportunities arise. This system-building process will take decades, punctuated by periods of rapid change. It will involve businesses and politicians, economists and lawyers, citizens and opinion leaders at all levels. To find our way to a better future, we'll need a vision. That vision should be: *whenever possible, protect and enhance the commons.*

—*Peter Barnes*

Business Based on the Common Good

A Latino entrepreneur returns to his roots with a local food cooperative

"Common sense" is a term Reginaldo Haslett-Marroquin repeatedly uses with ever increasing enthusiasm to describe the local food cooperative he is creating with Latino farmers in Minnesota.

"I come from the commons," declares Haslett-Marroquin, who grew up in Guatemala, where his family still farms communal lands, "and I am going back to the commons."

Since 2007 he has been the director of Rural Enterprise Center in Northfield (population: 17,000), which, like many small Midwestern communities, has attracted growing numbers of Latin American immigrants. Typically they work in low-paying farm-labor and factory jobs.

But where many see a problem, Haslett-Marroquin sees an opportunity that can benefit both the immigrants and the community as a whole. "Commons sense," he calls it.

The Need for Commons-Based Development

The idea for the cooperative was born when Haslett-Marroquin realized that many people around Northfield were unable to find

Reginaldo Haslett-Marroquin is creating a win-win solution for immigrants and small-town residents in Minnesota.

or afford healthy locally raised food. At the same time, new immigrants lacked the financial means to capitalize on their experience as sustainable small farmers. The solution was obvious. Find a way to get Latino farmers back on the land and connect them with consumers seeking wholesome food, which is exactly what Haslett-Marroquin is doing. He's calculated that with four acres a family can support itself raising free-range poultry.

"The project took a long time to put together, plan, secure resources, et cetera, but we now have three immigrant families raising free-range, naturally grown chickens and two families are growing vegetables." It's a small start, but the co-op is already laying plans to expand to eight counties over the next several years, and Haslett-Marroquin hopes eventually to operate in thirty-eight counties across southern Minnesota.

This small-farmer co-op is a shining example of an emerging idea known as commons-based development—a strategy that strengthens the commons by making sure that economic-expansion projects help the community as a whole. While commons work is often seen as an activist or community cause more than a business model, Haslett-Marroquin's projects embody many of the fundamental commons principles: a commitment to future generations, a focus on sustaining the earth, and a means of providing a benefit to everyone. As Haslett-Marroquin says, "The commons is a very straightforward common-sense approach to creating systems that sustain society and sustain life on the planet."

—*Jay Walljasper*

Chapter 6

Reinventing Politics

The Commons Moment Is Now

How a small, dedicated group of people can transform the world—really

SOCIAL CHANGE IS NOT SOMETHING easily diagrammed on a chart. Sweeping transformations that rearrange the workings of an entire culture begin imperceptibly, quietly but steadily entering people's minds until one day it seems the ideas were there all along. Even in our age of instantaneous information—when a scrap of information can zoom around the globe in mere seconds, people's worldviews still evolve quite gradually.

Learning from the Right

This is exactly how the paradigm of corporate power came to rule the world. First articulated in large part by an obscure circle of Austrian economists, it surfaced in the United States during the 1950s as a curious political sideshow promoted by figures such as novelist Ayn Rand and her protégé Alan Greenspan.

The notion of the market as the bedrock of all social policy entered mainstream debate during the Goldwater campaign in 1964, which appeared to mark both its debut and its demise. Despite Republicans' spectacular defeat in elections that fall—which extended from the White House all the way to local races—small bands of pro-market partisans refused to accept the unpopularity of their theories. Instead, they boldly launched a new movement that would eventually turn American life upside down.

Bankrolled by wealthy backers who understood that modern politics is a battle of ideas, market champions shed their image as fusty reactionaries swimming against the tide of progress and gradually refashioned themselves as visionaries charting a bold course for the future.

Their ranks swelled throughout the late 1970s as an unlikely combination of libertarian dreamers, big-business opportunists, and anxious defenders of traditional values signed up for the cause. The successive elections of Margaret Thatcher in Britain, Ronald Reagan in the United States, and François Mitterrand in France confirmed market fundamentalists' global ascendancy. Thatcher and Reagan, each in her and his own distinct way, became effective advocates for the idea that the market should be the chief organizing principle of human endeavor. Mitterrand, on the other hand, was a dedicated socialist but soon discovered that the growing influence of international capital rendered him powerless to carry out promises of his 1981 election campaign. This was final confirmation that we had entered a new age of corporate domination.

Ever since then, our world has been shaped by these forces. Alan Greenspan became the most influential economic policy maker in recent history during eighteen years as chairman of the U.S. Federal Reserve. And the market paradigm is now seen by many— a lot of whom did not begin as right-wingers—as an indisputable truth on the same level as the Ten Commandments or the laws of physics.

Today, it feels as though everything is for sale to the highest bidder—from the names of sports stadiums to DNA sequences that make human life possible. Since the 1980s, reform movements of the left and center successfully resisted certain extreme elements of the radical right agenda, but many Americans still believe a free-market blueprint for the future is inevitable. Progress, once viewed as the gradual expansion of social equity and opportunity, is now widely viewed as the continual expansion of economic privatization and unchecked corporate power.

Andy Singer

Introducing the Commons Paradigm

There are emerging signs that market fundamentalism has passed its peak as the defining idea of our era. In the United States, the first glimmer of hope was when the Bush administration's plan to partially privatize Social Security funds in the stock market gained little traction in Congress and public opinion. Painful financial upheavals around the globe revealed the glaring weaknesses of the current economic model for all to see, leaving some market true believers scrambling to embrace new policies. Yet old ideologies don't quietly fade, especially when they enjoy sizable support in the corporate world. We've seen a fierce backlash against Barack Obama's admittedly modest departures from rigid market thinking.

At the same time, a group of activists, thinkers, and concerned citizens around the world who are rallying support for the idea of a commons-based society. At this point, they're a scrappy bunch—many with backgrounds in various social movements, community causes, and Internet initiatives—not so different from the dedicated market advocates of the 1950s, except in where they place their hopes. These commoners, as they call themselves, see possibilities for large numbers of people of diverse ideological stripes coming together to chart a new, more cooperative direction for modern society.

The volatile political mood of our era bears some resemblance to the late 1970s when liberalism was losing its footing and conservative policy makers refashioned their old political rhetoric, based on social exclusion and apologies for capitalism, into a shiny new philosophy: "the market." Previously the thrust of right-wing thought had been focused on what they were against (civil rights, labor unions, social programs, et cetera), but by claiming the market as their mission, they were able to emphasize instead what they were for. The success of that rebranding has led to many of the problems we now grapple with today.

• • •

A New Political Dawn?

In the same way, commons-based thinking could eventually shift the balance of politics in the United States and the world. Yet unlike market fundamentalism, the commons is not just old wine in new bottles; it marks a substantive new dimension in political and social thinking.

A commons-based society holds considerable appeal for progressives after a long period in which the bulk of their political work has been in reaction to initiatives from the right. Activists across many social movements, now aware that an expansive political agenda will succeed better than narrow identity politics and single-issue crusades, are starting to experiment with the language and ideas of the commons. This line of thinking also makes sense to some traditional conservatives who regret the wanton destruction of our social and environmental assets carried out in the name of a free-market revolution. In the truest sense of the word, the commons is a conservative as well as progressive virtue because it aims to conserve and nurture all those things necessary for sustaining a healthy society.

Growing numbers of citizens—including many who never before questioned the status quo—now seem willing to explore new ideas that once would have seemed radical. Millions of Americans are now making shifts in their personal lives such as buying organic foods, using alternative medicine, collaborating online, and searching for something beyond consumerism that offers a sense of meaning in their lives. They may not yet be sprinkling their conversations with the word *commons*, but they are looking for changes in their lives.

Now is the time to introduce a decisive shift in worldview. People everywhere are yearning for a world that is safer, saner, more sustainable and satisfying. There's a rising sense of possibility that even with our daunting economic and environmental problems, there are opportunities to make some fundamental improvements. Everyone deserves decent health care. The health of the planet should take precedence over the profits of a few. Clean water, adequate food, education, access to information, and economic opportunity ought to be available to all people. In other words, a commons-based society. Let's transform that hope into constructive action.

—Jay Walljasper

You May Already Be a Commoner

The emerging movement draws diverse support

The commons is still an embryonic vision with no single unified political program. But it is a vision with great potential, because it is not being advanced by an intellectual elite or a political party but by a hardy band of resourceful irregulars on the periphery of conventional politics. These commoners are now starting to find each other, a convergence that promises great things.

At this early stage, the emerging commons movement is picking up particular support from these groups:

- *Environmentalists* trying to protect wilderness areas, stop pollution in its many forms, and win fair compensation for private use of public lands.

- *Local communities* trying to prevent multinational companies from privatizing their public water works or devastating their Main Streets with big-box stores.

- *Hackers and corporate programmers* who are building GNU Linux and thousands of other free software and open-source computer programs.

- *Artists, musicians, and bloggers* who use Creative Commons licenses to enable the legal sharing and reuse of their works on the Internet.

- *Scientists, academics, and researchers* sharing databases and trying to prevent corporations from patenting basic knowledge in medicine, high technology, and other fields.

- *Farmers*, especially in developing nations, who are trying to prevent biotech companies from imposing upon them genetically modified crops whose seed cannot be shared and whose ecological effects are troubling.

- *Ordinary citizens* rallying to defend public spaces by opposing intrusive commercialism in civic settings, sports venues, public schools, and personal spaces.

—*David Bollier*

New Hope for Bridging America's Economic Divide

How to compensate for decades of affirmative action for privileged whites

THE CIVIL RIGHTS MOVEMENT ENDED the legal basis of white supremacy in the United States several decades ago yet vast inequalities of wealth still persist, making equal rights a stubbornly elusive goal. There have been modest advances in reducing the black-white income gap. But if African American incomes continue to rise in the future at the same rate as they did between 1968 and 2001, it would take 581 years for black America to reach income parity with white America.

In 2004, the median family net worth of African Americans was $20,400, only 14.6 percent of the median white family net worth of $140,700. The median net worth for Latino families was $27,100.

Our nation needs to make a dramatic reinvestment in broadening wealth and opportunity for Americans who have been historically left out of prosperity. Massive government investments of the past that helped reduce the income gap, such as the nineteenth-century Homestead Act and post–World War II veterans and housing benefits, were effectively "whites only." Since the end of legal discrimination in the 1960s, there has not been a similar mass investment in economic opportunity that African Americans and other people of color could benefit from as equal citizens.

Where Wealth Originates

One barrier to new programs that could elevate the economic standing of lower-income Americans is a widespread misunderstanding of how private wealth is created. Both the media and popular mythology extol rich people as the best and brightest, with the assumption that they made it on their own. Yet no one amasses wealth entirely alone. In truth, many, if not most, wealthy Americans inherited a substantial portion of their net assets. And even for those who did not, private wealth (savings, home ownership, investment wealth) was created from a combination of individual enterprise and the commons.

The story of wealth creation in the United States needs to be revisited from the perspective of both race and the commons. There is a long and unseemly history of

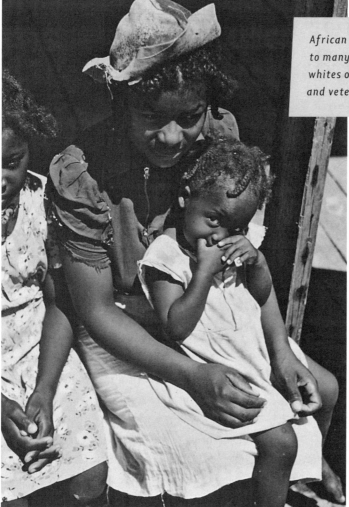

African Americans were denied full access to many benefits that lifted millions of whites out of poverty, including New Deal and veterans programs.

propriated the resources of foreign people.

Black laborers—first slaves, later sharecroppers and low-wage workers—have generated immense wealth for the richest white Americans and gotten very little in return. While workers of all ethnicities have been exploited, African Americans, along with other minorities, were systematically singled out for the lowest pay, worst working conditions, and greatest environmental impact on their communities. We can look back at the robber-baron fortunes of the industrial revolution, which were amassed by white elites who gained free access to the nation's commons resources to exploit for personal enrichment. Companies, buildings, and charitable institutions still carry the names of the individuals who cornered markets built on the natural commons, including oil, timber, and minerals, as well as socially created wealth, such as railroads and the stock markets.

But even the historical government programs most celebrated for boosting the

the U.S. government channeling common wealth to expand the individual wealth and opportunity of the most privileged citizens, almost all of them white.

Even before the existence of the United States as a nation, Europeans confiscated and enclosed land and natural resources from indigenous peoples, creating the base of wealth on which our modern economy was built. Similarly, the United States—often through military intervention—ap-

fortunes of ordinary citizens generally excluded Latinos, Asians, Native Americans, and especially African Americans. The Homestead Act, the most extensive nineteenth-century program for creating family wealth, expropriated indigenous people's lands and enclosed large tracts of common property to grant private property titles to white homesteaders.

Affirmative Action for White People

In the twentieth century, the programs of the New Deal and GI Bill are often praised as bold initiatives to expand the American middle class. But as Ira Katznelson chronicles in *When Affirmative Action Was White*, Social Security, the educational benefits of the GI Bill, and home-ownership programs of the 1950s all deepened the racial wealth divide.

These programs were designed by a Congress in which white supremacists still wielded wide power, and in many states they were implemented so as not to upset local white rule. As a result, the first two decades of Social Security excluded agricultural and domestic workers, occupations disproportionately held by African Americans. During World War II, African Americans faced unequal treatment in the segregated military and were less able to access the bountiful benefits of the GI Bill upon their return.

The postwar economic boom was fueled by subsidized housing assistance to more than 35 million Americans between 1948 and 1972 in the form of VA and other federal loan subsidies. The biggest beneficiary was "whites only" suburbia, which also benefited the most from mortgage interest tax deductions.

Due to economic inequality and various racist practices—such as redlining, bigoted realtors, and outright racist violence used to maintain segregated neighborhoods—most African American families were excluded from this huge infusion of government investment in the middle class. By 2004, 76 percent of whites owned their own home, compared to 49.1 percent of blacks and 48.1 percent of Latinos.

Today, the children and grandchildren of GI Bill recipients benefit from intergenerational wealth transfers that enable them to purchase homes, attend top colleges, and start businesses. But they probably don't think of themselves as beneficiaries of "white affirmative action."

It will be difficult to overcome this gaping racial economic divide if we ignore the role of the commons in creating wealth. We must start with the seldom recognized premise that much of what we consider personal wealth derives from common wealth.

Yet the American myth endures that people's level of wealth is a reflection of their individual effort and achievement. As long as privileged whites believe their wealth derives largely from their own effort, it will be difficult to build political support for an inclusive initiative to spread economic opportunity more widely.

In *The American Dream and the Power of Wealth* (Routledge, 2006), sociologist Heather Beth Johnson interviewed more than two hundred privileged white families about their attitudes toward family wealth. While these individuals acknowledged the role that financial support from their parents made in providing their children and themselves with tremendous educational advantages, they still deeply believed that one's station in life is determined by individual effort. These interview subjects saw no relationship between the privileges offered by their own wealth and the inability of others to achieve the American Dream.

Anyone who boasts that they are self-made is ignoring the crucial role of common wealth in creating personal riches. Individual initiative matters, of course, but is often akin to adding the cherry and whipped cream to the top of the existing sundae of common wealth.

Our best hope for eliminating the historical racial wealth divide lies in people recognizing that each of us has a birthright to share in the bounty of the commons for our sustenance and livelihood. People chafe at the notion of "giving people something for nothing." Yet we don't think twice about corporations and generations of privileged families growing rich from the commons for nothing.

Even white middle-class achievement needs to be understood in the context of preferential access to government programs and common wealth that was built on behalf of and through the efforts of all Americans, some of whom have not benefited from their own efforts.

Common Wealth for the Common Good

While private wealth is distributed unequally, common wealth belongs to all, and its benefits should, wherever possible, be universally shared. Income from commons-based resources should be used to reduce inequality and expand opportunity.

At the same time, common wealth should be managed not just on behalf of those living now, but also on behalf of future generations. Each generation has an obligation to preserve its shared inheritances and pass them on, undiminished, to the next.

Collectively we have a pretty good sense of what needs to be done to broaden opportunity and at the same time remedy the inequality created by whites-only programs, which were successful in improving the opportunities for a segment of the population. Here are some practical ideas on how we can share the wealth of the commons, which rightfully belongs to *all* Americans:

✦ Debt-free higher education, like the earlier GI Bill and Pell grants that enabled millions to graduate from college without deep debts.

✦ KidSave accounts, such as the proposal to grant every child born in the United States a tax-free inheritance of $5,000. Something similar is already done in the United Kingdom. When the child reaches eighteen, these funds (which have earned interest over nearly two decades) can be withdrawn for education, first home purchase, or starting a business.

♦ Expanded home ownership, through various first-time home owner programs, such as soft second mortgages and subsidized interest rates.

♦ Annual dividends to supplement wages. Alaska residents receive an annual dividend from the Alaska Permanent Fund, a portion of the state's oil wealth. Other sources of commons wealth could be used to fund similar state or federal programs.

♦ Establishment of "community wealth-building" funds—pools of capital to provide support for community development corporations, nonprofit housing organizations, employee-owned firms, social enterprises, community land trusts, and other efforts that help people in underprivileged communities gain financial assets.

♦ Commons-based revenue invested in programs that expand opportunity. In Texas, a percentage of oil wealth contributes to several trust funds that pay for K-12 and higher education.

> To speak bluntly, the rich are rich because, through corporations, they get the lion's share of the common wealth; the poor are poor because they get very little.
>
> —Peter Barnes, entrepreneur

How to Pay for Justice?

How will we pay for these wealth-broadening initiatives? It makes sense to fund these efforts by harnessing income from commons-based sources.

Paying the Owners (All of Us) for Using Natural Resources. Historically, polluters have dumped their waste into the natural commons without cost. If we charge for the use of our shared natural resources, we create both incentives to reduce pollution and a revenue stream for programs like those described above. This is at the heart of the commons-based cap-and-dividend proposal to curb climate change.

Common Wealth Recycling Program. If we recognize that large accumulations of private individual wealth came from using the commons, then it's obvious that we should tax inheritances more aggressively. There is also a moral rationale for taxing inheritances. Wealth created from the bounty of the commons may be temporarily claimed by individuals, but at some point much of it should return to society as a whole to be recycled into opportunities for others. Inheritance taxes could be dedicated to a Wealth Opportunity Fund to serve as a source for several of the uses described above.

Socially Created Wealth Captured by Corporations. The wealth of most corporations, like individuals, was generated thanks to commonly held resources. Peter Barnes, author of *Capitalism 3.0*, outlines the many often unacknowledged ways this happened. First, we grant them special privileges that are not available to real human beings, such as limited liability and perpetual life. We supplement these gifts with other socially created privileges, such as patents and copyrights that enable them to charge higher prices than a truly competitive market would allow. On top of that, society provides public infrastructure—roads, the Internet, regulated capital markets, and trade policies—that greatly enhances corporate wealth. And even more, we often give corporations commons resources worth billions: land to railroad companies, minerals to mining companies, the airwaves to broadcasters, pollution rights to polluters.

We rationalize these lavish gifts by arguing that corporations create jobs and strengthen our economy. But in reality, most of these benefits flow to privileged elites who own most of the corporation's stock and are disproportionately white. Corporations historically paid back a portion of this through corporate income taxes, but over recent decades this contribution has shrunk to almost nothing for some of the country's most profitable enterprises. Barnes proposes a levy on corporate wealth, placing a percentage of stock into an American Permanent Fund, to be managed on behalf of the common good.

The idea of the commons provides us with a new lens and a host of practical measures to reduce the racial wealth divide and remedy centuries of exclusion of African Americans and other people of color from America's common wealth.

—Dedrick Muhammad
& Chuck Collins

Hyde Square Task Force

A Boston youth organization offers lessons in democracy

The Hyde Square Task Force, a youth organization working in the Jamaica Plain section of Boston, made an extensive assessment of how people wanted to improve the community. The Task Force then raised money, hired staff, and created new programs to fulfill the commons-based goals articulated by the community:

Hyde Square Task Force members perform at a neighborhood event.

- Murals and other forms of public art
- Health-related education and training for youth
- Strong literacy among young people
- Community organizing efforts to address local problems
- Dance performances and other cultural events

The Hyde Square Task Force employs between 75 and 125 high school students part-time to foster and create these common assets. Beyond the value of what is produced, the community also "gains from the work we're doing because the young people are developing, they're becoming better students, they're becoming more informed and knowledgeable members of society," says Chrismaldi Vásquez, the Task Force's coordinator of organizing and policy initiatives.

Vásquez's introduction to community organizing began at age fourteen when she helped block a Kmart slated to take over a vacant lot in the community and secured funding to put a Youth and Community Center there instead.

Through an entirely youth-led effort, the Task Force campaigned to reinstate civics as a required course in Boston's public high schools. Organizing a citywide campaign, they lined up support from the city council, then turned out more than three hundred students for a public hearing on the proposal. "The high school students realized they were learning a lot of things through their work with the Task Force—the importance of voting, how government works—that they weren't learning in school but should be," Vásquez says. The Boston Public Schools is running a pilot version of the course in two schools, using a curriculum developed by Task Force members.

—Phillip Cryan

Saving the Planet, One Block at a Time

The neighborhood is a powerful—but often overlooked—tool for social improvement

NEIGHBORHOODS ARE THE MOST FAMiliar form of commons in most people's lives. Nearly every one of us is part of one, and they usually play a central role in our lives whether we realize it or not. If your home is burglarized while you're away, it's your neighbor who calls the police. Even more likely, your neighbor's presence strolling down the sidewalk or switching on her lights when she hears an unusual noise at your home discourages criminals from breaking in at all.

But crime is only one of many serious issues that can be effectively addressed at the level of the neighborhood commons. So can problems related to the environment, economic decline, and social alienation. All of us are more likely to pitch in to help improve things in our own backyard. Destruction of the rain forest upsets us, but a threat to the trees in our community gets us off the sofa and out into the streets to circulate peti-

Get something started in your community by throwing a party for the neighbors.

Will Taxes Always Be a Dirty Word?

Not if citizens have a direct say in how government spends their money

The chief cause of antagonism toward government over recent decades is frustration over taxes. People feel they are given no choice in deciding where their money goes as taxpayers compared to their role as consumers in the market economy.

Yet taxes are different than shopping. Ideally they are a collaborative way of solving problems and pursuing opportunities that can't be accomplished efficiently or equitably through individualized action. So it is important that we discuss taxes in a new light.

One promising way to do this is bringing a greater spirit of democracy and the commons into how taxes are spent. Citizens, after all, are the ultimate experts on how government funds should be invested in local communities. The Brazilian city of Porto Alegre (population 1.3 million) decided to do exactly that after the leftist Workers' Party was elected to office in 1989. The new officials invited everyone into the process of decision making with an innovative "participatory budget" that is credited with lowering unemployment, improving public transit, and revitalizing poor neighborhoods. Municipal health and education investments more than doubled in the years after participatory budgeting was implemented.

The idea has since been picked up in hundreds of other communities around Latin America and others in Europe, Asia, Africa, and North America.

—*Jay Walljasper*

tions, organize protests, and negotiate with the folks wielding chain saws. When we can see the direct effects of our actions, we are much more likely to stay involved with an issue and might broaden our focus from local to global concerns.

The notion of the neighborhood as an important social institution might seem old-fashioned to some (as is the idea of the commons itself), like nostalgic memories of the corner soda fountain. Actually, it's as up-to-date as an Internet café, where you find people e-mailing and Facebooking with folks in Morocco from their laptops, but also striking up conversations with neighbors at the next table.

Even as our social and cultural horizons expand in the twenty-first century, the local community is still where we lead our lives, where our toes touch the ground, where everybody knows our names. Neighborhoods remain the place where we can make the most positive impact. And when you look at what people all over the world are doing to improve life in their own backyards, the results add up to significant social change.

From Seattle to Holland, Neighbors Take Action

+ Grandmothers at the Yesler Terrace public housing project in Seattle drove drug dealers from their community by organizing a sit-in (complete with lawn chairs) at street corners notorious for crack traffic. They simply sat there knitting, and the dealers eventually cleared out, proving that old grannies willing to speak up for their community can sometimes accomplish more than SWAT teams taking over the neighborhood.

+ A group of frustrated neighbors in Delft, Netherlands, stopped autos from speeding down their street by dragging old couches and tables into the middle of the road, strategically arranging them so that motorists could still pass—but only if they drove slowly. The police eventually arrived and had to admit that this scheme, although clearly illegal, was a good idea. Soon the city was installing its own devices to slow traffic, and the idea of traffic calming was born—an innovative solution now used across the globe to make neighborhoods safer.

Neighborhood activism is often cast as a narrow, even selfish pursuit. "People are starving in Africa, and you're focused on starting a farmers' market!" But that ignores one of our chief assets for social change in the twenty-first century. Thanks to our amazing global communications networks, no good idea stays local for long. There's no better time in history to think globally and act locally.

—*Jay Walljasper*

Citizenship 2.0

How ordinary people are shaping the future

THANKS TO THE INTERNET AND ITS ability to help people connect with each other and manage shared resources—from blog posts and photos to videos and databases—commoners are inventing brand-new forms of civic action and leadership.

Citizens are no longer confined to the sidelines of world events. We don't need to plead with politicians or the news media for the chance to share our ideas and opinions. We now have the means and power to express ourselves on a global stage and to initiate political action.

Web Sites Heard 'Round the World

+ Bloggers did a more accurate job of covering the run-up to the Iraq War than the *New York Times* and the *Washington Post*. They helped counter reportage by the mainstream media, which, despite their army of reporters and commentators, gave us tragically misleading news about weapons of mass destruction. Independent bloggers did a better

job of sorting the facts from the government propaganda.

+ In 2006, everyone assumed Virginia governor George Allen would easily win a U.S. Senate seat. But at one campaign stop in rural Virginia, Allen called a college student of Indian heritage, who was videotaping his speech, a "macaca"—an ethnic slur. When posted on YouTube, the video became a key factor in Allen's loss—and in the Democrats' recapture of majority control in the U.S. Senate.

+ Then there are the students at Swarthmore College who exposed evidence of how simple it was to hack Diebold electronic voting machines. When Diebold tried to suppress the story by invoking copyright law, the students and other activists published the documents on the Web, triggering closer scrutiny of the matter. Eventually, many states banned the use of these Diebold voting machines.

+ Likewise, a group of activists, lawyers, and journalists created a public wiki to document the lethal side effects of Zyprexa, a bestselling antipsychotic drug.

The Internet puts power into our hands.

Prosecutors eventually sought more than $1.2 billion in fines against the drugmaker, Eli Lilly, for suppressing evidence of the drug's risks.

✦ This is a global phenomenon. After the Iranian presidential election in 2009, when the country's leaders shut down television and radio stations and censored newspapers, Twitter played a crucial role in enabling disenfranchised voters to challenge the political establishment and mount public protests. South Korean politics were changed when huge "flash mobs"—organized through the Internet and mobile phones—rallied to protest their president's meat import policies. In the same way, young Moldavian activists staged an immediate occupation of their national parliament in response to what they saw as an unfair election, and Egyptians mounted large protests against soaring food prices.

Power to the Commoners

As citizens using digital networks, we are acquiring an unprecedented ability to take action based on our own priorities, vision, and voices. In many instances, we have better, more reliable, and more timely knowledge than big institutions. We have access to a larger pool of talent—more eyes,

Lawrence Lessig

An expansive thinker about the digital commons

Lawrence Lessig is one of the first thinkers to appreciate the importance of the commons as a new model for the online world. In the mid-1990s, as a law professor at Harvard, he was pondering the future of this amazing new technology. Rather than seeing the Internet as a libertarian utopia of free-market principles (as many in the computer field did), Lessig came to see it as a democratic realm whose freedoms are highly vulnerable and must be actively protected.

But rather than just study the commons, Lessig wanted to do something to protect it. His big idea was to challenge the constitutionality of a copyright law that granted extraordinarily long terms of exclusive ownership of works before allowing them into the public domain—thus preventing people from using and sharing them freely online.

Working with a band of computer techies and law scholars, Lessig in 2002 founded a new organization, Creative Commons, which invented the Creative Commons licenses that let copyright holders make their work available without advance permission or payment. In 2008, he also founded Fix Congress First, which aims to restore public trust in our government by enacting campaign finance reform and a system of public financing of elections.

—*David Bollier*

Lessig, a Harvard law professor, wants to deploy the power of online communities to reform Congress.

ears, creative minds, in many more loca-tions—than the centralized institutions that report the news and make decisions at the highest level.

All these amazing developments are part of the emerging commons sector. Despite significant differences, each of these innova-tions offers citizens new ways of expressing themselves and organizing as a group with-out the sanction of big business, high-level political players, or the mass media.

I believe the recent emergence of com-mons citizenship represents a fresh new form of politics with the potential to rear-range the prevailing order. Working at the grassroots level around the world, com-moners are building new forms of power and institutions that can fight closed oli-gopolies, political elites, and media gate-keepers. Instead of being largely corralled by the well connected and the wealthy, citizenship—the freedom to participate in power, as Cicero put it—is becoming democratized.

It may appear that the free software hacker, blogger, tech entrepreneur, celebrity musician, college professor, and biologi-cal researcher have nothing in common. In truth, each is participating in social prac-tices that are incrementally and collectively bringing into being a new sort of democracy in action. This new polity is more open, participatory, dynamically responsive, and morally respected by the governed than the nominal democracies of nation-states. The bureaucratic state tends to be too large and remote to be responsive to local circum-stances and complex issues; it is ridiculed and put up with. But who dares to aspire to transcend it?

The commoners do. They are engaged in a struggle to invent a new epoch of "history-making citizenship"—one that is not domesticated and controlled by an aristocracy, political parties, or centralized media. It is instead an attempt to create a digital republic based on people's sincerest personal passions and interests and to tran-scend crude institutional imperatives and ideological shibboleths.

The American inventor and philoso-pher R. Buckminster Fuller once said, "You never change things by fighting the exist-ing reality. To change something, build a new model that makes the existing model obsolete." In their struggles to build new vehicles for citizenship, the commoners are doing just that.

—*David Bollier*

Chapter 7

Reclaiming Our Communities

Our Place in the World

In praise of sidewalks, parks, coffee shops, and other public gathering spots

THROUGHOUT EUROPE, FROM SICILY TO Stockholm, bustling squares and pedestrian zones are the pulsing heart of town. In Latin America, it's the plaza where people hang out in the evening to stroll and talk. In traditional African villages, it's a grassy patch set aside for kids to play and people to dance. In the Middle East, it's the souk or bazaar that stands at the center of community life. In Asia, it's the teeming markets that stay open late into the evening, drawing people from all walks of life. Even in North America, where our traditions of public life are less vital, we still gather in parks, town squares, and downtown streets.

As humans, we are hard-wired to seek out public spaces. David Burwell, a longtime environmental lawyer and activist in D.C., has been tracking research from the field of evolutionary biology and believes that we are instinctually drawn toward convivial places where we can comfortably connect with one another. In fact, public spaces are essential to the future of the species, he says, because that's where boys and girls have always met to talk, flirt, and eventually mate.

Public spaces are literally our common ground, a place where everyone is welcome. They are the most easily recognizable example of the commons—and provide the metaphor for the idea of what we share together.

Wonderful, Wonderful Copenhagen

Jan Gehl, a Danish architect who works throughout the world to improve the livability of cities, notes that "cultures and climates differ all over the world, but people are the same. They will gather in public if you give them a good place to do it."

Gehl has studied what makes public spaces work for most of his life. He began in 1962 by charting the progress of an experiment with shutting some streets in central Copenhagen to traffic. At that time, cars were overrunning the city, and a pedestrian zone was conceived as a way to bring vitality back to the declining urban center. "Shopkeepers protested vehemently that it would kill their businesses," Gehl recalls, "but everyone was happy once it started."

The pedestrian zone has been expanded a bit each year, with parking spaces in the city center gradually removed and biking and transit facilities improved. Cafés, once thought to be an exclusively Mediterranean institution, have become the hub of Copenhagen's social life. The pedestrian district is now the thriving center of a reinvigorated city.

Copenhagen's comeback gives hope to citizens around the world who want to make sure that lively public places don't disappear in this era of rampant traffic, proliferating malls, heightened security measures, overpowering commercialization, and the general indifference of many who think the Internet, television, and their little circle of friends can provide all the social interaction they need.

The Fall and Rise of Great Public Spaces

A century ago streets everywhere in the world were crowded with people. Many are now nearly empty, especially in the fast-growing suburbs sprouting all over the globe. Even in the crowded urban quarters of Asia and Africa, public spaces are suffering under the onslaught of increasing traffic and misguided development plans imported from the West.

The decline of public spaces represents a loss far deeper than simple nostalgia for the quiet, comfortable ways of the past. That's because they remain the best places to meet, talk, sit, look, relax, play, stroll, flirt, eat, drink, soak up the sunshine, and feel part of a broader whole. They are the starting

Copenhagen's bustling pedestrian streets are where everyone goes for a good time.

point for all community, commerce, and democracy. We have an inherent desire for congenial places to gather. That's why it's particularly surprising how much we overlook the importance of public places today.

"If you asked people twenty years ago why they went to central Copenhagen, they would have said it was to shop," observes Gehl, who runs the "urban quality" consulting firm Gehl Architects. "But if you asked them today, they would say it was because they wanted to go to town."

That small change of phrase represents the best hope for the future of public spaces. Historically, Gehl explains, public spaces were essential to everyone's lives. It's how people traveled about town, where they shopped and socialized. Living in cramped homes, often with no yards and certainly no cars or refrigerators, they had little choice but to use public spaces. Walking was most people's way to get around. Urban families depended on markets and shopping districts for the day's food. Parks were the only place for kids to play. Squares and churches and taverns were the few spots to meet friends.

But all that changed during the twentieth century. Cars took over the streets—which for millennia had been a commons belonging to all—first in industrialized nations and now in the developing world. Pedestrians and bicyclists were pushed out of the way. Towns and cities spread out, with many merchants moving to outlying malls.

"Some places have gone down the drain and become completely deserted," Gehl notes. "They even drive their *cars* to the health club to walk and get exercise!" he exclaims. "But other places have decided to do something about it; they fight back," he adds.

The key to restoring life to our public spaces—and our communities as a whole—is to understand that we have far more options for socializing and shopping than in the past. A trip downtown or to the farmers' market or the local library is now recreational as much as it is practical for most people.

"People are not out in public spaces because they have to but because they love to," Gehl explains. "If the place is not appealing, they can go elsewhere. That means the quality of public spaces has become very important. There is not a single example of a city that rebuilt its public places with quality that has not seen a renaissance."

Success Stories from Cities Around the World

Gehl ticks off a list of other places that have revitalized themselves by creating great public places: Barcelona, Spain; Lyon, France; Bogotá, Colombia; Vancouver, Canada; Portland, Oregon; Córdoba, Argentina; Melbourne, Australia; Curitiba, Brazil; and New York, New York.

Gehl relishes describing how Melbourne made great efforts to keep its streets pedestrian-friendly by widening sidewalks and improving pedestrian amenities, which ignited a spectacular increase in people going out in public. Córdoba turned its riverfront into a series of popular parks.

Hope in the 'Hoods of L.A.

In Los Angeles, transforming parks into community hangouts reduces gang violence

An investment in public space is reducing gang violence and increasing the sense of community in Los Angeles neighborhoods. The Summer Night Lights program, launched by antigang outreach workers and funded by private donations matched by the city, finances sports leagues, disc jockeys, lighting, and food to encourage residents to hang out at parks in their neighborhoods.

Summer Night Lights came to eight parks in violence-troubled neighborhoods during 2008, and the mayor's office credited the program with a 17 percent reduction in crime and 56 percent decline in homicides. In 2009, in the midst of severe cutbacks due to California's budget crisis, it was expanded to sixteen neighborhoods and was planned for twenty-four in 2010.

"These neighborhoods with gang problems don't have a lot of assets," notes Reverend Jeff Parr. "But there is a school, a park, and a rec center. Those are public assets. Let's use those to create social connections that replace gangs."

It is especially inspiring that the program welcomes known gang members in order to restore relationships between gang members and the neighborhoods they live in. The lack of safe public spaces has had major implications for young people, from obesity to crime rates. As one youth said, "You meet more friends here [than by] having nothing better to do and getting in trouble."

—*Sean Thomas-Breitfeld*

Curitiba pioneered an innovative bus rapid-transit system that prevented traffic from overwhelming the fast-growing city. Portland put curbs on suburban sprawl and transformed a ho-hum downtown into a bustling urban magnet, starting by demolishing a parking garage to build a town square. New York City is making bold strides to improve its public realm by opening up swaths of Times Square and Broadway as pedestrian space.

However, Gehl points to Barcelona as the best example of the power of public spaces. Once thought of as a dull industrial city, it is now mentioned in the same breath as Paris and Rome as an epitome of a great European city. The heart of Barcelona and of its revival is Las Ramblas, a pedestrian promenade so popular it has spawned a new Spanish word: *ramblistas*, meaning the folks who hang out in the area. In the spirit of liberation following the end of the

Franco dictatorship—when public assembly was severely discouraged—local citizens and officials created new squares and public spaces all across the city and suburbs to celebrate the return of democracy and heal the scars of political and civic repression. Some of them fit so well with the urban fabric of the old city that visitors often assume they are centuries old.

A Struggle to Keep Public Space Open to the Public

Matthew Blackett, one of the guiding lights behind Toronto's *Spacing* (one of the few local magazines in the world devoted to public space), became interested in public-space issues in a highly unusual way: he was tear-gased. It was at an antiglobalization rally in Quebec City where protesters were beaten back by police. "That galvanized me. I saw how the powers that be operate," Blackett remembers. "And it made me wonder: whose space is public space? How could they force us out of what was supposed to be public property?"

Blackett soon fell in with the Toronto Public Space Committee, which was formed in response to the city council's plans to ban people from hanging posters on all but a few lampposts and telephone poles around town. "At the same time they were trying to curtail community expression, notices about yard sales and music shows," Blackett notes, "they wanted to approve huge video billboards, which even city staff said cause traffic accidents."

The newly formed group won the fight against the poster ban and has broadened its focus to a whole range of issues: better transit, pedestrian rights, bike transportation, and homelessness, as well as the over-commercialization of public places. They emphasize positive solutions rather than just carping about what's wrong.

Blackett sees mobile phones, instant messaging, and wireless Internet as a boost to people's use and enjoyment of public spaces. Indeed, he believes they are sparking an evolution in our use of public places. Throughout the twentieth century technological innovations—telephones, radios, record players, televisions, VCRs, and computers—fueled a retreat from public places into our homes and cars. But new technology makes it increasingly simple to be plugged into the world while still enjoying ourselves in a park, café, or walking down the street. Blackett also sees passionate interest about public-space issues among younger people. More than previous generations, they seem conscious of the need to defend their favorite public spaces against encroachment from traffic, advertisers, unwanted development, and overblown security measures.

The Commons Comes to the Mall

If the idea of vital public spaces strikes you as a narrowly urban phenomenon, consider the Crossroads Mall in Bellevue, Washington. A standard-issue postwar suburb east of Seattle, Bellevue seems way off the radar as a place to promote lively public spaces. Especially Crossroads, a seventies-era enclosed mall surrounded by acres of parking a mile south of Microsoft's sprawling campus.

But look again. Whimsical public art dots the parking lot, a farmers' market is held weekly, and café tables flank the entrances—just like a classic downtown. An impressively well-stocked newsstand greets you in the hall of the main entrance, right next to a used-book store. Wandering through the mall, you find the local public library, a police station, and a branch of city hall. There are even comfy chairs stationed right outside the bathrooms and a giant-size chessboard where kids can push around pawns and bishops almost as big as they are. Some of the usual franchise stores are here, but you'll also find locally owned businesses, like a French bakery and the one-of-a-kind Common Folk Co. housewares store. The food court—where you can choose among Indian, Russian, Thai, Mexican, Japanese, Greek, barbecue, Vietnamese, Italian, a juice bar, or a burger joint—features local restaurateurs.

Many of the tables face a stage, where on this particular Thursday, Black History Month is being observed with an impressive program of music, theater, and dance—all of it first-rate. The audience is multi-ethnic, reflecting the changing demographics of American suburbia. The loudest applause comes from a delegation of preschoolers visiting from a nearby day-care center.

Ron Sher, who transformed Crossroads from a failing shopping center into a spirited gathering place, outlines the next phase of his vision. "I want a mix of upscale and affordable housing built on a part of the parking lot, so this could become a true town square that some people walk to. I want to get people together with the city to discuss how to step this up to be even more of a community center."

A number of shopping malls around the country invoke commons in their names as part of a PR effort to project a whiff of community spirit into what are essentially privatized bubbles wholly devoted to shopping. But Crossroads is one mall that truly resembles a commons, even if it is technically private property.

Now, of course, I would prefer to hang out in Copenhagen, or Barcelona, or the famous Pike Place market in downtown Seattle. So would many of the people in Bellevue. But the fact is, they live in Bellevue, and it's a great thing that they have a mall where they can take care of their errands, meet their neighbors, and have some fun. If a lively sense of public space and the commons can take root in a suburban mall, it can happen anywhere.

> **Public spaces are the only place where the rich and the poor meet on equal footing.**
>
> —Enrique Peñalosa

—*Jay Walljasper*

Roses Grow in Spanish Harlem

New York's guerrilla gardeners restore nature in the heart of the city

New York City today is dotted with beautiful community gardens that citizens created out of trash-filled vacant lots. These gardens sprouted in places that had become commons because the private real estate market wrote them off as worthless. In the 1980s, a group of self-styled "green guerrillas" began to take over the sites. "We cut fences open with wire cutters," said Tom Fox, an early activist. Soon, the City of New York began to formally allow residents to use the sites as community gardens, with the understanding that the property might eventually be sold.

More than 800 community gardens sprang up throughout the five boroughs, and, with them, an economic and social revival of the neighborhoods. "Ten years ago, this community had gone to ashes," said community advocate Astin Jacobo. "But now there is a return to green." Perhaps most important, the gardens gave neighborhood residents a chance to govern a segment of their lives. These spots became commons in every sense of the word.

The greenery and social vitality of these gardens boosted the fortunes of the surrounding neighborhoods, which ironically alerted the city to the growing economic value of the sites. When he was mayor, Rudy Giuliani proposed auctioning 115 of the gardens to raise $3.5 to $10 million. For city officials, the sites were little more than abandoned lots—underutilized sources of tax revenue that should be sold to private investors to boost the city's finances.

The mayor's plan ignited an uproar, as hundreds of neighbors demonstrated in numerous attempts to save the gardens. Determined to eke maximum revenue from the sites, the city rejected an offer by the Trust for Public Land (TPL) to buy 112 contested garden lots for $2 million. Then, one day before a planned auction of the sites, actress Bette Midler donated $1 million to help the TPL and other organizations negotiate a purchase of the lots for $3 million. Today, they thrive as green and lovely urban commons, giving hundreds of thousands of apartment dwellers a nearby patch of nature to enjoy and a place to gather.

—*David Bollier*

Can Private Property Be a Commons?

Often a place belongs to all of us even when it's owned by someone else

THE CULTURAL AND CIVIC LIFE OF A community is boosted by privately owned businesses such as coffee shops, corner taverns, bookstores, bowling alleys, union halls, places of worship, diners, beauty salons, and many other hangouts. Although privately operated, such establishments can function as a commons just as much as parks and community centers do.

More significant than whether a place is privately owned is whether it is *locally* owned. Out-of-town chains have no stake in boosting the overall social life of a community and so they rarely make the extra effort to become a hangout. Check out the local events bulletin board (if there is one) at Starbucks or McDonald's compared to ones at a homegrown coffee shop or diner. The walls and windows at the local joint will likely be overflowing with posters for art shows, handbills for concerts, notices

A sense of community is the most valuable product offered by many local businesses.

offering babysitting, and leaflets for other good causes. Not so at the chain.

But we can't take these important community hangouts for granted. Look at record shops, some of which are famously funky treasures where you can while away the afternoon rubbing shoulders with local musicians and receiving an unequaled edu-

cation from legendarily well-informed sales clerks. (Remember the movie *High Fidelity*?) According to the *New York Times*, 3,100 record stores around the United States closed between 2003 and 2008. And these weren't all boring chain stores at the mall; at least half were independents. But happily, the *Times* reports that some record stores are finding new ways to stay afloat, such as branching out into used CDs, vinyl, and hosting live performances.

Intense competition from national chains and online merchants is picking off many other kinds of local shops, too. Imagine what your community would feel like without that favorite local bookshop, coffeehouse, hardware store, or tavern. You'd still be able to buy novels, espresso, tools, and beer, but you might not meet your neighbors or know what's going on in the community.

Keep that in mind the next time you're ready to order online out of convenience or drive to the big box to save a few dimes. Local businesses are a commons, perhaps not in the precise definition of something that we own together but certainly in the spirit of something that enriches our lives. We'd be much poorer without them.

—*Jay Walljasper*

A Latin American Mayor
Makes Happiness
a Civic Cause

Rich and poor should both have access to life's pleasures

HAPPINESS ITSELF IS A COMMONS TO which everyone should have equal access.

That's the view of Enrique Peñalosa, who is not a starry-eyed idealist given to abstract theorizing. He's actually a politician who served as mayor of Bogotá, Colombia, and now travels the world consulting with urban leaders.

Peñalosa's ideas stand as a beacon of hope for cities of the developing world, which even with their poverty and immense problems will absorb much of the world's population growth over the next half century. Based on his experiences in Bogotá, Peñalosa believes it's a mistake to give up on these cities as good places to live.

"If we in the Third World measure our success or failure as a society in terms of income, we would have to classify ourselves as losers until the end of time," declares Peñalosa. "With our limited resources, we have to invent other ways to measure success. This might mean that all kids have access to sports facilities, libraries, parks, schools, nurseries."

Peñalosa uses phrases like "quality of life" or "social justice" rather than "commons" to describe his agenda of offering poor people first-rate government services and pleasant public places, yet it is hard to think of anyone who has done more to reinvigorate the commons in his or her own community.

Transforming Bogotá

In three years (1998–2001) as mayor of Colombia's capital city of 7 million, Peñalosa's administration accomplished the following:

+ Led a team that created the Trans-Milenio, a bus rapid transit (BRT) system, which now carries a half million passengers daily on special bus lanes that offer most of the advantages of a subway at a fraction of the cost.
+ Built 52 new schools, refurbished 150 others, and increased student enrollment by 34 percent.

- Established or improved 1,200 parks and playgrounds throughout the city.
- Built three central and ten neighborhood libraries.
- Built one hundred nurseries for children under five.
- Improved life in the slums by providing water service to 100 percent of Bogotá households.
- Bought undeveloped land on the outskirts of the city to prevent real estate speculation, ensuring it would be developed as affordable housing with electrical, sewage, and telephone service as well as space reserved for parks, schools, and greenways.
- Established 300 kilometers of separated bikeways, the largest network in the developing world.
- Created the world's longest pedestrian street, 17 kilometers (10.5 miles) crossing much of the city, as well as a 45-kilometer (28-mile) greenway along a route originally slated for an eight-lane highway.
- Reduced traffic by almost 40 percent by implementing a system under which motorists must leave cars at home during rush hour two days a week.
- Inaugurated an annual car-free day, when everyone from CEOs to janitors commutes to work in some way other than a private automobile.
- Planted a hundred thousand trees.

All together, these accomplishments boosted the common good in a city characterized by vast disparities of wealth. David Burwell—director of the energy and climate program at the Carnegie Endowment for Peace, who has long experience working on environmental and transportation issues—calls Peñalosa "one of the great public servants of our time. He views cities as being planned for a purpose—to create human well-being. He's got a great sense of what a leader should do—to promote human happiness."

Peñalosa of course didn't do this alone. Antanas Mockus, who both preceded and succeeded him as mayor, and Gil Peñalosa, Enrique's brother, who served as parks commissioner under Mockus, are among the many who deserve credit. Peñalosa ran again for mayor in 2008 (mayors can serve only one consecutive term), losing, according to some observers, because a leftist opponent also embraced his commons-style agenda.

Quality of Life Equals Common Wealth

Enrique Peñalosa has become an international star of sorts among green urban designers, so many assume he was trained as a city planner and inspired by long involvement in the environmental movement. But the truth is that he arrived at these ideas from a completely different direction. "My focus has always been social—how you can help the most people for the greater public good."

Growing up in the 1960s, when revolutionary fervor swept South America,

Peñalosa became an ardent socialist at a young age, advocating income redistribution as the solution to social ills. He studied economics and history at Duke University in the United States, which he attended on a soccer scholarship, and later moved to Paris to earn a doctoral degree in management and public administration. Paris was a marvelous education in the possibilities of urban living, and he returned home with aspirations of bringing European-style city comforts to the working class of Bogotá. Several years working in the business world moderated his ideological views but not, he is quick to point out, his quest for social justice.

"We live in the postcommunism period, in which many have assumed equality as a social goal is obsolete," he explains. "Although income equality as a concept does not jibe with the market economy, we can seek to achieve quality-of-life equality."

Taming the Auto

Peñalosa is proud of how his administration tamed the automobile in Bogotá in order to meet the needs of those who do not own cars. Nearly all cities around the globe accommodate motorists at the expense of everyone else. In the developing world, where only a select portion of people own motor vehicles, this is particularly unfair.

In Bogotá, Peñalosa used both carrots and sticks to reclaim the streets for everyone. The sticks—driving bans during rush hour and enforcement of long-ignored laws prohibiting parking on the sidewalks—drew howls of outrage. "I was almost impeached by the car-owning upper classes," Peñalosa recalls, "but it was popular with everyone else."

The carrots, however, were popular with everyone. The pedestrian streets, greenways, and bike trails he created are well used by commuters, recreational bikers, and walkers out enjoying the Latin custom of a paseo—an evening stroll.

Another hit is the Ciclovía, in which as many as 2 million people (30 percent of the city's population) take over 120 kilometers of major streets between 7 A.M. and 2 P.M. every Sunday for bike rides, walks, and public events. This weekly event began in 1976 but was expanded by Peñalosa. It now has spread to many Latin American cities as well as San Francisco, El Paso, and Las Cruces, New Mexico; it is being explored for Chicago, New York, Portland, and Melbourne, Australia.

Peñalosa's proudest achievement is TransMilenio, the BRT system that enables buses to zoom on special lanes that make mass transit faster and more convenient than driving. There are now nine TransMilenio routes crisscrossing Bogotá. Oscar Edmundo Diaz, senior program director for the Institute for Transportation and Development Policy (ITDP), who was Peñalosa's chief mayoral aide, proudly notes that even wealthy people who own cars are now enthusiastic users of the BRT. "You don't want to build a transit system just for the poor," Diaz counsels. "Otherwise it will be stigmatized, and even poor people will look down on it. If everyone uses it, it will help the poor more."

Public Passion

"Economics, urban planning, ecology are only the means. Happiness is the goal," Peñalosa says, summing up his work. "We have a word in Spanish, *ganas*, which means 'a burning desire.' I have *ganas* about public life.

"The least a democratic society should do," he continues, "is to offer people wonderful public spaces. Public spaces are not a frivolity. They are just as important as hospitals and schools. They create a sense of belonging. This creates a different type of society—a society where people of all income levels meet in public space is a more integrated, socially healthier one."

—*Jay Walljasper*

Minnie Fells Johnson

A public official who brought new life to downtown Dayton

Just a few years ago, the center of Dayton, Ohio, resembled a ghost town. Go there today, however, and you'll see a downtown full of life. A new transit hub, Wright Stop Plaza, serves as a town commons, with businessmen on their way to work grabbing coffee next to kids waiting for a bus to school. People gather for events at RiverScape, a new waterfront park that offers pedestrian access to the Great Miami River. A performing arts center attracts everyone from opera buffs to stand-up comedy fans. And crowds cheer wildly at the Dayton Dragons' baseball games.

These destinations, which have brought the Dayton community together in unexpected ways, all have one thing in common: they were made possible by Dr. Minnie Fells Johnson's pioneering work with the Greater Dayton Regional Transit Authority (RTA).

As head of the public transit agency, she championed the unorthodox idea that public transportation should do more than move people from place to place; it should create lively places—commons—where people can connect with each other. She has accomplished

As head of a public transit agency, Johnson saw her job as more than running buses.

this by greatly expanding the role of the RTA beyond that of a simple bus operator. The agency has become what Johnson calls "a connecting machine"—linking people to local institutions by creating attractive public spaces along transit routes.

"The idea has to be rooted in the interest of the larger community," Johnson says. "We never did anything that was out of step with what people said were their dreams."

Johnson has pursued social change since the 1960s, when, as a member of the Student Nonviolent Coordinating Committee, she participated in the Freedom Rides and sit-ins that confronted racial segregation. After retiring from the Greater Dayton Regional Transportation Authority after fifteen years in 2005, she became the board chair of Project for Public Spaces, a leading nonprofit organization in the field of revitalizing communities.

—Ben Fried

Reverend Tracey Lind

Nourishing the spirit of the commons in Cleveland

There is a profound spiritual dimension to the commons, notes Reverend Tracey Lind, dean of Trinity Episcopal Cathedral in Cleveland. Indeed, one of the most enduring forms of commons in the world today are the sacred places that play an essential part in all religions: temples, shrines, ritual sites, burial grounds, pilgrimage paths, holy springs, holy forests, holy mountains.

The religious nature of these places means they are generally open to everyone for prayer, ceremonies, and socializing. For example, Lind points out, "The famous Gothic cathedral of Chartres did not belong to just priests and bishops. It was a part of the whole community. Even today everyone in town can claim it as theirs and feel proud of it.

"What would happen if we made all houses of worship in this country into commons?" asks Lind, who trained as a city planner. She answered that question with Trinity Commons—the most ambitious new development in decades for the inner-city neighborhood where her church is located. She has brought a coffee shop, independent bookstore, Ten Thousand Villages fair-trade store, art gallery, labyrinth, and public square to the grounds of Trinity Cathedral. Anyone can come to browse, relax with a cup of

Lind transformed church grounds into a neighborhood plaza.

coffee, pray, reflect, read, check their e-mail on the cathedral's Wi-Fi system, or take part in one of the many events—religious and secular—that go on at the church. "Last year we had eighty thousand people come here for public events," Lind proudly notes.

—Jay Walljasper

Take Back the Streets

Once used by all, roads are now the exclusive domain of cars. But citizens everywhere are fighting to change that

THERE IS AN IMPORTANT COMMONS right under our noses that people seldom recognize: the street. For centuries, roads and streets served as a pathway for all forms of transportation: carriages, wagons, streetcars, bicycles, and, most of all, pedestrians. It's where children played, dogs slept, teens flirted, and adults gossiped.

During the twentieth century, streets were seized for the exclusive uses of motor vehicles—a dramatic shift in human civilization that's changed the fabric of people's daily lives all over the world. Even though laws in most countries, including the United States, grant pedestrians and bicyclists the same right to use city streets as motorists, that's not how it plays out. Here's how reporter Frank Tatu describes street life in Bangkok: "Crossing a thoroughfare is generally a life-threatening undertaking. . . . For the most part, pedestrians stand on street corners, with intense and strained faces, gauging the traffic and darting between lanes when the flow temporarily wanes."

Similar scenes occur everywhere. You're in the crosswalk, a short way into the street, and the DON'T WALK sign starts flashing.

You freeze. Back to the curb or hurry to the other side? A car horn blares. An impatient driver making a turn is headed right at you. You jump out of the way, but there's another car whipping around the corner at full throttle. Darting back to the sidewalk, you take a deep breath, thankful to be alive.

"We are in danger of losing a basic human right," says Michael Replogle, transportation policy director at the Environmental Defense Fund, "the right to walk in your own neighborhood."

Walter Hook, executive director of the Institute for Trade and Development Policy, notes that this is not merely a personal and environmental issue, but a question of social justice. "Remember that owning a car is out of reach for all but the upper 20 percent of people in the developing world," he says. When automobiles come to dominate a nation's streets, nonmotorists—even if they comprise an overwhelming majority of the population—suffer in terms of both mobility and safety. Hook notes that more than 50 percent of road fatalities in some developing nations are pedestrians.

Andy Singer

Who Stole Our Streets?

The chief culprits for this sorrowful situation are several generations of transportation planners, who built highways and revamped city streets to slavishly accommodate the growing rush of vehicles. The speed of traffic, more than the volume, is responsible for making streets into danger zones for humans. A comprehensive study by the U.K. government (translated from metric to mph) showed that at 20 mph, only 5 percent of vehicle-

Detroit's Surprise

A town common springs up in an unlikely place

Back in the 1970s, in the wake of devastating riots, Detroit tried to revive its downtown through a high-rise corporate complex called Renaissance Center. The Ren Cen was built as a walled fortress, and downtown continued to decline. Then in the late 1990s, a civic group in Detroit proposed the opposite approach: namely, an inviting public space. The result was Campus Martius, which expanded what was essentially a concrete traffic island into a small but lively public square. This was accomplished through what before had been unthinkable in the Motor City, displacing cars to make room for people.

People now flock to Campus Martius to hear music, go ice skating, admire the floral displays, watch outdoor movies, splash their hands in the fountain, meet a date at the café, or just relax and watch the passing scene. The place is drawing suburban residents back into the city for an agreeably urban experience not available near their homes. Investment is coming too—over half a billion dollars' worth and growing. The Compuware computer firm, for example, moved its offices and four thousand employees from the suburbs to a new site near the square.

—Jonathan Rowe

pedestrian collisions result in a fatality, but at 40 mph, 85 percent claim a pedestrian's life. Sixty years of traffic "improvements" on America's streets have rendered wide stretches of the country hostile to pedestrians. We now depend on cars to accomplish the simplest human acts—going to school, visiting friends, getting groceries. People drive today even to take a walk, because the streets around their homes feel inhospitable.

Children, old people, and the disabled are the biggest losers, because they usually don't drive and therefore live under a form of house arrest, depending on someone else to chauffeur them everywhere. But we all feel the effects. With fewer places to safely and pleasurably walk, we miss out on the world's simplest and most satisfying form of exercise. Our communities feel less neighborly. Social alienation and fear of street crime loom large in our lives.

The commons was sacrificed in countless ways to achieve this auto-cratic dream of speed, privacy, and convenience. Untold billions of dollars of public money were spent to enshrine the private car as essential to modern living. Public transportation systems were starved to feed the frenzy of road building, and since World War II our communities have been designed as if bicyclists and pedestrians don't exist. The air was polluted, the climate altered, land-

Make Paradise, Take Over a Parking Space

A grassroots movement converts parking into parks

A huge portion of American cities and suburbs is reserved solely for parked cars. Yet the land occupied by on-street parking actually belongs to all of us, and some of it could be used to bring some much-needed public space to our communities.

That's the idea behind PARK(ing) Day celebrated in a growing number of cities. In San Francisco people plug the parking meters, set out potted plants, and sit back to enjoy a day in their makeshift paradise. In Minneapolis, folks roll out turf and fire up the grills to cook bratwurst.

It all started in 2005, when the San Francisco–based art and activist studio Rebar decided to draw attention to the fact that 70 percent of outdoor space in downtown San Francisco was for the exclusive use of vehicles, not people.

"The hope is that the unusual sight of a parking spot transformed into a small public park will lead people to question how public space is allocated between cars and people," noted Streetsblog editor Ben Fried. Now, the idea has spread as far as Trapani, Italy.

Some permanent public space is sprouting in places once ruled by Fords and Toyotas. In addition to New York's well-publicized new public squares carved out of parking and traffic lanes along Broadway, San Francisco launched a Pavements to Parks program in 2009 that returned sections of the streets in three neighborhoods back to the people. It is now being expanded.

—Jay Walljasper

scapes paved over, neighborhoods ripped apart, and the very nature of our social connections turned upside down. Our public life precipitously declined as people began to move about town isolated behind their windshields. It's hard to make friends when your only interaction is honking at one another as you drive past.

• • •

But happily, after decades of second-class citizenship on the streets, North Americans are following the lead of Europeans and some Latin Americans by asserting their right to travel on foot or bike.

In Atlanta, a public rally marked the fiftieth anniversary of the killing of *Gone with the Wind* author Margaret Mitchell by a speeding taxi driver. In Boston, protests

Our Right to Street Life

forced city officials to abandon plans for a ten-lane highway to be built atop the Big Dig project in favor of a landscaped four-lane boulevard. Californians are busy mapping safe ways for kids all over the state to walk to school.

Bicycle use is on the rise in most cities, with two-wheelers now accounting for 17 percent of all commuter traffic in Davis, California, and 15 percent in Boulder, Colorado. Even in outlying suburbs, easy access to walking and bike paths has become the latest status symbol. In New York, the city has opened up sections of Times Square and Broadway as pedestrian-only zones with great success.

A key tool citizens use to reclaim their streets is traffic calming, an elegantly simple idea now being applied everywhere around the world to reinforce the message to motorists that streets are not their private property. Proven ways of doing this include narrowing traffic lanes, widening sidewalks, adding bikeways, rebuilding streets with gentle curves, painting pedestrian crossings, extending sidewalks a few feet into intersections, closing streets to traffic, installing speed bumps (also known as "sleeping policemen"), restricting right turns on red lights, and replacing stoplights with four-way stop signs. A number of cities in the Netherlands and elsewhere are dispensing with traffic controls altogether, a counter-intuitive but surprisingly effective idea that slows vehicle traffic by making drivers negotiate right-of-way with walkers and bikers.

Opponents of traffic calming complain that these measures simply increase traffic somewhere else. But numerous studies have shown that traffic is not a zero-sum game. When Greenwich Village's Washington Square Park was closed to traffic in the 1960s, traffic engineering studies showed that vehicle use on nearby streets decreased. Transportation officials in Nuremberg, Germany, documented the same phenomenon decades later when they closed a major street. Traffic often evaporates as people drive less often.

Many see traffic calming as more than just a way to promote safer streets. "Traffic calming involves a revised emphasis on quality rather than quantity of life. Some may even see the ultimate goal as the calming of society itself," says Australian urban planner Phil Day.

—*Jay Walljasper*

Everything I Need to Know
I Learned at the Library

Reflections from a lifetime spent in the stacks

WITH INFORMATION PLENTIFUL ONLINE and well-stocked big-box bookstores complete with children's story hours, who needs libraries anymore? Aren't they relics of a pleasant but no longer useful past, just like telephone booths?

Not at all. First, a surprising number of North Americans—not to mention billions of people in the developing world—don't have convenient access to the Internet, nor the budget to purchase every book that happens to interest them or their children.

The truth is: libraries are packed these days. New York, Los Angeles, and many library systems in between set all-time user records last year, as people flocked there to research jobs, use the Internet, and simply have someplace to go that costs no money. In San Francisco, attendance at story hours was up a whopping 43 percent. In St. Paul, Minnesota, and its suburbs, computer usage climbed 38 percent while use of the libraries' free wireless networks jumped 61 percent and attendance at computer classes increased 24 percent.

In many communities, this rise in library use began before the economy sank. Circu-

lation figures at Minneapolis's public libraries jumped 37 percent from 2000 to 2008. And the library system in surrounding suburbs saw a 23 percent rise in circulation during the same period.

The Power of Serendipity and Spontaneous Encounters

I myself would seem to be a prime example of a person who no longer needs the library. With a high-speed Internet line at home and a huge personal library thanks to many years of work as a book reviewer, why would I bother going to the library? Well, here's why. I go there to do research—the Internet doesn't have all you need to know. And, of course, it doesn't have librarians, who in my experience know everything and are remarkably generous in sharing it.

I also go to the library to find out what's going on (thanks to the most comprehensive bulletin board of events in the neighborhood) and the chance to run into my neighbors. Libraries stand as a prime example of

social capital, which more and more observers see as the secret sauce that makes the difference between a community that thrives and one that struggles. Just as monetary investments make things happen in the marketplace by capitalizing businesses, social capital makes things happen throughout society with investments of people's time and energy. Financial capital is measured in dollars, yen, and euros, while social capital is measured in civic organizations (the PTA, garden clubs, bowling teams, activist groups) and public institutions that bring people together (senior centers, youth centers, sports leagues, libraries).

Libraries in many towns are where people make informal connections as well as gather for specific purposes. For instance, the Iowa City Public Library hosts three thousand citizens' meetings a year—that's more than ten a day in a city of 67,000.

My Debt of Gratitude to the Librarians of Linden Hills

I credit libraries, and one library in particular, with boosting my journalism career. The longest sustained period of hanging out in libraries in my life was not in college but during the years I was editor of *Utne Reader*. I joined the now nationally recognized magazine in its infant days when a staff of four was crammed into a tiny office where every phone conversation become a communal experience. And don't ask about the bathroom, barely concealed behind a folding partition right next to my desk. Editing and writing articles was almost impossible in such close quarters, so I fled for hours each day to the nearby Linden Hills branch of the Minneapolis Public Library. That became my other "office," and for years I edited nearly every word in the magazine right there, cheered on by a distinguished crowd of investigative reporters, essayists, novelists, and other authors sitting on the shelves all around me.

I owe a huge debt of gratitude to Linden Hills Library and its knowledgeable and accommodating staff. It was a proud moment for me to be asked to speak at a neighborhood celebration of the library's sixtieth anniversary.

But at one point it looked as if the library would never see seventy. A budget crisis, brought on in part by cuts in state aid, threatened to swamp the Minneapolis library system. The lovely, popular Linden Hills Library ended up on a list of those to be shut down. An outpouring of community support saved it, but three other libraries, despite similar outpourings of support in their communities, were closed. And they remained closed for several years. All local libraries have seen their hours cut, and they are locked up tight on Sundays when many

The Little Library That Could

Frankfort, Indiana, boasts a community resource center dedicated to the idea that life is a work of art

In Frankfort, Indiana, a town of sixteen thousand between Chicago and Indianapolis, the public library has established itself as the focal point of community life by offering a range of activities emphasizing art, performance, and creativity. Library director Bill Caddell cites the life and work of Kentucky artist Harlan Hubbard as the inspiration for the library's mission. Hubbard ditched consumer culture, living simply with his wife, Anna, in a house on the banks of the Ohio River and aspiring to "make life a work of art."

The library followed Hubbard's example by responding to requests from local residents for lessons in everything from bread baking to belly dancing. As Caddell recalls, "We had so many classes that we ran out of room." So in 1988 it established the Hubbard School of Living—a new wing of the library that includes galleries, studios, and a two-hundred-seat theater. It is indeed a living work of art.

—*Cynthia Nikitin & Josh S. Jackson*

Mark Lakeman

Every neighborhood needs its own piazza

Returning home from world travels enchanted by the bustling public squares he saw in Europe, North Africa, and Central America, architect Mark Lakeman was fired up about the idea that all neighborhoods need their own piazzas—small squares found in traditional Italian towns. Often little more than a wide stretch in the street, the piazza exerts a magical quality in attracting people of all ages and incomes to come together and enjoy each other's company.

But how could something like that be created in his own largely blue-collar neighborhood in Portland, Oregon, without tearing down someone's house or radically redesigning existing streets? Lakeman and some neighbors put their heads together, coming up with a bold plan for the intersection of Southeast Ninth Avenue and Sherritt Street.

They began by setting up a portable teahouse, which drew dozens of people out of their homes on Monday nights to mingle. The next step was to paint the intersection in vivid colors, sending a clear message to passing motorists that this was not your ordinary corner. As social activity began to move out into the street, drivers and pedestrians instinctively learned to share the space, thus the intersection became known as Share-It Square.

But what did the neighbors think? Challenging the dominance of automobiles on American

Lakeman works with communities across North America to revive street life.

streets is a brazen act, especially to older people who came of age in the car-crazy 1950s. Lakeman worried about angry opposition arising to quash the experiment, until he talked with Brian Shaw, who lived right at the corner.

"Brian said that his father had fought in Italy during World War II and would tell stories about how when they liberated a village, everyone would automatically gather in the piazzas to celebrate," Lakeman recalls. "He said his dad always used to sing an Italian song with lyrics

(continued on page 152)

Mark Lakeman *(continued from page 151)*

saying, 'If you don't hear voices in the piazza when you wake up in the morning, then you know something is wrong.'

"Something is wrong with too many places in America today," Lakeman adds.

Projects similar to Share-It Square are popping up at dozens of Portland intersections. Lakeman and his collaborators went on to found City Repair, a nonprofit organization promoting a whole host of initiatives to help communities create new public spaces. And these ideas are spreading across the continent, with new "piazzas" sprouting in at least fifteen cities from San Diego to Rochester, Minnesota, to Toronto. Lakeman is now planning to take the idea of "block repair" global with his design firm Communitecture and with the launch of a new initiative to be called Planet Repair.

—*Jay Walljasper*

working families have the most free time to visit.

In this era of continuing budget crisis and "no new taxes," numerous libraries around the country face reduced hours or being closed altogether. What a tragic loss. Some kids will miss out on the chance to learn as much as they want about the world. People will be denied information that could change their lives. And, saddest of all, those communities lose an important common ground where people cross paths.

—*Jay Walljasper*

Chapter 8

Our Planet, Ourselves

Commonskeepers

Robert F. Kennedy Jr. describes how local citizens clean up rivers, bays, and lakes

ENVIRONMENTAL INJURY IS AN ATTACK against a basic human right, and the injury always lands hardest on the backs of the poor. Four out of every five toxic waste dump sites in America are in a black neighborhood. The nation's largest toxic waste dump is in Emelle, Alabama, where 90 percent of the residents are black. The highest concentration of toxic waste dumps in America is on the South Side of Chicago. The most contaminated zip code in California is heavily Latino East Los Angeles. Why? Because polluting industries go where they can most easily dominate the local political landscape.

Public trust assets—or commons—are those resources that are not readily reduced to private property and by their nature belong to the community. They include oceans, lakes, flowing rivers, aquifers, fisheries, wandering wildlife, parks, and public spaces. All are held in trust by the government for the people. They help define us as a community; they underpin our economy and culture and are the source of economic vitality. The first sign of tyranny is government's complicity in privatizing the com-

mons for private gain. Because the public trust is our community's life-support system, its theft is arguably the gravest threat to human rights.

The fundamental responsibility of government is to protect the commons on behalf of all the people. The best measure of how a democracy functions is how it distributes the goods of the land. Does it keep the public trust assets, the commons, in the hands of all the people, rich and poor alike, or does it allow them to be privatized and concentrated in the hands of a few wealthy or influential individuals?

The Waterkeeper Movement

This struggle for control of the commons defines the Waterkeeper movement. We recognize that we're not protecting these waterways for nature, the fishes, or the birds. We protect them because we understand that nature is the infrastructure of our communities. If we want to meet our obligation as a generation, a nation, and a

Residents of blue-collar towns along the Hudson River founded the organization Riverkeeper to revive the once-filthy waterway.

civilization to provide our children with the same opportunities for dignity and enrichment as our parents gave us, we must start by protecting our infrastructure: the air we breathe, the water we drink, the wildlife, the public lands—all of which enrich us and connect us to our history, provide context to our communities, and ultimately are the source of our values, our virtues, and our character as a people.

For those of you who are not familiar with the Waterkeeper movement, let me tell you a little bit of history. Hudson Riverkeeper was established in 1966 by blue-collar commercial and recreational fishermen who mobilized to reclaim the Hudson River from polluters. The Hudson is home to a 350-year-old commercial fish-

ery, one of the oldest in North America. Many of our members come from families that have been fishing the Hudson continuously since Dutch colonial times. They use the same traditional methods taught by Algonquin Indians to the original Dutch settlers of New Amsterdam and then passed down through the generations.

Blue-Collar Greens

One of the enclaves of the Hudson's commercial fishing is Crotonville, New York, a little village thirty miles north of New York City on the east bank of the river. Crotonville's residents were not prototypical affluent environmentalists; they were factory workers, carpenters, laborers, and electricians. Many made their living, or at least some part of it, fishing or crabbing the Hudson. Most had little expectation that they would ever see Yellowstone or Yosemite or the Everglades. For them, the environment was their backyard—the bathing beaches and the swimming and fishing holes of the Hudson River.

Richie Garrett, the first president of Riverkeeper, used to say about the Hudson, "It's our Riviera, it's our Monte Carlo." Richie Garrett was a gravedigger from Ossining, New York. He often told his followers, "I'll be the last to let you down."

In 1966, Penn Central railroad began vomiting oil from a four-and-a-half-foot pipe in the Croton-Harmon railyard. The oil blackened the beaches and made the shad fish taste of diesel, leaving them unsalable at New York City's fish market. In response, the people of Crotonville gathered in the only public building in the town, the Parker-Bale American Legion Hall. This was a very patriotic community; Crotonville had the highest mortality rate of any community in America in World War II. Like Richie Garrett, a Korean War vet, almost all the original founders, board members, and officers of Hudson Riverkeeper were ex-marines. These were not radicals or militants; their patriotism was rooted in the bedrock of our country.

> **The best measure of how a democracy functions is how it distributes the goods of the land.**
>
> —Robert F. Kennedy Jr.

But that night they started talking about violence. They saw something that they thought they owned—the abundance of the Hudson's fisheries that their ancestors had used for generations and the purity of its waters—being robbed from them by corporate entities over which they had no control. They had been to the government agencies that are supposed to protect Americans from pollution: the Corps of Engineers, the state Conservation Department, and the Coast Guard. And they were given the bum's rush.

Richie Garrett and a pilot named Art Glowka paid some twenty visits to an Army Corps of Engineers colonel in Manhattan, begging him to do his job and shut down that Penn Central pipe. Finally, the colonel told them in exasperation, "These [the Penn Central board of directors] are important people. We can't treat them this way." In other words, we can't force them to obey the law.

Bold Action to Protect Their Home

By March 18, 1966, virtually everybody in Crotonville had come to the conclusion that the government was in cahoots with the polluters. The only way they were going to reclaim the river was to confront the polluters directly. Somebody suggested that they

Rajendra Singh

Bringing rivers back to life in an arid region of India

Rajendra Singh, founder of Tarun Bharat Sangh (TBS, or Young India Association), always wanted to be a farmer. Bowing to family pressure, he studied to be a doctor of traditional Indian Ayurvedic medicine. After school, he moved to the Alwyn district in the arid state of Rajasthan. Singh was not just practicing medicine; he wanted to test some ideas about healing ecosystems.

Singh shows off a johad, a tiny reservoir that catches water in the rainy season to replenish the hydrological cycle.

The local Arvari River had dried up during the 1940s when the surrounding hills were stripped of trees. It flowed only during the monsoon season. Since that time, most people fled local villages to seek a livelihood elsewhere. When Singh arrived in 1985, he noticed that only the oldest and poorest residents were left in the area.

Drawing on indigenous Indian knowledge of geology, hydrology, and ecology, he began building tiny dams with *johads* (reservoirs) on streams flowing to the river in the hopes of reviving the natural water flow of surface and underground water in the region. The local elders chuckled as they watched him do back-breaking labor with very little results for two years. Only then, he remembers with a chuckle, did they decide he was sincere in trying to help them and begin offering tips on the right spots to place dams and *johads*.

It worked. The water captured in the *johads* during monsoon season slowly rejuvenated vegetation, which helped refill the aquifers from which people drew their drinking water and restore the water-retaining capacity of the hillsides.

The Arvari River came back to life and now runs all year, as do four other once dry rivers in the region. Groundwater levels have risen by an estimated twenty feet, and crucial forest cover, which helps to maintain the water-retaining capacity of the soil, has increased by 33 percent. People who abandoned the district are now moving back to farm and start businesses, Singh says.

(continued on page 158)

Rajendra Singh (continued from page 157)

In addition, the Young India Association challenges plans to privatize and deplete freshwater resources. In the Alwar area, where Singh began his work, activists have prevented forty water-intensive industrial companies (including bottled water and soft drink makers) from setting up factories.

Villagers are creating their own "river parliaments" to sustain the water commons. Each is governed by two leaders—one who is responsible to the community and one who is responsible solely to the water and nature.

"Water is a very emotional, spiritual thing," Singh explains, noting that the once lost river is now sacred again to local people. He says that many of the older residents now ask that when they die their ashes be sprinkled into the Arvari rather than the Ganges.

—*Adam Davidson-Harden*
& Jay Walljasper

put a match to the oil slick coming out of the Penn Central pipe. Somebody said they should jam a mattress up the pipe and flood the railyard with its own waste. Someone else suggested floating a raft of dynamite into the intake of the Indian Point Power Plant, which was sucking in and killing close to a million fish each day and taking food off their family's tables.

Then another ex-marine took the microphone. Bob Boyle was the outdoors editor of *Sports Illustrated* magazine. He was a world-famous angler and the author of several books on recreational fishing. Two years earlier, he had written an article for *Sports Illustrated* about angling in the Hudson. His research had brought him across a federal Navigation Statue called the Rivers and Harbors Act, a law from 1888 that made it illegal to pollute any waterway in the United States and provided for high

penalties. Surprisingly, the law included a bounty provision allowing anybody who turned in a polluter to keep half the fine. Boyle had sent a copy of the law over to the Time Inc. libel lawyers asking, "Is this still a good law?" They sent him back a memo saying, "It's never been enforced, but it's still on the books."

That evening, before three hundred men and women angered to the point of plotting violence, he held up a copy of that memo and said, "We shouldn't be talking about breaking the law, we should be talking about enforcing it." They resolved that evening that they were going to organize themselves as the Hudson River Fishermen's Association—which later became River-keeper—and that they were going to go out and track down and prosecute every polluter on the river.

Eighteen months later, they collected the

first bounty in United States history under the nineteenth-century statute. They shut down the Penn Central pipe. They used the money that was left over to go after Ciba-Geigy, Standard Brands, and American Cyanide, many of the biggest corporations in America. One after the other, they shut those polluters down. In 1973, they collected the highest penalty in United States history against a corporate polluter: $200,000 from Anaconda Wire and Cable for dumping toxics into the river in Hastings, New York. They used the bounty money to build a boat and hire a commercial fisherman, John Cronin, as the first full-time paid Riverkeeper. In 1984 John Cronin hired me using bounty money to be Riverkeeper's prosecuting attorney.

River Reborn

Since then we've brought four hundred successful lawsuits against environmental polluters on the Hudson, and we've forced polluters to spend almost $4 billon on remediation. The Hudson today is an international model for ecosystem protection. This river, a national joke in 1966, is today the richest body of water in the North Atlantic region. It produces more pounds of fish per acre and more biomass per gallon than any other waterway emptying into the Atlantic Ocean north of the equator. It's the only river system on both sides of the Atlantic that still has strong spawning stocks of all its historical species of migratory fish. The miraculous resurrection of the Hudson has inspired the creation of over 150 Waterkeepers—Riverkeepers, Baykeepers, Soundkeepers, and others—all across the country and around the world.

Waterkeeper Alliance issues licenses to use the Waterkeeper name after determining that a new program meets our strict standards. Each Waterkeeper has a patrol boat, they have a full-time paid Waterkeeper, and they sue polluters. They make sure nobody steals our water from our communities and that those waterways stay in the hands of the public, where they belong.

—*Robert F. Kennedy Jr.*

Water for All

*Activists around the planet proclaim
H$_2$O as our common property*

A FIERCE RESISTANCE TO THE ABUSE OF water and watersheds as well as to the corporate takeover of public water utilities is growing in all corners of the globe, giving rise to a new global movement. "Water for all" is the rallying cry of local groups in hundreds of communities around the world fighting to protect their water resources from pollution, destruction by dams, and outright theft from corporations.

These struggles for the basic right to water have galvanized a water justice movement that draws on the principles of the commons to articulate a new vision for the future. To the question, Who owns water? they answer, No one—it belongs to the earth, all species, and future generations. The goals of the movement (also known as the water commons movement) are simple but powerful: keep water public; keep it clean; keep it accessible to all.

This movement has already had an impact on global politics, forcing global institutions such as the World Bank and the United Nations to address the inadequacies of their water policies and helping formulate new policies in dozens of countries. New debates are now under way about control of water resources.

All over the world, the water commons is used as a dump site for our wastes. Ninety percent of the wastewater produced in the global South is discharged untreated into rivers, streams, and coastal waters. Seventy-five percent of India's and Russia's surface waters should not be used for drinking or bathing. The UN has reported unprecedented water quality deterioration in all of Africa's 677 major lakes and every one of its major rivers. Only about 2 percent of Latin America's wastewater receives any treatment at all.

The situation in the global North is better but not good. Twenty percent of all surface water in Europe is "seriously threatened," and 40 percent of U.S. rivers and streams are too degraded for swimming, fishing, or drinking, as are 46 percent of all lakes, due to massive toxic runoff from industrial farms. This unparalleled environmental crisis can be reversed only through the realization that water is a commons that belongs to everyone, and therefore harm to any water is harm to the whole—earth and humans alike. All over the world, communities are confronting the twin engines of water pollution: industrial agriculture and industrial production.

The move to local, sustainable agriculture is growing as people question the wisdom of dousing our vegetables and grains with chemicals and our meat animals with drugs, then shipping food thousands of miles to our dinner tables.

Groups are forming to fight the power of agribusiness and the water-guzzling practices of factory farms. Beyond Factory Farming, a Canadian network devoted to sustainable and humane farming, is working with local municipalities to establish regulations that would limit the amount of water available to large livestock operations.

Mining companies are also major culprits in the contamination of groundwater in the global South, but an emerging North-South network is challenging these compa-

nies. Activists in Canada and Chile teamed up to force Canadian mining company Barrick Gold to abandon a plan to remove the top of three glaciers on the Chile-Argentina border in order to get at the gold deposits underneath them. Massive amounts of glacier water that serves as the only source for seventy thousand farmers would have been destroyed.

From all over the world come stories of reclamation of polluted water. Europe's Lake Constance, once almost lost to phosphorus and other pollutants, has now recovered and provides drinking water to 4 million people. The recovery of Lake Constance was begun in 1954 by the three countries that surround the lake—Germany, Austria, and Switzerland—in a joint effort to save the third largest lake in Europe. Only by seeing the lake as common property, belonging to all, were the countries, local municipalities, and residents able to bring it back from ecological ruin.

Water is a life-giving resource to share—not a commodity to sell.

Waterkeepers, an alliance of 177 groups that began in North America, empowers local communities to protect their shared ecosystems. In the last several years, the Hudson Riverkeepers went to court to require power plants and industrial facilities to use closed-cycle cooling systems, stopping the disruption of aquatic species by thermal pollution. The Delaware Riverkeepers stopped army plans to dump by-products of deadly chemical weapons in the river. And the San Francisco Baykeepers forced the state of California to adopt a tough plan to slash mercury pollution in the bay.

While there is less money for pollution cleanups in the global South, success stories can still be found. In Colombia, sixteen large wetlands along the Bogotá River have been restored to pristine condition. This is the first step in cleaning up the contaminated river that supplies water for the 8 million people of Bogotá. True to principles of the commons, the indigenous peoples living on the wetland sites were not removed, but rather have become caretakers of these protected and sacred places.

Citizens (especially students) of many countries of the global South have become involved in the annual Clean Up the World Campaign. Held on the third weekend of September, it was started in 1993 by an Australian sailor upset about water pollution. It now involves more than 35 million people in 120 countries in an annual ritual of commons protection. The United Nations Environment Program has adopted Clean Up the World Day and now promotes it around the world.

Protecting Watersheds and Ecosystems

As a result of destroying so much of our water commons, we are quite literally running out of water. Right now, humans use more than half of the earth's accessible runoff water, leaving little for nature and other species. In the United States, industrial agriculture guzzles four fifths of the nation's total water use and is the leading source of pollutants in the country's rivers and lakes. In the global South, irrigation consumes more than 85 percent of total water use and is draining many rivers. As our demand for water grows, the strain on the earth and other living creatures accelerates. Humans have always assumed that we would never run out of water. But the truth is that less than one half of one percent of the world's water is available for our use without drawing down the water stock needed to replenish this cycle. We are depleting our water commons in six crucial ways:

Aquifer and Groundwater Mining. Sophisticated technology pumps groundwater far faster than it can be replenished by nature.

Virtual Water Exports. Export-oriented agricultural and trade policies mean that a large share of water is sent abroad in the form of food and other products.

Pipeline Diversions. We shift water from where nature provides it (and where it is needed for ecosystem health) to where we want it to grow food in deserts or serve massive urban areas.

Jesús León Santos

Transforming barren lands into green fields and forests

Mexico's food supply is undergoing a dramatic transformation: 40 percent of the nation's corn—a staple at dinner tables—is now being imported from the United States. The Mexican government meanwhile is pursuing agricultural policies designed to discourage small farmers in favor of large, industrialized operations. This holds huge repercussions for the environmental and economic balance of North America.

According to Octavio Rosas Landa, an economics professor at the Autonomous University of Mexico, current policies will drive 22 million of Mexico's 25 million peasants (40 percent of whom are indigenous people) off the land in the next few years, pushing many of them unwillingly to Mexican cities and the United States. When families who have farmed parcels of land for centuries depart the countryside, Mexico will lose irreplaceable local knowledge that could help solve its agricultural and environmental challenges.

You get a sense of what is being lost in Oaxaca province, where Jesús León Santos, a forty-four-year-old farmer of Mixtec Indian heritage, is leading efforts to transform barren landscapes into green fields and forests. (A UN study found 83 percent of the region is severely eroded.) His secret: reviving traditional Mixtec farming methods in order to restore local ecosystems. Working with an organization he founded called CEDICAM (in English, the Center for Integral Small Farmer Development in the Mixteca), León Santos is fighting rampant erosion by reintroducing trees, rainwater collection practices, contour drainage ditches, and stone terraces on hillside plots.

CEDICAM has worked with more than 1,500 small farmers, who have planted more than 1 million trees across 2,500 acres and reclaimed 2,000 acres of farmland. The trees help retain rainwater, which can be used to revive unproductive fields. León Santos encourages farmers to use organic compost instead of chemical fertilizer, which has doubled in price over

(continued on page 164)

Jesús León Santos, a Mexican farmer, introduces indigenous farming techniques to reverse erosion.

Jesús León Santos (*continued from page 163*)

recent years. He teaches them to plant crops in traditional *milpa*—an indigenous practice in which small plots of corn, beans, and squash are planted together to return nutrients to the soil and provide a natural defense against pests. He also counsels farmers to use oxen rather than tractors, which compact the soil, making it unable to absorb rainfall.

These traditional agricultural methods are becoming increasingly attractive to small farmers today as they struggle with the rocketing cost of artificial fertilizer, pesticides, machinery, and gasoline. "The Green Revolution displaced our local resources," he told the *New York Times*, using a phrase once coined to describe chemical, industrialized agriculture. "Our dependence on the outside—that led to our ruin."

In 2008, León Santos was awarded the prestigious Goldman Environmental Prize for his imaginative grassroots activism.

—*Jay Walljasper*

Deforestation. Clear-cut forests disrupt natural hydrological cycles, eventually leading to a reduction in the amount of rain in an ecosystem.

Urban Heat Islands. Impermeable pavements raise temperatures, thus reducing the ability of ecosystems to retain water, creating desertification.

Climate Change. Global warming is causing greater evaporation of surface waters.

Slovak hydrologist and Goldman Environmental Prize winner Michal Kravcik's groundbreaking research shows that when water cannot return to fields, meadows, wetlands, and streams because of urban sprawl and the removal of water-retentive landscapes, the actual amount of water in the hydrologic cycle decreases, leading to desertification of once green land. Kravcik is spearheading a movement to view water in the hydrologic cycle as a commons even before it has fallen from the clouds. He believes restoring ecosystems and watersheds by collecting and storing rainwater is key to the restoration of the hydrologic cycle upon which we all depend for life.

This kind of rainwater harvesting is a natural, as opposed to an expensive high-tech, solution to the water crisis that could employ millions of people in what Kravcik calls "community sustainable development programs." This kind of harvesting has been done in arid areas for millennia, but now is being done in other areas running out of clean water. China and Brazil have extensive rooftop rainwater harvesting programs, and Bermuda has a law that requires all new construction to include rainwater-gathering facilities. The Centre for Science and Environment in Delhi, India, runs several dozen such programs around the city and has trained thousands of practitioners from all over India to renew this ancient technique.

Water bottling facilities, which pay nothing to take millions of tons of water yearly from a community, are also a focus for the growing water commons movement. Brazil's Citizens for Water Movement traveled all the way to Nestlé's headquarters in Vevey, Switzerland, to protest the damage the company is causing to the ancient mineral springs of São Lourenço. Friends of the Earth Indonesia is fighting government concessions to several bottled water companies in central Java.

In Michigan, the Sweetwater Alliance and others have taken Nestlé to court for diminishing their local water supplies through the bottling of the Ice Mountain water brand. They won an important court victory, but the company is appealing the ruling. The action was inspired by a similar case in Wisconsin, where local residents stopped plans for a Nestlé bottling works. Residents of Fryeburg, Maine, are fighting to save their aquifer from Nestlé subsidiary Poland Springs, and local communities are adopting ordinances to assert their control over local water sources. A citizen's group in McLeod, California, successfully stopped Nestlé from a major water taking from Mount Shasta.

International Rivers is a powerful network on five continents working to protect rivers from the destruction of big dams. It offers legal advice, training, and technical assistance and helps in dealing with governments. One sign of success is that the number of big dams being built around the world has steadily declined since International Rivers was set up two decades ago.

Fighting for Water Justice

One of the definitions of a commons is that it is accessible to all without discrimination. The greatest indictment of current water policies is the water apartheid now imposed on people throughout the global South. Almost 2 billion people live in water-stressed regions of the planet; of those, 1.4 billion have little or no access to clean drinking water every day. Two fifths of the world's people lack access to basic sanitation, leading to a return of communicable diseases such as cholera. The World Health Organization reports that contaminated water is implicated in 80 percent of all sickness and disease worldwide.

The average North American uses almost 600 liters (150 gallons) of water a day. The average African uses just 6 liters (1.5 gallons). However, poverty and water apartheid are not relegated to the South. Water cutoffs have spread to the United States, where the Detroit Sewage and Water Department cut off water to thousands of residences unable to pay their (rising) water bills. To make matters worse, the city's Social Services Department removed many children from homes because they now had no access to clean water.

The Commons Solution

Water apartheid will not end until we declare water to be a public commons accessible to all. The global water justice movement declares that water must be seen as a basic human right and must not be denied to anyone because of the inability to pay.

In communities all around the world, local groups have resisted the privatization of their water services and won. In response to intense public pressure under the leadership of a grassroots group called FEJUVE, the Bolivian government of Evo Morales ousted the private water company Suez from the capital, La Paz, after a disastrous ten-year contract to manage the city's water. Suez was also forced out of Buenos Aires and Santa Fe, Argentina. Local groups celebrated when the municipality of Adelaide, Australia, took back its water from a private consortium after years of being engulfed in a "big pong" (stench) caused by leaking sewers. Recently, a powerful mobilization led by Food and Water Watch has successfully fought or reversed water privatization in Atlanta, Georgia; New Orleans, Louisiana; Laredo, Texas; and Stockton, California.

Citizens are not waiting for their governments to take the lead in asserting water as a human right. In 2004, the citizens of Uruguay became the first in the world to declare that everyone has a right to water. Led by Friends of the Earth Uruguay and the National Commission in Defense of Water and Life, the groups first had to obtain almost 300,000 signatures (which they delivered to Parliament as a "human river") in order to get a referendum placed on the ballot calling for a constitutional amendment on the right to water. It won and is now enshrined in the country's constitution.

The Indian Supreme Court recently ruled that protection of natural lakes and ponds is akin to honoring the right to life—the most fundamental right of all, according to the court. Activists in Nepal are going before their Supreme Court arguing that hiring a private firm to manage the drinking water system in Kathmandu violates the right to health guaranteed in the country's constitution. The Coalition Against Water Privatization in South Africa is challenging the practice of water metering before the Johannesburg High Court on the basis that it violates the human rights of Soweto's poor. Bolivian president Evo Morales has called for a "South American convention for human rights and access for all living beings to water" that would reject the privatized market model on water distribution imposed in many global trade agreements.

The water commons movement has forced open debate over the control of water and challenged the corporations and privatization advocates who set themselves up as the lords of this dwindling resource. The growth of this global water-justice movement is critical in bringing accountability, transparency, and public oversight to the mounting water crisis as conflicts over water loom on the horizon.

—*Maude Barlow*

Winning One for the Commons in Akron

Voters reject privatization of their sewer system

In February 2008, the mayor of Akron, Ohio, proposed leasing the maintenance and operation of the city's sewer system to a private company for ninety-nine years. Local activists from Northeast Ohio American Friends Service Committee and AFSCME Ohio Council 8 contacted the D.C.-based organization Food & Water Watch about the proposed privatization and asked for help with research and strategy development.

The two local organizations brought together two different constituencies to form a broad coalition of labor, religious, and community organizations known as Citizens to Save Our Sewers and Water (Citizens SOS).

Part of the success was their quick response. They were on the street before the mayor had produced any details about leasing the sewers. To raise awareness and educate their own constituencies, they organized screenings of the film *Thirst*, a 2004 documentary about problems resulting from privatization of a public water utility in Stockton, California.

In addition, they informed residents that 86 percent of U.S. water systems are publicly owned, and these are rated as more efficient and 13–50 percent less expensive than privatized systems.

Citizens SOS decided that the best way to counter the mayor's proposal was to require voter approval before the privatization of any public utility, which would mean passing a ballot referendum. By mid-July 2008, Citizens SOS had collected nearly four thousand valid signatures, more than enough to get their issue on the ballot. The mayor meanwhile created his own ballot proposal favoring privatization.

The local media favored the privatization plan, so Citizens SOS had to use alternative means to get their message out: door-to-door canvassing, phone calls, billboards, ads, letters to the editor, literature drops, parades, and political forums. The group also brought an activist from Stockton, California, where privatization of the local water utility had recently been overturned, to speak about the negative experience of privatization.

When Election Day 2008 finally came, residents overwhelmingly rejected the mayor's privatization plan and approved the measure requiring a vote on any municipal privatization by a margin of two to one.

—*Wenonah Hauter*

A Commons Solution to Climate Change

Cap-and-dividend could become the most popular government program since Social Security

IN 2006, NASA'S TOP CLIMATE SCIENTIST warned that we have, at most, a decade to turn the tide on global warming. After that, James Hansen said, all bets are off. Temperature rises of 3 to 7 degrees Fahrenheit will "produce a different planet."

If Hansen is right—and most scientists think he is—then every year lost is a year closer to the precipice. In more positive terms, we have a last chance—but only one chance—to save the planet.

For many decades, human emissions of greenhouse gases have exceeded the atmosphere's capacity to safely absorb them. To avoid disruption of the climate and human society, we need to create a system that steadily and permanently reduces those emissions all across the economy.

The Atmosphere Is Ours

The atmosphere itself is a commons—a gift of creation to all. It performs many vital planetary functions, including maintaining a livable climate. The trouble is, we humans—and especially we Americans—are disrupting it with our pollution. Even though we know we're causing long-term problems, we don't stop. Indeed, we *can't* stop as long as the current economic arrangement for using the atmosphere persists. That system—first come, first served, no limits, and no prices—is clearly dysfunctional. We need a new economy-wide system to reduce atmospheric disturbance. But the design of that system spurs great debate.

At the core of this debate is the question Who owns the sky? This is a philosophical and moral question, but, more important at the moment, it is a trillion-dollar economic question. Ownership of rights to the sky will determine who pays whom to use the atmosphere's limited carbon-storage capacity. Many large and powerful companies—what I call the legacy industries—are happy with the current arrangement, in which polluters pay nothing. But pollution has real costs, and if we want to fix the climate crisis, someone must pay them. If polluters don't pay, the rest of us will. We'll pay them in the form of higher energy prices, which will transfer huge amounts of our money to polluting corporations and substantially reduce our disposable incomes.

The alternative to corporate ownership of the sky is common ownership—that is, ownership by all. Under common ownership, polluters would pay to dump carbon into the atmosphere, and this "rent" would be returned to everyone equally—one person, one share.

It may be helpful to think of the atmosphere as a parking lot for carbon dioxide emissions. In any parking lot, when demand for parking exceeds capacity, we limit use to short time periods by installing meters. If the lot is owned by a public entity, the money paid by parkers is used to benefit all. In the case of our shared atmosphere, we must also limit parking and charge for it. And the money polluters pay should benefit all.

Why Cap-and-Dividend Is the Most Politically Practical Plan

How might this be done? In recent years, the climate policy debate has focused on the notion of *capping carbon*—that is, putting a physical limit on the total amount of carbon that can be dumped into the air each year. A cap would be enforced by requiring carbon emitters to acquire permits and then

The money energy companies pay to pollute should not be traded among themselves but given back to those who own the sky—all of us.

steadily reducing the number of permits issued.

The crucial economic question is whether polluters will be given carbon permits for free or required to buy them in auctions. Legislation has been introduced in both the U.S. House and Senate to create a cap-and-dividend system in which all carbon permits would be auctioned and the proceeds returned in equal monthly dividends to every American with a Social Security number. The money would be wired electronically to people's bank accounts or debit cards, just like Social Security. As carbon prices rise over time, so—automatically—would dividends. In this way, household purchasing power would be protected during the carbon phase-down no matter how high fuel prices go.

A cap-and-dividend system (also known as cap-and-refund) has many benefits. It is simple, transparent (it's easy to see where the money goes), and creates the right incentives. The more fossil-fuel energy you use, the more you pay in higher carbon prices. Since everyone gets the same amount back, you gain if you conserve and lose if you guzzle. The winners are thus everyone who conserves fossil fuel—plus our children, who inherit a stable climate.

What's more, cap-and-dividend has a progressive effect on income distribution. Its central formula—from each according to their use of the atmosphere, to each an equal share—is fair to poor, middle class, and rich alike, but the poor benefit most because they pollute the least.

> At the core of the climate debate is: who owns the sky?
>
> —Peter Barnes

A Boost to the Poor and Middle Class

And it's not just the poor who would benefit. A 2007 study by James Boyce and Matt Riddle at the University of Massachusetts— (*Cap and Dividend: How to Curb Global Warming While Protecting the Incomes of American Families*—found that because upper-income people use so much more energy than everyone else, over 70 percent of Americans would come out ahead under cap-and-dividend. That's good news for the middle class, which has seen its income fall in recent decades.

From a political perspective, a carbon cap with monthly dividends would be the most popular federal program since Social Security. It would lock in public support for emission reductions no matter how high fuel prices rise. And on top of that, it would be popular with politicians who would be off the hook for rising prices. If voters complain, politicians can say, "The market sets prices, and you determine by your energy use whether you gain or lose. If you conserve, you come out ahead."

Unfortunately, under intense pressure from polluting industries, Congress is

Darryl Birkenfeld

Home on the Ogallala Commons

For Darryl Birkenfeld, the commons is not just an environmental and economic issue—it's a spiritual and ethical challenge. A former Roman Catholic priest and part-time farmer in the Texas panhandle, Birkenfeld directs Ogallala Commons (www.ogallalacommons.org), a small nonprofit community resource network with a visionary agenda: to help people in the Great Plains recognize their well-being depends upon the commons.

Ogallala Commons refers to the region that lies atop the vast High Plains–Ogallala Aquifer—the largest (by volume) freshwater aquifer on the planet, which covers 174,000 square miles spreading across eight states from New Mexico to South Dakota. This part of Mid-America receives relatively little rainfall, making the underground source of water essential, and its continual depletion is a serious question mark for the future of the region.

So far, twenty-five communities or counties in Texas, Oklahoma, Colorado, New Mexico, and Kansas have partnered with Ogallala Commons in pursuing a commons-based vision of community development. These "commonwealth communities" pursue a holistic approach to development that combines sustainable agriculture and business development with plans to promote stable communities and a sense of history and culture.

"We are a collaborative network," explains Birkenfeld. "We don't have a membership. Everyone in the region is already a member—three million of us! They just don't know it yet."

But Birkenfeld is no dreamy idealist; he is a pragmatist trying to get things done. On the dry plains, responsible stewardship of water is always a major concern. Ogallala Commons has led an effort to help protect more than sixty thousand seasonal wetlands known

(continued on page 172)

Birkenfeld, a farmer and former priest, aims to get people across Mid-America thinking about what they share.

Darryl Birkenfeld *(continued from page 171)*

as playas. "People have no idea that so many forms of life are dependent upon these playa wetlands," says Birkenfeld. "There are any number of agencies in Texas, Oklahoma, and Kansas that are responsible for these wetlands, and still 70 percent of them are degraded, and they're getting worse."

To educate people about water, Ogallala Commons has organized a series of "water festivals" for schoolchildren. Going beyond "turn off the faucet while brushing your teeth," the project teaches kids about the intricate water cycles in the central and southern Great Plains, and how humans need to actively work with nature to sustain the water supply and the environment.

The economic woes of the Great Plains make it difficult for many communities to keep their young people, who tend to leave for big cities once they are finished with school. So Ogallala Commons has helped start a series of summer community internships to help young people envision new possibilities for themselves in their hometowns. One student intern who is studying landscape architecture, for instance, wants to find ways to protect the prairie landscape. To date, with help from CHS Foundation and local communities, Ogallala Commons has created eighteen internships in four states.

—David Bollier

focused on cap-and-trade legislation that auctions only 15 percent of carbon permits and gives most of the rest to a variety of corporations. The bills have some good features but are so full of loopholes and giveaways that many environmentalists and consumer groups urged that they be fixed or rejected. I hope by the time you read this that the politics will have shifted toward cap-and-dividend.

—Peter Barnes

In Trusts We Trust

*A **proven form of common ownership** that preserves resources for the public good*

TREBAH GARDEN IS A SPECTACULAR PIECE of paradise in Cornwall, England, a verdant ravine with a huge variety of trees and shrubs that winds its way down to a beach on the Helford River. Several years ago, I visited this garden to enjoy its beauty. But I learned that its history and management structure are as interesting as its flora.

The property is first recorded in the Domesday Book of 1086 as belonging to the Bishop of Exeter. It passed through the hands of many squires and farmers until it was acquired in 1831 by a wealthy Quaker family, which developed the extraordinary garden. In the twentieth century, the property changed hands several more times, and the garden gradually deteriorated. The last private owners sank a small fortune into restoring the garden, then donated it to a trust so it could be opened to the public and preserved for future generations.

Today, anyone can become a lifetime member of this trust by making a donation of £250. Members get free access to the garden (other visitors pay an admission fee) and elect a council to manage the property. They receive an annual report, audited accounts, and notices of meetings at which they may vote and submit resolutions. At present, there are about a thousand voting members of the trust.

Gardens of Change

As I wandered through the acres of ferns and rhododendrons, it struck me that Trebah is a microcosm for the larger transformation we need to make. It has passed from private ownership to a form of common ownership that enables it to be shared and preserved. If we think of the world as a collection of gardens—that is, of ecosystems in which humans play active roles—the Trebah Garden Trust model becomes extremely interesting. It illuminates both a process by which natural gifts can shift from private to common ownership and an institutional model—the trust—for managing such gifts as permanent parts of the commons.

Trusts are centuries-old institutions devised to hold and manage property for beneficiaries. Neither trusts nor their trustees may ever act in their own self-interest;

they're legally obligated to act solely on behalf of beneficiaries.

Trusts are bound by numerous rules, including the following:

✦ Managers must act with undivided loyalty to beneficiaries.

✦ Unless authorized to act otherwise, managers may spend income from the trust's activities but are not to diminish principal.

✦ Managers must ensure transparency by making timely financial information available to beneficiaries.

These rules are enforceable. The basic enforcement mechanism is that an aggrieved beneficiary or a state attorney general (in the United States) can bring suit against trustees. When that happens, the trustees must prove they acted prudently; if there's any doubt, they are fined or fired.

I believe each generation has an obligation to pass on the great gifts of creation undiminished to those not yet born. If we are to accomplish this, someone must act as trustee of nature's gifts, or at least of the most endangered of them. The question is, who?

Government is one possibility, but not the only one or necessarily the best one. Governments have protected some of our most scenic treasures as national parks and wilderness areas, but governments are continuously subject to political pressure to exploit natural resources for the benefit of the living, and there is nothing that legally requires them to be loyal to future generations.

The other possibility is trusts.

The Trebah Garden Trust isn't a rarity. Throughout Britain, the National Trust—a nongovernmental charity founded in 1895—owns over six hundred thousand acres of countryside, six hundred miles of coastline, and two hundred historic buildings and gardens. It has more than 3 million members, who elect half of its fifty-two-person governing council (the other half are appointed by nonprofit organizations that share the trust's goals). In the United States, there are now over 1,500 Trebah-like trusts, protecting over nine million acres. On top of that, the fifty-five-year-old Nature Conservancy protects more than 15 million acres spread across the country.

Saving the Family Farm in Suburbia

Another kind of trust can help save family farms and open space around cities. For ex-

This Land Is Community Land

Community land trusts showcase a new model of cooperation

An increasingly popular form of commons-based management system is the community land trust, a form of land tenure that separates the value of the land from the value of improvements made to the property. A nonprofit community land trust acquires a site by gift or purchase and then develops a land-use plan that may include affordable housing, agriculture, open space, recreation, or commercial uses important to the community. The land is leased on a ninety-nine-year agreement for the purposes defined. Leaseholders may own buildings (and make improvements on them), which they can sell. But they can't sell the land itself, which is owned by the trust. To prevent capitalization of land value, the resale price of improvements is limited to replacement costs.

The first U.S. community land trust was created in 1967 in Albany, Georgia, by Robert Swann and Slater King in order to provide African American farmers with access to land. There are now more than two hundred in the United States, according to the E.F. Schumacher Society, which provides resources for community land trusts.

—Susan Witt

ample, in Marin County, just north of San Francisco, family-owned dairy, sheep, and cattle ranches have survived. A big reason is that ranchers there have an option beyond selling out to developers: selling conservation easements to the Marin Agricultural Land Trust (MALT).

A conservation easement is a voluntary agreement between a landowner and a trust that permanently limits uses of the land. The owner continues to own and use the land and may sell it or pass it on to her heirs. However, the owner gives up some of the rights associated with the land— for example, the right to build additional houses on it or to clear-cut trees. The trust that acquires the easement makes sure its terms are followed by the current as well as future owners.

In Marin County, MALT has preserved nearly forty thousand acres of farmland by buying conservation easements from ranchers. This represents about a third of the land currently farmed. The ranchers receive the difference between what the land would be worth if developed and what it's worth as a working farm. In effect, they're paid to be stewards of the land and to forgo future capital gains.

Most of MALT's money comes from government sources. What the public receives isn't a place to graze livestock like the commons of old, but a lasting pastoral landscape and a viable agricultural economy that makes fresh, local food possible. That's not a bad alternative to suburban sprawl.

• • •

Other Forms of Trusts

The trust model is not limited to land. Many types of commons can be managed with trusts to benefit the public as a whole and future generations. Here are some examples.

✦ Air or sky trusts acknowledge that everyone has a stake in the atmosphere and that those who pollute it are robbing us of something valuable. This is the basis of the cap-and-dividend proposal, a commons-based solution to global warming that has been introduced in the U.S. Congress.

✦ Watershed trusts limit the amount of fertilizers and pesticides that can be used within a watershed. This would protect streams and rivers from noxious runoff and boost incentives for organic farming. Such trusts could also hold water and development rights.

✦ Aquifer trusts would protect underground water sources, which are being depleted faster than rain replenishes them. Millions of people around the world depend on aquifers for their drinking water.

✦ City street trusts would help curb pollution and congestion by charging drivers for using crowded streets at peak times. The revenue could be used for mass transit and bike paths. Such policies are now used in London, Norway, Stockholm, Singapore, and other places, usually under the name of congestion pricing.

Pacific Forest Trust

Protecting our stake in private woodlands

A forest is more than a timber supply or future subdivision: it's an ecosystem bursting with life. Forests supply us with an array of vital services, from keeping our waters clean to providing habitat for wildlife to regulating the climate.

About 80 percent of America's forests are privately owned, and many are under threat. Lumber companies own a lot of this land and focus on clear-cutting trees for quick profit, neglecting the other functions of forests that are important to all of us. Meanwhile, owners of smaller tracts of forests are often tempted to sell to real estate developers planning subdivisions or vacation homes.

Until recently, there was no one to speak for the trees. Then Connie Best and Laurie Wayburn—like Dr. Seuss's Lorax—decided that it was their job. In 1993, they founded the Pacific Forest Trust, an organization that protects forests by acquiring conservation easements. Under these arrangements, private forest owners sell or give up their rights to subdivide, clear-cut, or develop their forests in any other unsustainable way—restrictions that continue even when the land is sold. Owners can harvest trees sustainably, and they often receive cash or tax benefits, plus the peace of mind that comes from knowing their forests will be managed responsibly forever.

The Pacific Forest Trust has so far protected fifty thousand acres of trees in California, Oregon, and Washington.

—Peter Barnes

✦ An airwaves trust would charge commercial broadcasters and telecommunications companies for using the airwaves, which belong to us all. The revenue would support noncommercial broadcasting and the media budgets of political candidates, boosting democracy by curtailing the power of wealthy campaign contributors.

—Peter Barnes

John Bunker

A modern-day Johnny Appleseed rediscovers some of the 10,000 varieties that once flourished in the United States

Biodiversity—the biological commons that sustains life on earth—is increasingly threatened as industrial society marches into remote corners of the planet. To many, the extinction of wondrous and valuable species of plants and animals is simply inevitable. Yet some people will not quietly accept this loss. They organize to protect genetic treasures in the rain forests of the Amazon, the savannas of Africa, and even the farmyards of Maine.

John Bunker is one of those people. Bunker enlists people all over Maine to help preserve endangered varieties of apples. They search out abandoned farm sites looking for fruit from long forgotten apple trees, sending it to Bunker. In the nineteenth century, many New England towns boasted of their own unique apples. He hopes to revive some of the more than ten thousand varieties that were grown throughout America 120 years ago.

That cornucopia now has been reduced to the dozen or two apple varieties we find in our grocery stores. And it's important to note that these apples did not thrive because they were the best. In many cases, like the criminally bland Red Delicious, they were specially bred to sur-

Bunker enlists volunteers all over New England to search for heirloom apple trees.

vive long-distance shipping or to look, rather than taste, good.

Bunker likes to rhapsodize about the Black Oxford, a tasty purple-skinned apple with cream-colored flesh that was the first almost-lost variety he came across years ago when a farmer brought in a bushel to sell at a food co-op where he worked. It was the start of his career as a modern-day Johnny Appleseed and is now one of many varieties that Bunker grows and sells through his company Fedco Seeds.

—*Jay Walljasper*

How to Win Full Health Care Reform

Americans look to Canada's system of a health care commons

IT'S RELATIVELY EASY FOR AMERICANS to understand that parks, sidewalks, the environment, and the Internet are all part of the commons. That's because no one owns them.

But it's more of a stretch when it comes to elements of the commons that have traditionally been under private ownership. Access to health care, for instance, rightly belongs to all of us the same as air, water, sunshine, or other things we depend upon for life. We are, after all, morally bound to help anyone who needs medical attention. And our tax money funds much of the research that results in new medicines and procedures. Yet these simple truths are clouded by the fact that in the United States, even after the passage of President Obama's health care reforms, a large share of health services is operated on a for-profit basis—a unique situation among wealthy nations, which means our health care is more expensive and many people have limited access.

If health care were more widely recognized as a commons, the idea of a public health care option—or even a single-payer system—would not seem so controversial to Congress members. In fact, a look right across the border at the Canadian health care programs shows how well a health care commons works.

How Canadians Created a Health Commons

The seeds of the current Canadian health system were sown in rural Saskatchewan in the early twentieth century when small cities with no doctors began to subsidize a physician to come and set up practice. Several communities then joined together to open publicly funded hospitals.

In the 1930s, a new Canadian political party, whose name reflected its philosophy, the Cooperative Commonwealth Federation (CCF), came to power in Saskatchewan. In 1946 the province enacted legislation that guaranteed free hospital care. Premier Tommy Douglas had hoped to offer universal health care, but the province lacked the financial resources.

In 1958, building on a decade of success in Saskatchewan, the Canadian federal government used the power of the purse to coax other provinces to introduce public hospital insurance. Ottawa promised to pay 50 percent of the cost of provincial programs that satisfied the following rules, which were shaped by the idea of health as a commonwealth, or commons.

1. *Public Administration*: The plan must be run by a public authority and be nonprofit.
2. *Comprehensiveness*: All necessary medical services must be covered.
3. *Universality*: Every resident of a given province or territory must be entitled to the same level and extent of coverage.
4. *Portability*: When insured persons travel or move within or outside Canada, their coverage must be maintained.
5. *Accessibility*: All insured persons must have access to hospital and physician services

By 1961 all provinces had adopted a hospitalization insurance program.

Taking the Next Step Toward Universal Coverage

Since Saskatchewan had been paying 100 percent of the cost of its program, the 50 percent federal match allowed it to extend public health coverage to physicians' visits. A promise to do so by Tommy Douglas, who still led the CCF, became the principal issue in the 1960 provincial elections. The CCF won, and on July 1, 1962, the new system went into effect. That day 90 percent of the province's doctors went on strike.

It was a defining moment in Canada's health care history. Aided by the American Medical Association, Saskatchewan's doctors used some of the same rhetoric that has proven so effective in U.S. health care debates: socialized medicine is communistic and would limit a patient's choice of doctors.

But by 1962 Saskatchewan residents had been served by a commons-based health care system for more than fifteen years. When the doctors called a mass public demonstration against socialized medicine, expecting forty thousand to attend, only 10 percent of that number showed up. The strike ended two weeks later.

In 1964 came further evidence of how deeply rooted the idea of a health commons had become in Saskatchewan. The CCF party lost the elections. The incoming Liberal Party had opposed public insurance for physicians' services, but it did not try to overturn the 1962 law.

In 1966 Ottawa offered to fund provincial health plans for doctors under the same conditions as it had funded provincial health plans for hospitals. By 1972 every Canadian was covered by the new Medicare insurance.

Thirty years later, a Commission on the Future of Health Care summed up the process thus: "The principles of the Canada Health Act began as simple conditions attached to federal funding for medicare.

Over time, they became much more than that. . . .The principles have stood the test of time and continue to reflect the values of Canadians."

Lessons in Defending the Commons

The Canadian experience also shows that the price of defending a commons, as with liberty in general, is eternal vigilance. Once created, a commons will face continuing challenges from two major forces. One is the ingenious ability of individuals and corporations to find loopholes that allow them to maximize their income at the expense of the commons. The other is the tendency of governments during difficult economic times (or when driven by market ideology) to starve the commons, which undermines public support by reducing its effectiveness.

Canada's health commons has had to defend itself against both forces. The loophole it faced was that Canada's Medicare legislation permitted doctors and hospitals to charge patients extra for better service. The law required universal access. But it did not specifically prohibit doctors and hospitals from charging additional fees or allowing patients to pay to jump ahead on the waiting lists. In 1984 Canada responded to this threat by passing a new Health Act that effectively eliminated user charges or surcharges on publicly insured services.

More recently, Canada's health commons has had to deal with shrinking federal support. By the early 2000s, the federal share of the provincial health care budget was down from 50 percent to 20–30 percent. Ever longer waiting lines resulted in ever broader public grumbling and ever more aggressive lobbying by for-profit companies to be allowed to deliver the same health services.

In 2005, the issue came to a head when the Supreme Court of Canada voted 4–3 that Quebec's prohibition against private health insurance for medically necessary services violated the Quebec Charter of Human Rights and Freedoms. Chief Justice Beverly McLachlin wrote, "Access to a waiting list is not access to health care."

Quebec responded in two ways. In 2007 it allowed private insurance for the three surgeries that had the longest waiting times: knee and hip replacements and cataract surgery. At the same time, it improved the delivery structure of its health system to reduce waiting times. In March 2009, Quebec's health minister announced that nearly all patients seeking knee and hip replacements in the public system were beginning treatment within three months, down from nine months or more.

At the time, CBC News reported, "More than two years after Quebec legalized private medical coverage for select surgeries, the insurance industry says it has not sold a single policy."

In appreciation for their health care systems, Canadians in 2004 voted Tommy Douglas as "the Greatest Canadian" in a national poll sponsored by the Canadian Broadcasting Company.

—*David Morris*

Germs We Share

Public health is a commons we can't afford to ignore

It's a simple fact of medicine that our good health depends on the good health of others. You cannot seal yourself away from germs, contamination, unsanitary conditions, or disease vectors.

Infection defies all attempts at enclosure. Borders between nations and divisions between economic classes are meaningless in the face of disease. No amount of money or privatization can ensure your safety. We are all connected to each other through the viruses and bacteria we exchange.

This is true as ever in an age when a problem like AIDS, SARS, or H1N1 can erupt suddenly into a global pandemic. Public health threats are not a historical footnote from the days when raw sewage poured into our water supply. In fact, it was an understanding of public health as commons that allowed us to eradicate many deadly diseases through the creation of public sewers and water systems. The same approach is necessary today to prevent deadly new outbreaks. This means studying all our social and environmental interconnections and coming up with plans that protect the weak and vulnerable of the world in order to protect us all.

—*Jay Walljasper*

Andrew Kimbrell

Early voice for the commons

Throughout the 1980s and '90s, Andrew Kimbrell—a D.C. public interest lawyer, environmental activist, and author—championed the commons as a breakthrough that could change how our society views the environment and social justice. Many people at the time had no idea what he was talking about or, if they did, considered it an arcane detail plucked from the pages of history. But Kimbrell persisted in raising the issue, pointing out that environmental destruction and economic inequity is simply the modern version of medieval lords seizing resources that rightfully belong to everyone.

Kimbrell is the founder of the D.C.-based International Center for Technology Assessment and the Center for Food Safety, as well as the author of *The Human Body Shop: The Engineering and Marketing of Your Life* and *Fatal Harvest: The Tragedy of Industrial Agriculture*. He has filed numerous lawsuits and organized political campaigns addressing global warming, biological warfare, food irradiation, factory farming, genetic engineering, and preserving the integrity of organic food standards.

"The commons is a promising model to help us think about the kind of world we want for the next generations," Kimbrell suggests. "It helps us think beyond the commodification of everything in the world as a sign of progress, which in the short term creates wealth, but in the long term creates catastrophe."

—*Jay Walljasper*

An attorney and activist, Kimbrell challenges genetic engineering, factory farming, and biological warfare.

Privatization Harms Our Health

Patent restrictions on genes and drugs hamper access to medical cures

THE U.S. PATENT AND TRADEMARK Office grants patents for genes as well as inventions. With the sanction of the U.S. Supreme Court, which recognized the patenting of life-forms in 1981, pharmaceutical and biotech companies can legally assert exclusive control over who may study, test, or look at a gene, in case such activities interfere with the profit potential of their patent.

Granting property rights in genes is defended by the industry as a necessary incentive to spur medical innovation and cure diseases. But in practice, it is now clear that exclusive patents on genetic knowledge are actually a form of monopoly that grant patent holders the ability to thwart competitive research, squelch innovative products, and charge exorbitant prices. The end result, as some women are discovering, is dangerous to their health.

Myriad Genetics, a private company in Salt Lake City, owns a patent on genes known as BCA1 and BCA2. Women who have these genes have a significantly higher risk of contracting breast and ovarian cancer. But because of its patent Myriad is the only source of diagnostic testing for the genes. Myriad is also the only research center that is allowed to study the BCA genes. Everyone else needs formal permission, which may require a license fee. If you happen to be a medical researcher at Harvard or UCLA or a respected European medical center, don't bother trying to study these genes. It would violate Myriad Genetics' patent.

And if you want to get a diagnostic test to see if you have BRCA gene mutations, again, you can only go to Myriad Genetics. Its BRCAnalysis® test costs $3,000.

The problems from patenting genes are not confined to breast cancer. Across the board, gene patents have gummed up scientific research and diagnostic testing by fencing off knowledge and limiting what can be done with it. In March of 2010, the American Civil Liberties Union and the Public Patent Foundation won a lawsuit charging that patents on two human genes associated with cancer are unconstitutional and invalid. The lawsuit—brought on behalf of four scientific organizations representing more than 150,000 geneticists, pathologists, and laboratory professionals—calls into question the legality of existing patents on thousands of human genes.

"Patents are meant to protect inventions, not things that exist in nature like genes in the human body," said Chris Hansen, a staff attorney with the ACLU. "Genes isolated from the human body are no more patentable than gold extracted from a mountain."

Privatizing Taxpayer-Funded Research

The privatization of medical cures is even more infuriating, if that is possible, when applied to patents arising out of publicly funded research. Until thirty years ago, there had been a broad consensus that the intellectual property rights of federal research should stay in the public domain or at least be licensed on a nonexclusive basis. That way, taxpayers could reap the full measure of value from their collective investments. In the late 1970s, however, large pharmaceutical, electronics, and chemical companies mounted a bold lobbying campaign to revoke the public ownership of federal research. Since enactment of Bayh-Dole Act of 1980, which authorized universities to patent the fruits of federally funded research, we have seen a land rush to propertize and sell academic research that was once freely available to all.

Between 1980 and 2000, the number of patents secured by universities grew tenfold, bringing in more than $1 billion in royalties and licensing fees—a windfall enjoyed mostly by a dozen top research uni-

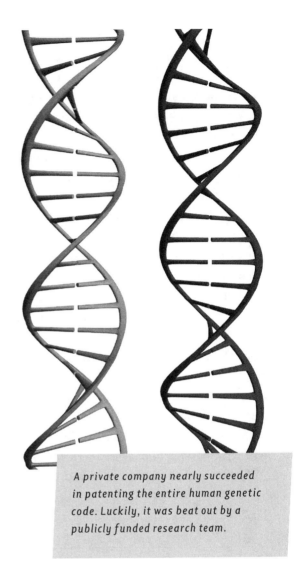

A private company nearly succeeded in patenting the entire human genetic code. Luckily, it was beat out by a publicly funded research team.

versities. In reality, this is a privatization of the public's investments. Even though the public pays for the lion's share of risky basic research for new drugs, the long-term equity returns tend to go to drug companies and a handful of universities. In the United States, we have seen this with the cancer drug Taxol, the antidepressant Prozac, the hypertension drug Capoten, and a number of HIV and AIDS therapies.

The upshot is that citizens often have to pay twice for pharmaceuticals and other medical treatments—first as taxpayers who finance the research and second as consumers who pay monopoly prices for drugs. This is a pure giveaway, because it's not even clear that companies *need* exclusive patent rights as an incentive to commercialize new drug research.

Multinational corporations are no longer content to simply claim ownership of commons knowledge at home. Now they scour the developing world to claim patents on the botanical and ecological knowledge acquired by indigenous people through the centuries, a practice known as biopiracy. They move into Madagascar, Brazil, Guatemala, and other poor countries to find plants and microorganisms that might be used in making new medicines and genetically engineered crops. But as Seth Shulman writes in his book *Owning the Future*, "Who, if anyone, should be able to claim ownership rights to the globe's genetic and cultural inheritance?"

Who Owns Our Chromosomes?

A few years ago, we almost lost ownership of the entire human genome—a sequence of 23,000 genes that is the code of human life itself. A private start-up company, Celera, was aggressively trying to privatize genomic sequences and put them in one big privatized database. That way, it would have a monopoly over future use of the genomic data by licensing access to its database. Fortunately, a coalition of public-sector scientists decoded much of the genetic data first, which ensures that much of the human genome—a source of innumerable future medical breakthroughs—is now in the public domain.

—*David Bollier*

Chapter 9

Liberating Information and Culture

The Alchemy of Creativity

How cooperation boosts art, science, and everything else

THE FOUNDERS OF THE UNITED STATES embraced the commons when it came to ideas. They understood that the best fresh ideas are generated out of previous ideas, and therefore should remain in the public domain (a cultural commons). Indeed, copyright and patent law in the early days of the nation expressly aimed to move new cultural creations into the public domain as soon as possible. In 1790, copyrights lasted fourteen years with a chance to renew for another fourteen. Today, after passage of the 1998 Sonny Bono Act by Congress, copyrights last for seventy years beyond the life of the original creator, or 120 years from creation in the case of corporate ownership.

It's only very recently that the rise of intellectual property law has tipped the scales toward private ownership of every conceivable aspect of what we create, from breakthroughs in science and other academic fields to traditions in art and pop culture. Today people are attempting to claim exclusive rights to spices, healing herbs, or yoga poses that have been used for centuries. Compare that to Benjamin Franklin, one of the founders of the U.S. Patent Office, who refused to patent the famous Franklin stove. Why? Because he said he was merely build-

COMMONERS

Larry Gonick

ing on ideas of stoves that came before. "As we enjoy great advantages from the inventions of others," he wrote, "we should be glad to serve others by any inventions of ours."

Novelist Jonathan Lethem documented how the free exchange of ideas works in art in an essay for *Harper's Magazine*, "The Ecstasy of Influence," in which he traced patterns of borrowed influences through music (Delta bluesman Son House to Chicago bluesman Muddy Waters to British rock bands), animation (without Fritz the Cat, there would be no *Ren & Stimpy Show*), and literature (Ovid's telling of the story of Pyramus and Thisbe was the inspiration for Shakespeare's *Romeo and Juliet*, which in turns was the inspiration for *West Side Story*). To prove his point about the mutually collaborative nature of new ideas (as opposed to the "eureka" theory, in which ideas are concocted out of thin air), he strove to footnote the influence of every line of his essay.

The Scientific Commons

A great example of a cultural commons from the field of science is the Human Genome Project, a massive collective effort on the part of scientists around the globe to decode all human genes. New information discovered in the project was shared for all to use and to improve upon in their own research. The project was competing with a private venture that sought to sell the data that were produced. The private ven-

ture didn't succeed in decoding the genome ahead of the Human Genome Project, and thankfully so, because the high cost of their data may have stymied many subsequent scientific and medical advances.

The Human Genome Project used a commons approach that was based on two assumptions: 1) genes are part of nature and thus belong to all of us, and (2) sharing information would be more productive than privatizing it.

Busting Out of the Market Mind-set

Examples of thriving systems managed according to the principles of the commons rather than the privatized market exist all around the world today, from fisheries off the coast of Greece to forests in Tanzania and Indonesia to the open-source software movement.

But most of us have been taught that the commons began to fade away in seventeenth- and eighteenth-century England, when private landowners claimed and enclosed (literally, with fences) land used by commoners to graze livestock. Yet the commons endures to this day throughout the British countryside in the form of legally protected rights-of-way that entitle anyone to cross private property on tens of thousands of miles of paths throughout England, Scotland, and Wales. This is also true in the cultural realm, where we make imaginative journeys thanks to stories, songs, ideas, knowledge, and research belonging to all of us. It is not trespassing to take advantage of the creativity of Plato, Buddha, Leonardo da Vinci, Shakespeare, Bach, Darwin, Florence Nightingale, and many others.

Those fences of eighteenth-century England give us a powerful image and metaphor for the "enclosure" of culture going on today at an alarming pace. Here are a couple of examples. Media companies want to slow down your access to Web sites that don't pay a premium fee for their place on the Internet, a troubling violation of the commons principle of net neutrality that will allow huge enterprises to dominate the flow of information. Another example is the Walt Disney Corporation, which has built its empire on appropriating and ultimately copyrighting material from the public domain—from "The Little Mermaid" and *Robin Hood*, all the way back to Mickey's first cartoon, "Steamboat Willie," which was taken directly from Buster Keaton's character Steamboat Bill. But try using an image of Mickey Mouse in your own work and you'll soon hear from the Mouse's lawyers.

Creative Commons

No one wants to deny people the chance to make an honest living off their creative work. But the recent proliferation of copyright and intellectual property privileges means that many artists, scientists, and other creators are denied access to material they need to do their most valuable work— an even graver threat to their livelihoods and to the needs of society as a whole. I'm making a film called *What We Got: DJ Spooky's Journey to the Commons* to highlight all that we share, from air, water, and land to our art, culture, and discoveries. I want to practice what I preach by sharing the movie we make online so that others can remix and repurpose it under the terms of a Creative Commons license.

—Brad Lichtenstein

Disney Loots the Public Domain

And gives nothing back in return

Some of the stories the Disney Corporation has borrowed from the public domain since 1937:

Aladdin	King Arthur
Alice in Wonderland	Little Mermaid
Around the World in 80 Days	Oliver Twist
Atlantis	Pinocchio
Beauty and the Beast	Pocahontas
Cinderella	Robin Hood
Chicken Little	Snow White
Christmas Carol	Sleeping Beauty
Davy Crockett	Swiss Family Robinson
Legend of Sleepy Hollow	Three Musketeers
Hercules	Treasure Island
Hunchback of Notre Dame	Wind in the Willows
Jungle Book	

Stories the Disney Corporation has contributed to the public domain since 1937:

None

When Knowledge Becomes Private Property

Overuse of patents, copyrights, and trademarks locks up what belongs to everyone

OVER THE PAST TWO DECADES, MODERN culture has become infatuated with the idea that knowledge should be owned like real estate or stock shares. The original idea, of course, is that copyrights, trademarks, and patents reward people for their creative labors and thereby boosts the common good.

This fundamentalist approach shuts down a broader discussion about how knowledge ought to circulate in our culture. Its adherents are intent on snuffing out any idea that valuable knowledge can be produced and disseminated without locking it behind the doors of rigid copyright and patent monopolies.

I believe in copyrights and patents. In some cases, they provide significant and necessary incentives to invest in new works. But today copyrights and patents are going far beyond their original goals—such as the one stipulated by the U.S. Constitution, to "promote progress in science and the useful arts"—and are becoming ends in themselves. Instead of carefully balancing private interests and public needs, copyrights and patents are becoming crude, antisocial instruments of control and avarice.

Silent Campfires

One alarming story about the expansion of copyright law involves ASCAP, the American Society of Composers, Authors and Publishers, the body that collects performance licensing fees from radio stations, restaurants with jukeboxes, and other places where recorded music is played.

ASCAP decided that its domain should be extended to summer camps. Why shouldn't boys and girls singing around the campfire be considered a "public performance" obligating them to pay royalties? ASCAP approached the American Camping Association in 1996 and said it wanted blanket performance licenses from hundreds of summer camps—something on the order of $300 to $1,400 per season per camp.

This caused quite a ruckus. When it was discovered that ASCAP wanted money for the Girl Scouts to sing "This Land Is Your Land" and "Puff, the Magic Dragon," the press went nuts. There were stories about camps where kids were actually dancing the macarena without music and resorting to noncopyrighted songs like "The Bow-

Legged Chicken." An ASCAP official heart-lessly told a reporter, "They [camps] buy paper, twine, and glue for their crafts—they can pay for the music too." Eventually, after a huge public outcry, ASCAP backed down. But its claim to legal authority to charge summer camps for their "public performances" of copyrighted songs remains intact.

Lawsuit Barbie

The issue in so many of these battles is: who shall control the "public mean-ing" of familiar images? Mattel is legendary in trying to protect the cultural "meaning" of Barbie. It has gone after any unauthorized uses of Barbie. It went after a series of pho-tographs by Mark Napier called *Distorted Barbie*, which dared to depict Barbie as fat or as having Down syndrome. Even highly distorted images of Barbie that were essen-tially unrecognizable were deemed unac-ceptable by Mattel.

Mattel has gone after a magazine that caters to adult collectors of Barbie dolls. Mattel even pressured the Seattle publisher of a book, *Adios, Barbie: Young Women Write About Body Image and Identity*, to change the title. This extreme clampdown on free expression has spurred culture-jammers, such as the self-styled Barbie Lib-eration Organization, which swapped GI

> People don't pay royalties to use a colorful expression of speech or get a license to tell fairy tales to their kids.
>
> —*Jonathan Rowe, commons activist*

Joe voice boxes with those in Barbie dolls, so that GI Joe would say, "Let's plan our dream wedding," and a baritone Barbie would yell, "Vengeance is mine!"

I am happy to report that a U.S. feder-al circuit court has put a damper on Mat-tel's bullying litigation. Utah photographer Tom Forsythe made a series of seventy-eight photos of Barbie for his *Food Chain Barbie* exhibit. It featured Barbie stuffed into a blender and in other kitchen poses. Only a few of Forsythe's photos sold. He spent about $5,000 to mount the exhibit, and lost money.

No matter; Mattel wanted to send a message that you can't mess with Barbie. It spent years liti-gating the case, requiring Forsythe to find pro bono legal counsel, which spent nearly $2 million defending him. Forsythe pre-vailed in the circuit court, which delivered a stinging rebuke to Mattel for bringing a "groundless and unreasonable" trademark dilution claim.

Watch Your Words

The privatization of words is another dis-turbing trend. The Japanese corporation that owns the Godzilla trademark has a habit of threatening all sorts of people who use the suffix *-zilla*, including a Web site called Davezilla, which featured a lizard-like cartoon character.

McDonald's claims to own 131 words and phrases. The San Diego–based corporation actually claims to own the Irish prefix *Mc*. It has successfully prevented restaurateurs from naming their restaurants McVegan, McSushi, and McMunchies.

Ralph Lauren, the clothing line, went after the U.S. Polo Association Polo magazine, claiming it was a trademark infringement for the organization to use the word

Creative Commons Licenses

The new symbol of global sharing

Until recently, writers, artists, and other creators interested in continuing the rich tradition of the cultural commons faced a dilemma when they released their work to the public. They could place it in the public domain and lose all control over how it was used (including the opportunity to make money if a large media conglomerate picked it up), or they could protect it under copyright. If they chose copyright, anyone who wanted to reproduce their work would need their permission, which would prevent most people from using it even for noncommercial purposes that would not deny the creator any income.

To address this problem, Harvard law professor Lawrence Lessig and colleagues at the Creative Commons organization devised a system that allows noncommercial users to freely share and modify creative works. Creators can affix a Creative Commons symbol to their works and thereby alert others that the works can be shared in specific ways—for example, only in noncommercial settings or only if the author is properly credited. Musicians, filmmakers, and authors can authorize free sharing of their works online while retaining the copyrights for commercial sales. Many scientific disciplines are now using the CC licenses to sidestep commercial publishers and start their own "open access" scholarly journals.

Over the past decade, more than fifty countries and several large-scale legal jurisdictions (such as Scotland and Puerto Rico) around the world have adopted the Creative Commons licenses. More than 150 million works now carry Creative Commons licenses, and many important projects and companies rely on the CC licenses, including Wikipedia and the photo-sharing Web site Flickr. The CC logo itself has become a symbol of the sharing culture.

—David Bollier

polo on its line of clothing. MasterCard went after Ralph Nader for using *priceless* in his campaign ads when running for president in 2000. Nader's free-speech rights ultimately prevailed, but the gay athletes who wanted to host a series of athletic competitions in San Francisco could not use the name Gay Olympics because the word *olympic* is owned by the U.S. Olympic Committee, which gets to decide who can use it. Special Olympics for disabled kids is OK but not Gay Olympics.

TV demagogue Bill O'Reilly reportedly went ballistic when he learned that comedian Al Franken was using the words "fair and balanced" in the subtitle of his book that mocked various right-wing pundits, including him. The federal court laughed Fox News's case out of court and Franken won. But pity the people who can't afford to hire expensive attorneys to represent them. A woman from Los Angeles dared to name her neighborhood newspaper the *Beechwood Voice*. She was threatened with legal action by the *Village Voice*, which claimed that use of the word *voice* as a newspaper name diluted its trademark.

These stories illustrate that many prominent corporations want to commodify all culture as private property. This fundamental market approach, not coincidentally, favors the Disneys, Time Warners, and Rupert Murdochs because it protects the market value of large inventories of copyrighted and trademarked works. It directly stifles expression that is local, amateur, small-scale, or noncommercial—the kind of expression that almost anyone outside

a powerful corporation would engage in. This amounts to a wholesale privatization of our cultural commons.

Commons Hero Jonas Salk

Things were not always this way concerning valuable knowledge. Contrast these stories with Jonas Salk, the inventor of the polio vaccine. When journalist Edward R. Murrow asked him, "Who owns the patent on this vaccine?" Salk replied, "Well, the people, I would say. There is no patent. Could you patent the sun?" This story helps us remember that current notions about ownership of knowledge are not inevitable and universal; they are the result of mounting market pressures to make our scientific and cultural commons into private property.

The privatization of knowledge has only intensified as the courts—in the United States, at least—have lowered the standards for obtaining patents while broadening the scope of what is patentable. It is now possible to own mathematical algorithms embedded in software programs. The very tools needed to conduct scientific research are now private property, available only for a steep fee.

Imagine what might have happened to biotechnology and computer science if contemporary patent rules had been in place in the 1950s and 1960s. Neither the biotech nor the computer revolution would have occurred in the first place. Too much fundamental knowledge would have been off-limits due to patents.

Problem of the Anti-Commons

The over-patenting of knowledge sometimes results in an "anti-commons" problem, in which property rights for a given field are so numerous and fragmented that it becomes very difficult to conduct research. The transaction costs for obtaining rights are simply too numerous and costly. For example, there are thirty-four "patent families" for a single malarial antigen, and those rights, applying to different pieces of the research agenda, are owned by different parties in many different countries. One reason that a malaria vaccine has been so elusive is because the patent rights are so complicated and expensive to secure.

It is worth noting that sharing and the public domain do not harm the market. Quite the contrary. They invigorate it. In January 2005, I cohosted a conference called "Ready to Share: Fashion and the Ownership of Creativity." It explored the power of openness in apparel design. Precisely because no one can own the creative design of clothes—one can own only the company name and logo, as trademarks—everyone can participate in the design commons. The result is a more robust, innovative, and competitive marketplace. This is exactly the effect that Linux, the open-source computer operating system, has had on the software sector. It has opened up new opportunities for value-added innovation and competition in a marketplace once dominated by the Microsoft monopoly.

Yale professor Yochai Benkler argues in his magisterial book *The Wealth of Networks* that a great deal of knowledge production is more effectively pursued through a commons than through markets. Questions of ethics aside, why doesn't money simply "buy" the knowledge it needs? Because money tends to subvert the social dynamics that make the knowledge commons work, it can sabotage self-directed inquiry. It undermines the social trust, candor, and ethics that are essential to creativity and good research.

Once you start to talk about the commons, you open up a whole new vector of discussion. A market may serve atomized consumers and look to the bottom line, but a commons serves a community.

—David Bollier

Pat Mooney

A watchdog defending global biodiversity

Pat Mooney paints a sobering picture of just how far enclosures of the commons are proceeding. Companies are turning all sorts of agricultural crops and even basic elements of matter into proprietary products. As executive director of the Canadian-based ETC Group, Mooney has long fought the corporate consolidation, bio-technology abuses, and wrong-minded public policies that are accelerating these enclosures.

ETC Group fights corporate enclosure in agriculture and science.

"Industry concentration is driving a huge loss of biodiversity," he said recently at a commons meeting in Germany, noting that only ten companies now control almost 70 percent of the global seed market. Three companies—Monsanto, DuPont, and Syngenta—control half of the market. This market consolidation has in turn greatly strengthened the political clout of agribusiness, wiping out traditional sustainable farming practices and overpowering efforts to regulate risky new technologies such as genetic engineering.

The ETC Group also raises concerns about a number of other significant enclosures-in-progress stemming from fast-developing new technologies such as nanotechnology, which is manipulation of matter atom by atom to build microscopic materials and devices. Already Harvard University holds patents on the nanotechnological version of twenty-three elements of the periodic table, notes Mooney. What happens in the future if anyone wanting to use a synthetic form of an element as common as, say, copper must get permission from Harvard or another license holder?

Even more worrisome is the fact that scientists do not really know the environmental and other consequences of altering basic aspects of our planet, such as inventing new life-forms.

The commons can be a useful concept to defend against such enclosures, Mooney asserts, because it challenges the reasoning of the market paradigm that there should be no limits on the introduction of technologies nor on the power of corporations to make all the decisions regarding the future directions for science and our economy. But the public debate on these crucial issues is transformed when biodiversity, food, and the elements of the periodic table are seen as commons that belong to us all.

—*David Bollier*

If Not for Them: Bob Dylan's Debts

He's candid about what he owes Woody Guthrie, Robert Johnson, Kurt Weill, and many anonymous balladeers

BOB DYLAN'S AUTOBIOGRAPHY *CHRON-icles* offers a good demonstration that great artists are commoners. They succeed thanks in part to a vast inheritance, the cultural commons.

Would it be possible to map Dylan's own debts to that heritage? He himself tells us a lot about where to look—for instance, in the recordings of bluesman Robert Johnson.

"When Johnson started singing, he seemed like a guy who could have sprung from the head of Zeus in full armor. . . . Over the next few weeks I listened to [the record] repeatedly, cut after cut, one song after another, sitting staring at the record player. . . . I copied Johnson's words down on scraps of paper so I could more closely examine the lyrics and patterns, the construction of his old-style lines and the free association that he used."

Exactly the same thing had happened in Minneapolis a few years earlier when Dylan first heard Woody Guthrie's songs. He also describes large debts to Hank Williams and to the old English ballads as collected by Francis James Child in the late nineteenth century. He had been schooled in these by an English professor at the University of Minnesota. "I could rattle off all these songs without comment as if all the wise and poetic words were mine and mine alone."

Describing the day he first recorded songs for Leeds Music, his first publisher, he writes, "I didn't have many songs, but I was making up some compositions on the spot, rearranging verses to old blues ballads, adding an original line here or there, anything that came into my mind—slapping a title on it. . . . I would make things up on the spot all based on folk music structure."

"Pirate Jenny"

Perhaps the most striking example Dylan gives of his schooling concerns a time when his girlfriend took him to hear an evening of Bertolt Brecht–Kurt Weill songs. "They were like folk songs in nature, but unlike folk songs, too, because they were so sophisticated. . . . The song that made the strongest impression was a show-stopping ballad . . . , 'Pirate Jenny.' . . . Later, I found myself taking the song apart, trying to find out what made it tick, why it was so effective."

Dylan offers a list of his own early songs—"Mr. Tambourine Man," "Lonesome Death of Hattie Carroll," "A Hard Rain's A-Gonna Fall," and others—and then says, "If I hadn't . . . heard the ballad 'Pirate Jenny,' it might not have dawned on me . . . that songs like these could be written. In about 1964 and '65, I probably used about five or six of Robert Johnson's blues song forms, too, unconsciously, but more on the lyrical imagery side of things. If I hadn't heard the Robert Johnson record when I did, there probably would have been hundreds of lines of mine that would have been shut down—that I wouldn't have felt free enough or upraised enough to write."

In the same context, Dylan writes of reading French poet Arthur Rimbaud's line "*Je est un autre*," "which translates into 'I is someone else.' When I read those words the bells went off. It made perfect sense. I wished someone would have mentioned that to me earlier."

All great artists who live and work in the cultural commons might take that as their motto: "*Je est un autre*."

—*Lewis Hyde*

Bob Dylan

Woody Guthrie

DJ Spooky

Hip-hop remix master

Paul Miller, a beret-wearing hip-hop musician, is the living embodiment of collaboration. He performs and records as DJ Spooky (the name is taken from a character in William Burroughs's novel *Nova Express*). His CD remixes and deejay performances "steal" materials from every imaginable source—from Yoko Ono to Metallica to modern minimalist composer Steve Reich to Jamaican pop tunes of the 1960s to D.W. Griffith's movie *Birth of a Nation* to Pacific island folk traditions.

But he has earned his eclecticism honestly. He travels constantly to music-making subcultures around the world, from indigenous people to electronic music undergrounds, from Antarctica to Angola to a New Year's Eve party on the beaches of Rio—and then produces something new.

Miller deeply explores the philosophy and meaning of remix culture in his book *Sound Unbound*, an anthology of essays about music sampling by the likes of Sun Ra, Philip Glass, William Burroughs, and a few dozen others.

Miller points out the artificiality of authorship: in practice, no one creates something entirely new. Why should the most recent individual author get all the credit for the work, as copyright law mandates? He points out that societies that openly honor the reuse of works from the past are actually "keeping the past alive" through that reuse. New art becomes an ongoing conversation with our ancestors.

—*David Bollier*

Portrait of a sound artist as a commoner. (A still from the forthcoming movie What We Got: DJ Spooky's Quest for the Commons.*)*

The Rise and Fall of Two Key Information Commons

The government backs away from its traditional role of fostering a wide range of viewpoints

IN THE BEGINNING, THERE WAS THE POST office. Before the Internet, before cable, before TV, before radio, mail delivery was our major means of mass communication. The founders of the United States understood its importance and deemed that it must be a public institution. Article I, section 8, clause 7, of the U.S. Constitution states, "Congress shall have Power to establish Post Offices and Post Roads."

Congress wanted the U.S. Post Office to be a monopoly. In 1792, it prohibited the private transmission of any letter or packet "on any established post-road," as well as the establishment of any competing postal service by foot, horse, vessel, boat, or "any conveyance whatever, whereby the revenue of the general post-office may be injured."

But the Post Office still had to deal with private companies that found loopholes in these rules. In 1845, in response to private post companies cherry-picking the most profitable big-city routes, Congress closed loopholes and increased penalties for the private delivery of certain types of mail.

This was justified because the Post Office had a broader mission than simply deliver-

ing letters—it was dedicated to spreading information as widely as possible. Indeed, the way the Post Office historically set postage rates exhibited its qualities as a commons.

Information in the Public Interest

From the very first, Congress decided that political news was crucial to an informed electorate and a unified nation. The 1792 postal law allowed newspaper printers to send each other newspapers for free, which was important to the flow of information from national and international sources to rural villages. Throughout the early 1800s, the content of local newspapers consisted largely of national and foreign news stories clipped from other publications. The 1792 law also provided for the mail delivery of newspapers to subscribers at the relatively low rate of 1 cent for up to a hundred miles or 1.5 cents for more than a hundred miles. This policy led Alexis de Tocqueville to observe on his 1830s tour of the United

States that "nothing is easier than to set up a newspaper, as a small number of subscribers suffices to defray the expenses. In America there is scarcely a hamlet that has not its newspaper."

This special rule for newspapers slowly grew into the broader discounted rate classification of second-class mail, which expanded to cover other types of materials that the Post Office recognized as having educational and cultural benefits. Eventually, periodical pamphlets, magazines, non-profit publications, library materials, and books were included.

The Post Office's goal was not only to inform and unite the nation, but to strengthen local communities. In 1845, Congress granted free delivery for weekly newspapers within thirty miles of the place of publication. In 1852, Congress allowed small newspapers and magazines circulating in the state of publication to be mailed for half the regular rates.

From the very start, the Post Office charged more for advertising mailings. In the early twentieth century, when magazines and newspapers were turning into advertising vehicles, Congress devised a creative solution. Periodicals paid a low postage on their reading content and higher rates on their advertising pages.

The rise of Rush Limbaugh, along with right-wing talk radio and Fox News, can be traced to the repeal of the fairness doctrine in the broadcasting industry.

Privatizing the Post Office

The Post Office's role as an information commons was prone to the problems experienced by many public institutions, from schools to mass transit: a deterioration of service over time due to budget reductions, bureaucratic inertia, and fierce attacks from those favoring privatized services. The crisis came in October 1966 when the Chicago Post Office ground to a virtual halt under a mountain of mail. That stimulated

congressional hearings and a presidential commission, which concluded that "today the Post Office is a business. Like all economic functions it should be supported by revenues from its users. The market should decide what resources are to be allocated to the postal service." The report added that the Post Office should not be "allowed to discriminate unduly among its users in the pricing of its services." The idea that it should be allowed to discriminate at all defied the mission of the Post Office as a commons.

In 1970, Congress transformed the Cabinet-level Post Office Department into the independent United States Postal Service (USPS). Nine of the eleven members of the board of governors (BOG) are appointed by the president and confirmed by the U.S. Senate. Rates are set by another body, the Postal Rates Commission, with approval from the BOG.

The Post Office's role as a commons has been slowly eliminated. In 1979, the U.S. Postal Service allowed for the private delivery of "extremely urgent" letters. This helped launch Federal Express and other private courier services. In 1986 private delivery of international mail was permitted. But attempts by Congress to privatize the Postal Service or eliminate its monopoly were thwarted.

Since the 1970 reorganization, the USPS has been expected to be self-supporting. Mail classifications are no longer designed to reflect the value of the mail to its recipient and boost the flow of information. In 2007 the USPS dramatically increased the rates on nonprofit periodicals while giving substantial savings to larger media corporations that could install in-house technology to better prepare their publications for mailing.

From 1913 to 1955, the rate for the first ounce of first-class mail stayed at 3 cents, even though if the price had kept pace with inflation it would have been 8 cents. From 1955 to 2009, the rate has increased to 44 cents. If it had kept pace with inflation, a first-class postage stamp would now cost 24 cents.

Recent USPS "deficits"—caused in large part by a 2006 congressional requirement that it contribute $5 billion a year for ten years to fund future retirees' health benefits, a requirement that had less to do with actuarial necessity than with a political desire to make the national debt appear smaller—have spurred renewed calls to slash its information mission by closing post offices, eliminating one day of mail delivery, eliminating its monopoly on first-class mail and mailboxes, or privatizing its operations altogether. Throughout this debate, the public service nature of the post office has been largely ignored.

The USPS's information commons function is still important and should be supported, as it traditionally has, by general taxes. The vast majority of Americans still depend on the mail, especially those without the means to purchase home Internet connections or use expensive courier services. And contrary to all the jokes, the USPS is remarkably efficient and has widespread support. In 2007, a Gallup survey found that 92 percent of residential customers rated their postal service as excellent, very good, or good.

Airwave America

After newspapers and the mail, radio became the primary means of mass communication. It's easy to forget that the broadcasting airwaves are, and once were treated as, a commons, owned by citizens, not powerful media companies.

At the dawn of the broadcasting era, the free market prevailed. The government set no rules. The 1912 Radio Act authorized the federal Commerce and Labor Department to issue radio station licenses to U.S. citizens upon request. Which it did, resulting in chaos—564 broadcasting stations were operating by 1922, and their signals were often interfering with one another, which threatened to kill the budding industry in the cradle. Radio station owners asked the government to step in and fix the mess.

The question was how to do it. Several options were on the table. The U.S. Navy might have controlled all broadcasting, as it wanted to do. Frequencies could have been auctioned off to the highest bidders.

Or the United States could have created the equivalent of the British Broadcasting Company.

The original British Broadcasting Company was founded in 1922 by a group of six private telecommunications companies. In late 1926, the British Broadcasting Company became the British Broadcasting Corporation, with exclusive control of the

airwaves under the terms of a Royal Charter. The charter outlined the BBC's public services: sustaining citizenship and civil society, promoting education and learning, and stimulating creativity and cultural excellence.

The BBC is required by its charter to be free from both political and commercial influence and to answer only to its viewers and listeners. The Royal Charter also prohibits the BBC from showing commercial advertising on any services in the United Kingdom (television, radio, or Internet). It is funded from a license fee imposed on radio and TV sets sold in Great Britain. In order to justify the license fee, the BBC is expected to maintain a large share of the viewing audience in addition to producing programs that commercial broadcasters would not normally present.

The United States chose not to emulate Britain and went instead for commercial broadcasting on privately owned stations, but not privately owned frequencies. The Radio Act of 1927 declared the airwaves a public resource. Broadcasters paid no money for their station licenses, but in return they received no property rights to the frequency. The short-term license's renewal was supposed to depend on whether the station served the public interest. Broadcasters were deemed "public trustees." As the Federal Radio Commission (FRC), forerunner of the Federal Communications Commission (FCC), explained, "The station must be operated as if owned by the public. . . . It is as if people of a community should own a station and turn it over to the best man

The Great Facebook Rebellion

Commoners fought back when the Web site tried to grab ownership of what users post

When Facebook quietly tried to claim ownership in any content that users put on the site, it incited a revolt. It all started in February 2009 when Facebook changed the legal "terms of service" that users must agree to when they sign up. The TOS is that dense legal language that no one really reads but which everyone nominally consents to by clicking the button "I agree."

Essentially, the new TOS said that anything you upload to Facebook becomes the property of Facebook, even if you close your account. So your photos, your writings, your music, your blog (if reposted to your Facebook page) would belong to Facebook. Facebook could even choose to sublicense your content if it so desired. It presumably thought that it might make money by selling a viral hit or letting advertisers use amateur content or people's photos for commercial purposes.

While Facebook didn't call attention to this content grab, the Consumerist, a blog associated with Consumers Union, did. Soon Julius Harper, a Los Angeles video-game producer, joined others in organizing a Facebook group called People Against the New Terms of Service, which quickly attracted 136,000 people. After a *New York Times* article publicized the controversy, the Facebook rebellion exploded. On February 18, Facebook decided to restore the former terms of service.

The new TOS was a "mistake," Facebook later claimed. More likely, Facebook thought it could grab broader legal rights over a massive collection of user-generated content without attracting attention.

Once the controversy flared out of control, however, Facebook wisely beat a hasty retreat. It invited Facebook users to help formulate a "bill of rights" for users that would cover their "freedom to share and connect." But the company's enlightened response does not fully resolve the question of who shall ultimately control user-generated content. It is still Facebook's Web site.

—*David Bollier*

in sight with this injunction: 'Manage this station in our interest.'" The commission made it clear that there was no room for "propaganda stations" as opposed to "general public-service stations."

In 1930, the FRC made clear the meaning of public interest by denying a license renewal to a Los Angeles station used primarily to broadcast sermons that attacked Jews, Roman Catholic church officials, and law enforcement agencies. In 1949, the FCC again defined what it meant by the public interest when it introduced what later became known as the fairness doctrine. Broadcasters had to devote "a reasonable percentage of time to coverage of public issues; and [the] coverage of these issues must be fair in the sense that it provides an opportunity for the presentation of contrasting points of view."

In 1959, Congress reaffirmed that the fairness doctrine had statutory authority by amending the Communications Act of 1934. In 1969 the U.S. Supreme Court upheld the application of that doctrine, noting, "Congress need not stand idly by and permit those with licenses to . . . exclude from the airwaves anything but their own views of fundamental questions." In 1974 the FCC called the fairness doctrine "the single most important requirement of operation in the public interest."

In filing their applications for license renewal, stations had to provide detailed information on their efforts to seek out and address issues of concern to the community. The program listings became the basis for determining whether licenses should be renewed.

• • •

> I want politicians to know what they are giving away when they take away our commons.
>
> —Vel Wiley,
> *public access broadcaster*

Information Commons Dismantled

With the ascension of Ronald Reagan to the presidency in 1981, the rules for broadcasting licenses suddenly changed. The FCC eliminated the requirement that licensees provide detailed program information as the basis for license renewal.

In 1984, the FCC eliminated programming guidelines that set minimums for news and public affairs programming and also discontinued enforcing the fairness doctrine. When citizens groups sued to reinstate the doctrine, Appeals Court judges Robert Bork and Antonin Scalia, two Reagan appointees, concluded that the fairness doctrine itself, despite its congressional reaffirmation in 1959, was not a law but a guideline. In August 1987 the FCC unanimously decided that the fairness doctrine was contrary to the public interest.

This put the ball in Congress's court. The House, by an overwhelming three-to-one margin, and the Senate by a margin of almost two to one, passed a bill clearly reiterating that the fairness doctrine was indeed the law. Among those voting in favor of the fairness doctrine were leading conservatives such as Representative Newt Gingrich and Senator Jesse Helms. But Ronald Reagan

Vel Wiley

Helping everyday people broadcast their ideas

For twenty-seven years Vel Wiley, executive director of MATA Community Media in Milwaukee, Wisconsin, has been committed to the idea that everyday people should not simply be passive consumers of media, but creators of it too. MATA Community Media (formerly Milwaukee Access Telecommunications Authority) has a fully equipped television studio and two local channels on the cable dial, which offers people the chance to create their own video programming and see it play in thousands of Milwaukee living rooms. "It's a community resource," Wiley says. "Everybody owns it. Everybody can use it. It's a commons."

MATA Community Media has helped the region's Spanish speakers, community organizations, church groups, youth groups, schoolchildren, deaf people, blind people, social justice advocates, Boy Scouts, nonprofit organizations, and YWCA members to tell their stories and hone their video skills. One kid who cut his teeth at the MATA studio was George Tillman Jr., now one of Hollywood's leading African American moviemakers, director of *Soul Food*, *Men of Honor*, *Barbershop*, and *Notorious*, as well as producer of the *Soul Food* television series. Other MATA alums have gone on to careers as newscasters, producers, and engineers for commercial TV stations.

MATA Community Media, like public access channels all across America, was created out

Wiley fights for people's right to express themselves.

of a strong sense of the commons. Private cable TV operators depend upon public infrastructure to spread cable lines to customers' residences, and federal communications policy along with local legislation has long required them to offer people a way to create their own television programming.

In return for a lucrative cable contract for the Milwaukee market, Time-Warner Cable agreed to provide video production facilities and cable channels for the public at large. That's how MATA was born. But cable corporations came to resist the idea that they owe the public anything in return for making heaps of money on a publicly guaranteed monopoly, and they have vigorously attacked public access policies. First, swarms of cable and telecom lobbyists pres-

(continued on page 208)

Vel Wiley (continued from page 207)

sured Congress to repeal a federal law that ensured public access broadcasting in all fifty states, and then they hit state capitols to slash support for local public access programs.

"Our funding was cut 57 percent in 1999, and we went from training six hundred people to training a hundred," Wiley remembers. By 2012, all public funding for public access will be eliminated. Yet Wiley and MATA refuse to fold up. They now keep public access going in Milwaukee with the help of foundation grants and on-air appeals for financial support from viewers.

The cutbacks have not deterred Wiley in her ambitions for what public access can accomplish. She's now exploring a regular program that would be directly focused on issues of the commons. "I want people to understand the commons. I want politicians to know what they are giving away when they take away our commons."

—Jay Walljasper

vetoed the bill, and there were insufficient votes in the Senate to override the veto.

The failure of that effort transformed radio (and then television) into a potent and one-sided political voice. Until then, call-in talk radio had complied with FCC community service requirements by focusing on public-interest issues and presenting all viewpoints.

A few months after the FCC dropped the fairness doctrine, Rush Limbaugh's program, with its in-your-face attitude and one-sided perspective, was syndicated. Limbaugh marketed his show in unprecedented fashion, offering it free of charge to stations across the nation. Within weeks, fifty-six stations had picked up the show; within four years, over six hundred stations were carrying it—the fastest spread of any talk show in history. Others imitated Limbaugh's format. The number of radio talk stations more than doubled from 1987 to 1993.

In 1993, the nation discovered the political power of this new entity. The Democratic Congress and newly elected Democratic White House revived the effort to make the fairness doctrine law. Rush mobilized his listeners. The bill never came up for a vote. According to National Public Radio, "privately, top aides in both the House and Senate admit that efforts to reimpose the doctrine have been put on hold in large part due to the talk show hosts."

In 1994, talk radio made itself felt in national elections. When the Republicans stunningly captured the House of Representatives that year, for the first time in almost forty years, Newt Gingrich called it "the first talk radio election." In early 1995, the Republican Party held a special ceremony for Limbaugh, naming him an honorary member of Congress. They dubbed him the majority maker.

The new conservative majority approved waves of giveaways to powerful media corporations, the outright sale of frequencies, and the reversal of the foundational rules of the airwaves, nearly wiping out any acknowledgment that the airwaves belong to the people and should be managed as a public trust.

Fifteen years later, talk radio has changed the nature of political discourse. Some persuasively argue it has changed our very culture. Media scholar Henry Giroux describes a "culture of cruelty" increasingly marked by racism, hostility, and disdain for others, coupled with a simmering threat toward any political figure who comes into the crosshairs of what many now call hate radio.

Seventy-five years after the Federal Radio Commission declared there was no room on the public airwaves for "propaganda stations" and denied a license renewal to a station that attacked Jews and law enforcement agencies, the airwaves are filled with both propaganda and venom. Today the airwaves, stripped of commons rules, feed hatred.

—*David Morris*

How to Save Newspapers

The first step is seeing them as an information commons

According to almost everyone, including reporters and editors in most newsrooms, the era of the daily newspaper is over. They simply cannot compete with the Internet, which is scooping them on breaking news and rustling most of their advertisers.

But this obituary gets the facts wrong. Actually, the readership and reach of quality newspapers is stronger than ever because of the Web. Even as home deliveries and newsstand sales slide, the Internet is bringing huge numbers of new readers seeking the in-depth reporting that newspapers offer. It's not newspapers themselves that are outdated (presuming you still call them newspapers when "printed" online), but rather the business model that carried them through the twentieth century—slender profits from circulation on top of fat money from advertising.

To conceive a different business model for newspapers to survive, we must start by thinking differently about newspapers themselves—not as a business at all but as a public service, a part of the information commons. If we view daily newspapers as an essential public service that we cannot afford to lose, how do we keep them publishing? There's probably more than one answer but, in looking at how other important but not necessarily profitable institutions survive, here are some commons-based solutions.

- **Taxpayer Support Through an Independent Agency.** Search no further than NPR, PBS, and the Corporation for Public Broadcasting for successful examples of Americans receiving high-quality news and culture in return for a tiny portion of their tax dollars.

- **Reader Support and Sponsorships.** Public radio and television offer other practical ways for paying the high costs of providing information. Readers, foundations, civic organizations, and even private individuals could underwrite quality reporting.

- **Community Ownership.** No one owns the Green Bay Packers. Shares of the team are widely spread out among people of the community. Why not the *Los Angeles Times* or *Boston Globe*?

- **Nonprofit Status.** One of America's most respected newspapers, the *St. Petersburg Times*, has been owned for many years by the nonprofit Poynter Institute. A number of other nonprofit experiments are under way, including *MinnPost*, a new online daily in Minneapolis–St. Paul that boasts that it is the only news organization to open— rather than close—a Washington bureau recently.

—*Jay Walljasper*

Art for Everyone's Sake

Notes on creativity as a commons

IS ART A COMMONS? OR IS THIS SENSE of collective creativity a violation of the individualistic nature of artists themselves? That's a topic I've been exploring both in my art and in conversations with artists around the United States.

Most of the artists I've talked with welcome movement toward a commons-based society as a way to increase the meaning and value that art offers to all of our lives. The current status of the art market—the buying and selling of art at exorbitant prices as part of an increasingly privatized and exclusive sphere where art is out of reach, literally and figuratively—hurts us all. The relentless expansion of the market into the world of art calls us to protect access to making and participating in art. Preventing further encroachment of the market into the commons of art and culture can help ensure that people enjoy and partake of art in the broadest sense as well as protecting artists' ability to draw more freely from material, ideas, and ways of working in order to create anew.

* * *

An Artistic Commons Alive in China

My first encounter with art as a commons took place from 1998 to 2001, when I had the great fortune to live in China and study the traditional art of paper cutting. I traveled to many remote villages along the Yellow River where people still lived in cave homes. In the village of Yen Chuan, I met many aging paper-cut artists who make intricate designs with paper, using only a common household scissors and their strong hands. This was a tradition handed down from mother to daughter.

Each woman I visited would take out paper cuts, which were usually stored between the pages of their children's textbooks, and lay them out so I could look at them. Occasionally the same pattern would appear at a different woman's house. When I asked where the original pattern had come from, none of the women seemed to be able to answer or even comprehend the question. After repeated attempts to make myself understood, it suddenly dawned on me that there was no particular attention

paid to who first conceived a pattern in China.

Like the way quilting and other traditional women's crafts are taught, in a manner that not only encourages but also relies on sharing and copying, the tradition of paper cutting is an art commons. Young girls are taught to make paper cuts by first copying the patterns of others. Eventually, as this tradition is passed down through generations, the same patterns make their way into different homes. Parts of one pattern are incorporated into new ones, and different regions even become known for certain styles and motifs.

Here was the commons, alive and kicking. But what meaning might it provide for those of us living in a culture and artistic sensibility saturated by market-based thinking? For many of us, it is hard to imagine how things might be different.

Creative Expression as a Basic Human Inheritance

Creativity is inherent in all humans, something we are born with and share as a gift or an inheritance. Kris Maltrud, a dancer in New Mexico, describes it this way: "Any kind of art and expression—performance, literary, visual—is essential and belongs to everyone. I consider creativity a birthright—something that all of us have that we share."

A South Carolina Community Torn by Tragedy Discovers Its Common History

Sharing the past brightens prospects for the future

History is a form of commons that has a surprisingly strong influence on our lives. We all are entitled to draw our own lessons from what happened in the past, and fierce debates often unfold as people with opposing views grapple about what really happened.

History can become a form of healing, too, in which people who explore their common past realize they really do have a lot in common. That's what happened during a particularly difficult time in Union County, South Carolina. Struggling after the shutdown of several textile plants, the rural county found itself in national headlines in 1994 when Susan Smith, a disturbed mother, drowned her two young sons by driving a car into a local lake. She then concocted a story about a black man hijacking the car and killing her boys. At first, many folks believed her, opening old racial wounds that had divided the community. The incident gave everyone—black and white—a bad sense about their community that lingered for many years.

Eventually Art Sutton, who owned the local radio station, decided it was time to move beyond the tragedy, so he organized a group to put on a play about Union County's history. Working with Community Performance Inc., a theater company from Chicago, local folks produced *Turn the Washpot Down*, a pageant of local stories and historical events that didn't overlook unpleasant truths but at the same time instilled a sense of pride and hope. The show played eleven sold-out performances, and led to the formation of a local theater company, Boogaloo Broadcasting.

"Its potent impact is derived from its truth," wrote critic Linda Frye Burnham in *American Theater* magazine, "the resonance of shared ordeals and delights, its portrait of a place like no other." *Turn the Washpot Down* had a deep influence in the community. Burnham notes, "It has already saved its soul."

—Jay Walljasper

Lewis Hyde, a poet who has extensively explored the idea of the commons-based gift economy, talks about an artist's creative energy as the inner life of art, as something generated, in part, by inspiration or intuition, organically bestowed upon humans as a gift, through no effort on our part. Another way of saying this is that artistic expression emerges, in part, from an essential aspect of being human—something we

New Ways to Keep Artists from Starving

Commons-based ideas for supporting culture

Every civilization needs art—statues and paintings, myths and stories, music and dance, which should be available to everyone. But artists and cultural workers need to eat, and if they share their work freely or cheaply, how will they make a living?

In many countries, national governments proudly support the arts. But in the United States, public funding has never been strong and has declined a lot over recent years. Here are some commons-based methods for supporting the artists we depend upon, which could be expanded (ideally alongside more generous public funding).

- The Music Performance Trust Fund is one model. In the 1930s and '40s when radio stations started playing prerecorded music on the air, musicians had reason to worry. Not only were their individual livelihoods threatened, so was the future of live performance. After a strike in which many artists refused to record, the musicians' union and the record industry created the Music Performance Trust Fund. For every recording sold, record companies pay a small royalty into the trust, which uses the money to sponsor free performances.

Every year the fund pays musicians to perform as many as ten thousand free concerts in parks, schools, and hospitals across the country.

- The San Francisco Hotel Tax Fund is a similar idea that underwrites scores of community arts institutions, from the symphony orchestra to the outspoken San Francisco Mime Troupe.

- Harvard law professor William Fisher proposes a system that compensates artists with public funds based on how frequently their works are downloaded.

- Economist Dean Baker of the Center for Economic and Policy Research proposes a tax-credit-funded voucher system that pays artists who put their work in the public domain for everyone to use.

- Writer Lewis Hyde has proposed that a small percentage of royalties from big-selling artists in various genres should go into a fund that would help support the coming generation of performers, writers, and other talents.

—Peter Barnes

all have "in common." This is one way we can understand art as a commons.

But an understanding of art as a commons has broader significance when we begin to look at what happens when an artist's creative energies are expressed. Sal Randolph, a New York–based poet and new media artist, explains: "I think of art like any other human cultural activity—making dinner, science, music. All of what we do depends on our cultural context. We wouldn't know how to make scrambled eggs if a million people hadn't already done it. The idea of a painting—paint, brushes, stretching a canvas, what you might put on the canvas—these are all things that we do because of our culture. A simple way of looking at it is as social ecology or the way in which we live. We don't make any thing without being indebted to the commons."

This offers a look at another layer of how art is a commons. The commons is a place where we are linked with everyone else's creative expression: a treasure trove of history and culture that has come before us and which influences how we perceive, envision, and comprehend what is possible today. Something new emerges out of various combinations of cultural ingredients—traditions passed down from our families, rituals and ceremonies given to us by our communities, and interactions with popular culture that we receive on a daily basis.

Joy Garnett, a New York–based painter, reflects, "Art contains within it a multitude of cultural and historical references, symbolism, meanings, 'baggage,' as well as the seeds of that which has yet to come. Art is a bridge between contemporary culture and all that has passed before. It allows for a pooling of information, both past, present, and future, and hence extends the commons across time.

"Artists are only partially aware of all the different stuff that actually goes into making their work," she adds. "This newly created cultural material belongs to everyone. It came out of the commons; once released, it returns to it. . . . While we each may experience any given artwork differently, art is part of the glue that connects us."

Treasures Belonging to Us All

Art can help us see the commons as a resource that we draw from and give back to, consciously and unconsciously. It animates and describes other commons as well as being a commons itself. This important role gives us all, not just those calling themselves artists or cultural workers, a reason to worry about the mounting influence of the market in the art world. Don Russell, the executive director of the D.C.-based Provisions Library, an arts and social change resource center, sums it up well: "If you look at the history of human action, you can see that art is one of the first things we have—the fashioning of things and ideas for social purpose and survival."

Art as cultural, historic, and national treasures is something that we all inherit as a people. We all own it and have to figure out how to share it. Catherine D'Ignazio, a Boston-based artist who explores avenues of participation and distribution in art, notes, "The question about ownership opens up the notion of a civic sphere where we are participating—creating spaces where people can come together and share experiences and engage in a critical dialogue about the world we live in."

Catherine is also a founding member of the Institute for Infinitely Small Things, a research organization/artists collective in Boston that has a video you can see on its Web site titled *57 Things You Can Do for Free in Harvard Square*. This video shows individuals jumping up and down, playing games, and enjoying the park—a humorous artistic work that reminds us that simple nonmarket ways to enjoy ourselves still exist, even in one of America's most gentrified shopping districts. Here artists help us to see and name the commons and, in so doing, help us take a step toward reclaiming what belongs to all of us.

—Rachel Breen

Chapter 10

What You Can Do to Restore the Commons

Fifty-one (Mostly) Simple Ways to Spark a Commons Revolution

What you can do—alone and with others—to make a better world

Perhaps we cannot raise the wind. But each of us can put up the sail, so that when the wind comes we can catch it.

—E.F. Schumacher

Personal Life

1. Challenge the prevailing myth that all problems have private, individualized solutions.

2. Notice how many of life's pleasures exist outside the marketplace—gardening, fishing, conversing, playing music, playing ball, making love, watching sunsets.

3. Take time to enjoy what the commons offers. (As the radical Brazilian educator Paulo Freire once declared, "We are bigger than our schedules.")

4. Introduce the children in your life to the commons. Let them see you enjoying it and working with others to sustain it.

5. Keep in mind that security and satisfaction are more easily acquired from friends than from money.

6. Become a mentor—officially or informally—to people around you. (And be prepared to learn as much as you teach.)

7. Think about living cooperatively with housemates.

8. Don't be afraid to ask for help.

9. Have some fun. The best reason for restoring the commons is that it enriches our lives.

Community Life

10. Offer a smile or greeting to people you pass. The commons begins with connecting, even in brief, spontaneous ways.

11. Walk, bike, or take transit whenever you can. It's good for the environment but also for you. You meet very few people behind the wheel of your car.

12. Treat commons spaces as if you own them (which, actually, you do). Keep an eye on the place. Tidy things up. Report problems or repair things yourself. Initiate improvement campaigns.

13. Pull together a potluck. Throw a block party. Form a community choir, Friday night poker game, May Day festival, or any other excuse for socializing.

14. Get out of the house and spend some time on the stoop, the front yard, the street—anywhere you can join the river of life.

15. Create or designate a "town square" for your neighborhood where folks naturally want to gather—a park, playground, vacant lot, community center, coffee shop, or even a street corner.

16. Lobby for more public benches, water fountains, plazas, parks, sidewalks, bike trails, playgrounds, and other crucial commons infrastructure.

17. Conduct an inventory of local commons. Publicize your findings and offer suggestions for celebrating and improving these community assets.

18. Organize your neighbors to prevent crime and defuse the fear of crime, which often dampens a community's spirits even more than crime itself.

19. Remember that streets belong to people, not just automobiles. Drive carefully, and push for traffic calming and other improvements that remind motorists they are not kings of the road.

Money & the Economy

20. Buy from local, independent businesses whenever possible. For more information see www.amiba.net and www.livingeconomies.org.

21. Before buying something online from a distant vendor, see if you can find it or order it from a local merchant. That way, your money stays in the community.

22. Investigate how many things you now pay for could be acquired in more cooperative ways—checking out DVDs at the library, perhaps, or quitting the health club and forming a morning jogging club.

23. Form a neighborhood exchange to share everything from lawn mowers to child care and home repairs to vehicles.

24. Barter. Trade your skill in baking pies with someone who will fix your computer.

25. Look into creating a Time Dollars systems (www.timebanks.org) or locally based currency (www.smallisbeautiful.org).

26. Organize a commons security club (commonsecurityclub.org). You are not on your own when it comes to economic woes.

27. Watch where your money goes. How do the stores, companies, and financial institutions you use harm or help the commons?

28. Purchase fair trade, organic, and locally made goods from small producers as much as you can.

29. Join campaigns opposing cutbacks in public assets such as transit, schools, libraries, parks, social services, police and fire protection, arts programs, and more.

30. Support activists around the globe working for environmental protection, human rights, worker rights, sustainable development, indigenous people, and action on climate change.

31. Take every opportunity to talk with elected officials and local activists about the importance of protecting the commons. Do the same with citizens groups, nonprofit organizations, labor unions, professional societies, and business leaders.

32. Protest the private patenting of products created with research paid for by taxpayers. Demand that publicly funded research data be available to everyone on the Internet.

33. Write letters to the editor about the commons, post on local Web sites, call in to talk radio, tell your friends.

34. Learn from everywhere. What can Germany teach us about health care? India about wellness? Africa about community solidarity? Indigenous people about the commons itself? What bright ideas could be borrowed from a nearby neighborhood or town?

Environment

35. Pick up litter that is not yours.

36. Avoid bottled water whenever you can. Tap water is generally safer. If you still have concerns about the local water supply, get a filter and pressure local officials to clean it up.

37. Become a guerrilla gardener, planting flowers and vegetables on neglected land in your neighborhood.

38. Organize a community garden (www.communitygarden.org) or local farmers' market.

39. Roll up your sleeves to restore a natural area or beautify a vacant lot.

40. Remember everything going down your drain, on your lawn, in your garbage, or into your storm sewer eventually winds up in our water or air.

41. Seek new ways to use less energy and create less waste both at home and work.

42. Form a study group to explore what can be done to promote sustainability in your community.

43. Purchase goods—from beer to clothing to hardware—produced close to home whenever possible. Shipping, trucking, and flying goods long distances stresses the environment.

Information & Culture

44. Patronize and support your public library.

45. Demand that schoolchildren should not become a captive audience for marketing campaigns.

46. Contribute your knowledge to online commons such as Wikipedia, open-education projects, and open-access journals. Form your own online community to explore commons issues.

47. Use Creative Commons licenses for your own writing, music, videos, and other creative pursuits.

48. Conceive a public art project for your community.

Commons Consciousness

49. Think of yourself as a commoner and share your enthusiasm.

50. Launch a commons discussion group or book club with your neighbors and colleagues or at your church, synagogue, or temple.

51. Spread some hope around. Explain how commons-based solutions can remedy today's pressing problems.

—*Jay Walljasper*

How to Become a Commoner

It starts with commoning—the natural act of connecting with others to find security, comfort, and joy

AT A RECENT MEETING OF A COMMON security club in Boston—one of many groups around the United States in which people come together to discuss ways to help each other get along in these insecure economic times—someone raised the idea of a tool exchange. Neighbors could take inventory of who owns a snow blower, wheelbarrow, extension ladder, hedge shears, various drills, shovels, rakes, or other gear that folks could share.

One man in the group, who had grown up in the Virgin Islands, said that back home if he knew a neighbor owned a ladder, he naturally assumed he could use it. No one would think of buying something new if someone they knew already owned one. This is *commoning*, which means putting the ideas of the commons into practice in your personal life.

The people of the Virgin Islands are poorer than those of Boston in economic terms, but their tradition of sharing lets them enjoy a sense of abundance and security missing in even the swankiest American communities. Yet more and more people in North America and Europe are beginning to look around their neighborhoods and say, "I think we can solve this crime/environmental/social/economic problem if a bunch of people pitched in to help."

This represents a swing in the direction of commoning, and it reflects a broader shift in thinking from the prevailing YO-YO ethic ("You're on your own") to WITT ("We're in this together"). At the center of this trend is people joining together to become "co-creators" of the world they want to see. They aren't waiting for someone else to do it.

Commoning is a "third way"—not locked into the profit-driven mechanics of the market nor dependent on distant government agencies—that enables everyday citizens to actively make decisions and take actions that shape the future of their communities. (Though most folks who do it don't call it commoning. They simply think of it as common sense.)

The act of commoning is built upon a network of social relationships (based on the implicit expectation that we will take care of each other) and a shared understanding that some things belong to all of us and must be used in a sustainable and equitable way. This is the essence of the commons.

Commoning Has Always Been with Us

The term *commoning* has been popularized by historian Peter Linebaugh, whose book *The Magna Carta Manifesto* shows that the founding document of Anglo-American democracy repeatedly affirms people's right to use the commons for their basic needs. A majority of English people derived at least part of their livelihoods from the commons before the brutal onset of the industrial revolution. They were known as commoners. Hence the word *commoning* describes people living in close connection to the commons.

"I use the word because I want a verb for the commons," Linebaugh explains. "Commoning has always been with us, although we seem to notice it only when the commons are being taken away from us."

The loss of the commons robs people of their autonomy to meet basic needs for sustenance, economic security, and social connections. Thus, commoning involves taking your life into your own hands rather than depending on corporations and other outside forces to sell you what you need. It's a way to resist the dominant paradigm of modern life, which insists that what's bought and sold in the market economy provides meaning to our lives. It's a way to tap into a hidden chamber within our imaginations, which holds ideas for different ways to live.

"Much of commoning depends on mem-ory," Linebaugh offers. "We are resurrecting some forgotten traditions and cultural practices." But he is quick to note, "We are not just *discovering* the commons; we are inventing it is as well. We are learning how to interact and take responsibility in ways that are both old and new . . . discovering more elemental ways of interacting and organizing social and economic life."

—*Julie Ristau*

What Would a Commons-Based Society Look Like?

State of the Commons 2035

A special report from Fox News

From the Fox News–Wall Street Journal–
National Review Information Link

Posted: August 3, 2035, 2:38 P.M.

SOUTH BEND, INDIANA (USA)

Just a few years ago, the sight of downtown streets in South Bend thronged with shoppers, office workers, and entertainment seekers would have been shocking. Once upon a time, you could shoot a cannon down South Bend's Main Street at eight P.M. with little risk of casualties. But downtown is now bustling with people day and night, many who come not to work or shop but to be where the action is.

Over the past five years, 6,800 new housing units have been built in the area, along with a spate of new offices, restaurants, bars, stores, theaters, and galleries. South Bend's newly completed downtown farmers' market complex draws tens of thousands of visitors each day, and Lafayette Street is referred to as the "Wall Street of Credit Unions," with more than a dozen

cooperatively owned financial institutions headquartered along a three-block stretch. One of these, the Mondragon American Trust, which popularized the concept of transforming suburban subdivisions into eco-villages, is now larger than all but two Wall Street banks.

As much as anywhere in the United States, South Bend has prospered by capitalizing on the promise of the commons—which means assets belonging to all of us, from water and wilderness to the Internet and cultural treasures. The commons also refers to a new ethic of sharing and cooperation that can help solve pressing problems of the twenty-first century, advocates say. This spirit has come to influence decision making at all levels in South Bend, bringing big changes to city hall, business offices, and neighborhood groups.

While the ideas of the commons sound theoretical and abstract, commons-based policies show practical results. The South Bend unemployment rate hovers below 2 percent, and the city ranks high for the quality of its municipal services and the strength of its civic organizations. Because

Loyalty to the Notre Dame football team is about the only thing that hasn't changed in South Bend, Indiana, since the community seriously embraced the commons in the early 2010s.

such a sizable share of economic activity rests in the hands of locally owned businesses and cooperatives, South Bend's new wealth is spread around the community, not piped to corporate headquarters far away. The last of the area's six Walmart stores closed last year, while Target/Home Depot/IKEA/Gap announced layoffs last month accounting for 55 percent of their South Bend workforce.

High school graduation rates are the highest ever in the city's history, with 93 percent of students going on to college or to technical training programs. The St. Joseph River and local lakes are clean enough for fishing and swimming. Three light rail lines, coupled with policies to promote bicycling and pedestrian-friendly neighborhood businesses, give the once-gritty city an almost Parisian quality of urban charm.

Stuck in the Past?

Even with the city's impressive performance, some charge that South Bend is looking backward, paddling against the stream of economic progress that has powered human advancement and prosperity since the dawn of the industrial revolution. B. Dietrich Campbell, former president of the South Bend Area Chamber of Commerce, thunders about the "inanity of those who put their faith in shimmering, shadowy ideas about cooperation and community, when it has been proven over and over that the privatized workings of an all-out market economy is the only way to stay above water in a competitive world. The gimmicks being tried today in our city will soon collapse, leaving us worse off than ever."

Campbell, a fiery congressman from 1995 to 2007, was forced out of his chamber of commerce position six years ago, replaced by the owner of a family-run sporting goods store. This year, for the first time, the chamber signed on as a co-sponsor of South Bend's famous Common Wealth Festival, which was launched fifteen years ago by local activists as a celebration of what South Bend residents share in common—from parks and arts organizations to local online communities and loyalty to the Notre Dame football team. Last year, the Common Wealth Festival attracted eight hundred thousand visitors, making it the second-largest event in the state, behind the Indiana State Fair but ahead of the Indianapolis 500.

South Bend mayor Lakeesha Kluzynski brags that per capita income is now higher in once dilapidated inner-city neighborhoods than in the suburban areas, where middle-class people fled in the twentieth century. But she is quick to add, "We see the region as one unified community, and we make decisions based on what's best for everyone. There is very little disparity on key measures of social well-being between wealthier districts and poorer ones. This is because of our dedication to the common good."

"I don't know of another place that has done a more thorough job of bringing government, community groups, nonprofit institutions, and private business together to solve pressing problems and make sure that future generations enjoy the bounty of the commons in their daily lives," declares Salaam Sanchez, director of the prestigious E.F. Schumacher School of Business at the University of Puerto Rico. "South Bend is pointing us in the direction of a sustainable, prosperous, and—dare I say—pleasurable future.

"A few die-hard market zealots still complain that all this emphasis on the commons is a retreat from human progress," Sanchez adds. "But that only makes sense if you believe that progress inevitably means rising environmental disasters, increasing poverty, mounting social alienation, and the commercialization of almost everything in our lives. Only a fool would accept those terms."

As Goes South Bend, So Goes the Nation?

While South Bend has accomplished the most of any American community in promoting a vision of the commons—thanks to the enthusiastic work of citizens coming out of neighborhood organizations, social movements, labor unions, the business community, and religious congregations—you see similar policies being put into action everywhere, from Bangor to Berkeley, Ottawa to Oaxaca.

Nearby Gary, Indiana—once an economic basket case in anyone's eyes—is now thriving as the center of the revived Lake Michigan fishing industry. Hard-hit Buffalo, New York, flourishes as the home of world-renowned green engineering firms. Even after the closing of its military bases, San Antonio is booming, thanks to its emergence as a music and media capital known as the Tex-Mex Hollywood.

Even stalwart Republicans now concede that measures to boost the commons represent a necessary correction to the reckless privatization of public assets that started with Ronald Reagan and intensified under George W. Bush. No one, not even on the farthest reaches of the American right, wants to put lobbyists back in charge of writing energy, economic, and environmental legislation.

"Those were dark days, which thankfully are now in the past," declares Newt Gingrich III, president of the Theodore Roosevelt Institute (once known as the Heritage Foundation). "It was a huge mistake to equate belief in markets with obedience to corporations. Activists on the right can admit when we were wrong. Small, independent businesses, working with community groups, have been the salvation of our country, and we intend to make sure that the balance of power does not tip too far in the direction of government. The public

> **The future is already here, it is just unevenly distributed.**
>
> *—William Gibson, science fiction author*

sector can do some things very well—but not everything."

It's significant that the first Republican elected to the White House in more than a decade was very careful to voice her support for a commons-based society at every campaign stop. After nineteen months in office she has proposed no major changes to once controversial policies that mandated Community Impact Statements for all new development projects, launched a new Marshall Plan for Local Economies throughout the world, or granted national sovereignty to Native American tribes.

Of course, no political office holder today would dare attack overwhelmingly popular measures such as universal public health insurance and free college tuition, paid for by user fees levied upon companies using commons resources, or the Children's Trust Fund, which provides every U.S. citizen at age twenty-four with $150,000 to invest or start a business, paid for by service fees on all stock market transactions.

Political action, of course, represents only part of the overall thrust of the commons. Probably the greatest impact has come in the flowering of community and civic organizations dedicated to improving people's lives. Reverend Peggy Chang, a bestselling self-help author and Southern Baptist minister, notes, "From the rise of shared-family housing to the teen service corps and the creation of new neighborhood plazas in almost every town, the commons brightens our lives from morning to midnight. It amounts to a spectacular shift from 'me' to 'we.'"

Indeed, the daily rhythm of modern society has evolved dramatically since the harried days when demands of the market economy drove almost every aspect of life. Chang exults over the changes: "The long working hours, financial anxiety, and lack of time for family, fun, friends, and faith seem like a bad dream now. The rediscovery of the commons prompted people to think more about what really mattered to them."

Libertarian Paradise Lost

This cultural shift can be seen most vividly in a town like Cato, Texas. If you were looking for a place that once stood as the antithesis of a commons-based society, Cato would be it. This outer-ring suburb of Houston, founded as a gated community in 2002, gained widespread media attention for its almost complete lack of government services. The local water utility was a subsidiary of the Bechtel Corporation, and nearly all the community's children attended private academies. Even the police department was run as a for-profit business, with different levels of protection

Cato, Texas, pictured here in 2012, became world-famous as an experiment in extreme individualism. At that time, the town offered almost no government services and very few civic organizations.

available to households depending on how much in premiums they paid to a private security company. (Some lower-cost plans, for instance, did not cover house calls for nuisance crimes, burglaries, or domestic disputes.)

Cato never attracted anywhere the 125,000 residents projected by its developers. Today, the population stands at 4,200, down from about 11,000 in 2015. At one point there was serious discussion about leveling the place to create community gardens, but the town got a reprieve in 2022 when a station on Houston's expanding commuter rail system opened. The real turnaround began, however, with the formation ten years ago of People United to Build Livability in Cato (PUBLIC).

Buffy Ayn Beauchamp, one of PUBLIC's instigators, recalls, "At that time, all anyone could talk about was what's wrong with Cato—no sidewalks, no parks, no locally owned businesses, no one who knew their neighbors. No *there* there. And truthfully, it was hard to look beyond the endless strip malls, six-lane streets with roaring traffic, and shabby McMansions with rust streaks on the vinyl siding. But this community had some good things going for it too, namely that a lot of people living here were willing to roll up their sleeves to make things better."

Meeting weekly in the back room of a coffee shop, PUBLIC drafted an ambitious agenda to tackle the town's problems. A baby-sitting co-op, mentoring programs, neighborhood tool exchanges, car-sharing club, Mardi Gras parade, and annual harvest festival were the first orders of business of this hard-charging organization. Then came the new park, public school, recreation center, and recycling depot—all funded by federal grant money but built mainly by local volunteers. The site of a vacant mall was fashioned into a Main Street, and a Latino cultural center now occupies an Old Navy store. Local churches spearheaded construction of a community-owned grocery, café, hardware store, fitness center, and cantina. The Houston Park District took over management of the country club and deluxe spa, opening them to the public.

Strolling through the community on a spring evening, when the temperature has cooled to the mid-nineties, there are few reminders the town began as an experiment in creating a privatized utopia. Indeed, historical preservationists lost the battle to save the statue of economist Milton Friedman that stood next to the now demolished guardhouse at the town's main entrance, where today you'll find a memorial to victims of the Great Texas Heat Wave of 2021.

The Commons Goes Global

It astounded people around the globe—including many in the United States—that over the past decade most Americans have gradually come to think of themselves as "commoners." While Canada had social democratic sensibilities to build upon and

Mexico benefited from indigenous and peasant traditions that kept the spirit of the commons alive, the United States was long guided by the ideals of rugged individualism. No country believed more fervently in privatization and extremist market economics, no matter what the social cost. But over the past fifteen years, the country's political landscape has been reshaped and Americans have wholeheartedly embraced the principles of commoning—a network of informal exchanges and sharing that characterize community life today.

So what happened?

Scholars, bloggers, and everyday citizens offer many theories, all of which note the rise of the digital commons. Americans took advantage of the Internet and other new technologies to make closer contact with people in other countries, gaining exponentially more knowledge about what was happening around the globe. Ordinary citizens in places like South Bend and suburban Houston learned that the French enjoyed better—and less expensive—health care. They learned that Ecuador's national constitution protected the rights of ecosystems. They were shocked to discover the "workaholic" Japanese spent fewer hours on the job each year than Americans and enjoyed at least a week more vacation.

This learning process intensified into

> **Under the rule of the market economy, we can't see the forest for the lumber.**
>
> —*Jay Walljasper,*
> *commons commentator*

action during the second decade of the century as the ideas of the commons took hold globally. Indigenous people's successful claims for national autonomy in Colombia, Brazil, and Australia fueled similar efforts from the Yukon to the Yucatán. The "Free the Streets" movement that erupted first in China, and then in Jamaica and the UK, inspired citizens to organize for massive reductions in automobile traffic. The radical reenvisioning of patent and copyright laws pioneered in Bavaria was adopted in North America.

No great idea about how to improve our lives stayed in one place for long. Wilderness restoration practices pioneered in Madagascar took root across the Northern Hemisphere. Denmark's savvy strategies to care for an aging population were soon implemented throughout industrialized nations. The Common Wealth Festival dreamed up in Karachi, Pakistan, was imitated in South Bend, Pretoria, and hundreds of other places.

"Democracy took a great stride forward with the rise of the global commons," declares Fernanda Vasconcelos Ruiz, an outspoken librarian who became governor of the Mexican state of Jalisco. "Suddenly people had access to unlimited information, which before had always been controlled by the experts, the media, and the politicians. Now a plumber or a schoolteacher could propose a solution with the same expertise and data as a big shot. It inaugurated a new epoch of citizenship, with very positive results for the common man and woman."

The widening reach of global communications also paradoxically ignited people's passion for locally rooted culture. Hussein "Mahatma" Usmani, founder of the Karachi Common Wealth festival and now UN Commissioner for Commons Development, notes, "The hallmark of our era is that people have one foot in the wider world and one foot firmly planted in their own community. We live in the 'Glocal Age,' when people can enjoy the best of what's global and what's local.

"I think this is why we are experiencing fewer armed conflicts and large-scale terror campaigns these days, even as we cope with the ordeals of water shortages," Usmani continues. "The strong instincts all humans possess for group identification are now channeled into their own region or city, rather than into abstract allegiances like Pakistan or India, Muslim or Hindu or Christian. It's much healthier for us to fiercely believe that our local football team is the best or that our cheese tastes better than what's eaten in the next valley."

Around the World in Your Own Backyard

The glocal spirit of the commons is on full display here at the Common Wealth Festival in South Bend, which opened last night. At the TED (technology/entertainment/design) Bazaar, folks are urged to download the latest movies, music, blogs, software, greenware, smartware, slowware, poetry, architectural codes, news reports, video mash-ups, engineering specs, gaming templates, typographical styles, and fashion designs from everywhere across the planet. At the same time, festivalgoers can sample seventy-five different beers, forty wines, thirteen bourbons, thirty-one vinegars, a hundred and sixteen cheeses, fifty-six different kinds of sausage, and eight varieties of West African–style cassava brew, all made right inside the county line.

"South Bend is the center of the universe—to those of us who live here," exclaims Mayor Lakeesha Kluzynski, who admits to liking the Polish sausages best. "That's the great gift of the commons—letting us discover the wonderful things around us that we all share."

—*Jay Walljasper*

The Best Movies, Novels, Music, and Art That Evoke a Spirit of Sharing

What are your favorites? Let us know.

This is a work in progress—with a lot missing at this point, especially from non-Western sources. We seek your nominations for the best stories and art that convey a sense of the commons. Please send in an e-mail to jay@onthecommons.org.

Fiction, Poetry & Stories

Robin Hood. These tales of a principled English bandit who gives to the poor while protecting the commons have been told and retold since the fourteenth century.

"Stone Soup." This French fairy tale reminds us of the rewards of cooperation.

"Remembrances," John Clare (1832). An English Romantic poet's lament for the lost common lands of his youth and the culture they sustained.

Resurrection, Leo Tolstoy (1899). In his last novel, Tolstoy chronicles a repentant Russian prince who decides to return his vast estate to the peasants.

Cannery Row, John Steinbeck (1945). Overlooking the ocean, a raffish band of commoners inhabit the vacant lots behind Monterey's cannery.

Milagro Beanfield War, John Nichols (1974). A tale of magic in northern New Mexico, where community-owned acequia irrigation systems are central to local culture. Later, a great movie directed by Robert Redford (1988).

Danny, the Champion of the World, Roald Dahl (1975). A plucky nine-year-old prevents a wealthy landowner from destroying a local forest.

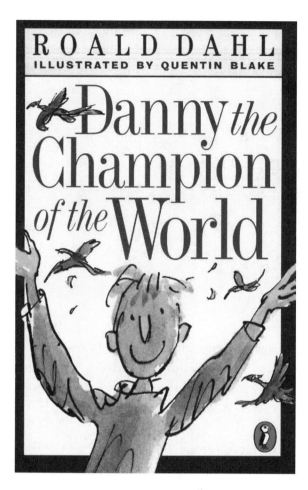

The Meadow, James Galvin (1992). A poetic portrait of a small patch of Wyoming: "The history of the meadow goes like this: No one owns it, no one ever will."

Music

"The Best Things in Life Are Free," Jack Hylton (1925). "The moon belongs to everyone," sang Frank Sinatra, Sam Cooke, and many others. "Flowers in the spring / The robins that sing / Sunbeams that shine / They're yours and they're mine."

"Fanfare for the Common Man," Aaron Copland (1942). A symphonic celebration of everyday people.

"This Land Is Your Land," Woody Guthrie (1944). Don't forget the seldom-sung lyrics from the original version: "As I went walking, I saw a sign there / And on the sign it said 'No Trespassing,' / But on the other side it didn't say nothing. / That side was made for you and me."

"Let's Work Together," Canned Heat (1969), Dwight Yoakum (1990). In both the acid-blues Canned Heat version and Yoakum's honky-tonk rendition, this catchy tune by Wilbert Harrison (who wrote the 1950s R & B hit "Kansas City") is an ode to commoning: "Together we'll stand / Divided we'll fall / C'mon now people / Let's get on the ball / And work together."

"The World Turned Upside Down," Billy Bragg (1985). Bragg made a hit of Leon Rosselson's song about England's seventeenth-century Diggers, who declared: "You poor take courage / You rich take care / This Earth was made a common treasury / For everyone to share."

It Takes a Nation of Millions to Hold Us Back, Public Enemy (1988). A landmark recording that loudly declared the political power of hip-hop through the electronic commons of sampling.

"Villanelle for Our Time," Leonard Cohen (1999). Cohen sings the hopeful

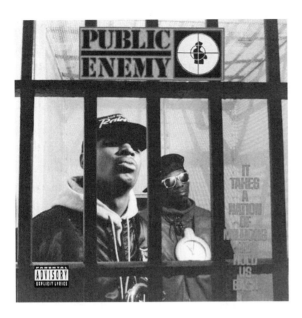

A pioneering public art movement brought sharp social messages to ordinary people throughout Mexico—and eventually the world.

Free Manifesta and **The Free Biennial,** Sal Randolph (2002). Randolph's work focuses on the importance of gift giving and the promise of economic alternatives, including these two shows open to any artist, which were held in the public spaces of Frankfurt and New York.

lyrics of poet F.R. Scott: "Quickened with passion and with pain / We rise to play a greater part / This is the faith from which we start: / Men shall know commonwealth again."

"The Revolution Starts Now," Steve Earle (2004). "In your own backyard / In your own hometown."

The Seeger Sessions and **Live in Dublin,** Bruce Springsteen (2006 and 2007). A rousing tribute to the folk tradition, in both its great songs (mostly from the public domain) and the tapestry of America's many musical styles.

Visual Arts

Mexican muralists Diego Rivera, José Orozco, David Siqueiros, and others

Movies

It's a Wonderful Life, Frank Capra (1946). It's hard to think of a Hollywood character that embodies the common good more than George Bailey.

Motor Mania, Walt Disney Studio (1950). A Disney cartoon starring Goofy—now on YouTube—depicts how America's streets were colonized by automobiles.

Chinatown, Roman Polanski (1974). A classic L.A. film noir about who owns the water.

Dersu Uzala, Akira Kurosawa (1975). The legendary Japanese director captures the stunning nature and culture of Siberia in a powerful tale about an indigenous man of the forest who saves a Russian survey crew in the early twentieth century.

Pathfinder, Nils Gaup (1987). A riveting adventure story based on a legend from the indigenous Sami people of Scandinavia, shot entirely in the Sami language.

Dances with Wolves, Kevin Costner (1990). An "ecological Western" about a U.S. Army lieutenant who adopts the ways of the Lakota Sioux.

The Navigators, Ken Loach (2002). A harrowing yet humorous British film about what happens to five railway workers when their jobs are privatized.

The Adventures of Greyfriars Bobby, John Henderson (2006). A terrier that refuses to leave the grave of his deceased master is cared for by the whole community. Based on a true story from Scotland.

WALL-E, Andrew Stanton (2008). Earth is governed and then abandoned by a megacorporation. In this animated adventure, a lonely robot sets in motion a movement to bring life back.

—*On the Commons*

From Acequias to Wiki

The growing vocabulary of the commons

acequia. Centuries-old cooperative irrigation systems in New Mexico communities.

aloha. In the traditional definition as defined by the state of Hawaii, *aloha* means "the essence of relationships in which each person is important to every other person for collective existence."

anti-commons. A dysfunctional situation that occurs when private property claims are so restrictive and fragmented that they result in an inability to share resources and innovate because the economic transaction costs are too high.

bienes communes. A rough Spanish translation for the commons.

biopiracy. The appropriation and privatization of genes, plants, and other traditional biological resources in developing countries by multinational corporations.

cap-and-dividend. A commons-based system of environmental regulation in which companies pay for pollution permits, and the proceeds are given back to citizens on an equal basis. Also known as *cap-and-refund*.

capitalism 3.0. A future stage of capitalism in which the economy's operating system is redesigned to protect the commons, the environment, and the welfare of people. Taken from the title of a book by entrepreneur Peter Barnes.

commodification. The process of converting noncommercial goods or services into commodities for sale.

common assets. Those parts of the commons that have a value in the market. Radio airwaves are a common asset, as are timber and minerals on public lands.

commoners. In modern use, people who are dedicated to reclaiming and restoring the commons.

common good. Policies and customs that are judged to be what is best for the public as a whole, even if such a policy might, at times, be inconvenient for some individuals.

commoning. A verb popularized by historian Peter Linebaugh to describe the social practices used by commoners in the course of managing shared resources and reclaiming the commons.

common pool resource (CPR). A finite resource that is available for everyone to use (e.g., fish from a lake or ocean, or irrigation water from a stream).

commons. What we share. Creations of both nature and society that belong to all of us equally and should be preserved and maintained for future generations.

commons-based society. A society whose economy, political culture, and community life revolve around promoting a diverse variety of commons institutions and the basic principles of the commons.

commons-based solutions. Distinctive innovations and policies that remedy contemporary problems by helping people manage resources cooperatively and sustainably.

commons paradigm. A worldview in which reclaiming and expanding the commons is central to the workings of society.

copyleft. A form of copyright licensing that authorizes reuse and modification of cre-

ative works so long as any derivative works remain available to others for further sharing and reuse.

cornucopia of the commons. A term that describes a "the more, the merrier" effect occurring in online commons that invite open participation. The term was coined by software programmer Dan Bricklin to rebut the "tragedy of the commons" mythology.

Creative Commons and Creative Commons licenses. A nonprofit organization based in San Francisco that provides a series of free public licenses that allow copyright holders to make their creative works legally available for copying, sharing, and reuse.

ejido. Commonly owned land in Mexico held by the state and distributed to individual families, which cannot be sold. Prescribed in the 1917 constitution.

enclose. To convert a commonly shared resource into private property. Similar to *privatize*, below.

externality. The social or ecological costs of economic activity that are not factored into market transactions.

faux commons. Online commons, such as YouTube, that are venues for user-generated content and appear to be self-governing commons but are actually controlled by for-profit companies.

free-software movement. Started by hacker Richard Stallman in the 1980s as a way to ensure that computer programmers could have the legal freedom to access, modify, improve, and share software code without the restrictions of copyright law. The General Public License (GPL) is the legal innovation that makes free software possible.

full cost accounting. A method of economic assessment that goes beyond the costs of a given marketplace transaction to include the costs borne by the commons, such as environmental destruction, community displacement, etc. See *externality,* above.

Gemeingüter. A German word for *commons.*

gift economy. Unlike the transactional relationships of a marketplace, a gift economy revolves around the voluntary giving of gifts to the community without any quid pro quo or strict accounting of individual entitlement.

hima. Literally "protected place" in Arabic. In Islamic tradition, it is a place that is taken care of by the entire community.

iCommons. A spinoff project of Creative Commons that advocates for commons-based sharing of culture and information.

intellectual property. A body of law that includes copyrights, patents, and trademarks. In recent years, corporations and other interests have sought to broaden their proprietary privileges by describing their rights as a form of "property," ignoring the fact that the public has always held rights in works protected under copyright, patent, and trademark law.

iriachi. Traditional commonly owned land in Japan.

land trust. A legal mechanism that enables private organizations to conserve and manage land for public goals, especially preservation of nature and affordable housing.

Linux. A highly popular open-source computer operating system.

market-based society. A society where most decision making is driven by the rigid dictates of the economic marketplace. Outside the United States, similar to the term *neoliberal.*

market paradigm. A worldview that holds up the workings of the marketplace not simply as an efficient economic tool, but as a moral code dictating how all elements of society should operate. The paradigm holds that the quest for profit should dictate all human endeavors, from education to health care to the arts.

net neutrality. A policy principle for the Internet that ensures open, nondiscriminatory access for all users. Net neutrality advocates insist that the Internet will no longer function as an open, innovative commons if the companies who control access to the Internet are allowed to favor certain Web sites and types of digital traffic.

open access. A term whose meaning depends upon the specific type of commons being discussed. In the context of a finite natural resource, such as timber or grazing land, an open-access regime means that anyone can use the resource, which may result in its overuse and ruin. In the context of an infinite resource, such as information, an open-access regime does *not* deplete the source, but more likely adds value to it.

open-access publishing. A burgeoning field of scientific and scholarly publishing that bypasses conventional commercial publishers and relies upon Creative Commons licenses to make journal articles and books freely available.

open business models. A new class of businesses that rely upon online communities and open digital platforms to provide goods and services at a profit.

open educational resources (OER) movement. A diverse movement of projects initiated by colleges, universities, scholars, and students to make educational software, books, journal articles, research, and other tools for learning more openly available, inexpensive, or free.

open science. A set of research practices and ethical norms that seek to make scientific findings as openly available as possible, reducing impediments caused by copyright law, patent law, and university rules.

open source. A type of software developed by volunteers and made widely available to the public at little or no cost. *Open source* is now frequently used to describe cooperative, volunteer efforts in a wide variety of fields. See also *peer production.*

open vs. free. On the Internet and other digital platforms, software or content that is *open* is accessible to everyone, but that does not necessarily make the software or content *free* to use as one wishes without restriction.

peer production. A new mode of economic and cultural production on the Internet that enables large numbers of people to collaborate in the production and maintenance of shared information resources. Prominent examples include free software, Wikipedia, and the Flickr photo-sharing Web site. See also *open source.*

privatize. To turn a commons or other public service or asset into private property. Similar to *enclose,* above. Privatization has been a key aim of libertarian and right-wing political movements over the past thirty years.

public assets. Elements of the commons that are publicly owned and usually managed by a government body: water utilities, public transit, libraries, schools, roads, sewers, and communications systems.

These are frequent targets for privatization efforts.

public domain. A body of creative and cultural works that are freely available for anyone to use, most often because the term of copyright protection for them has expired. Long considered a repository of essentially worthless works (because they have no market value), the public domain is now recognized as a vital resource for new creativity and innovation.

public goods. An economics term meaning goods and services that can be used by all without diminishing their availability.

public spaces. Places that are open to everyone and play a central role in the social and public life of a community: parks, sidewalks, plazas, civic buildings, downtowns, etc.

public trust doctrine. A legal principle dating back to Roman law that says that the state holds certain resources—notably access to bodies of water—in trust for its citizens, prohibiting any transfer of those resources to private interests.

semipublic spaces. Privately owned places that function very much like public spaces: coffee shops, vacant lots, houses of worship, museums, community gardens, etc.

standing. The ability of citizens to show in court that they have suffered harm or have a sufficient stake in a legal matter to bring a lawsuit challenging a law or court decision. In U.S. courts, legal standing that allows parties to sue in order to defend the commons can be exceedingly difficult to show, because the law generally protects individual rights and private property interests and is silent about or hostile to people's stake in commonly held resources.

taking. An act of government that seizes private property from an individual for public use. Many political conservatives regard environmental regulations and other government policies that may regulate the actions of private land owners as *takings*.

tragedy of the commons. A term popularized by biologist Garrett Hardin in 1968 to describe how exploitation and ruin of commonly shared resources is inevitable. Hardin later conceded that he was actually describing the tragedy of an *unmanaged* commons.

trust. A legal entity created to manage assets on behalf of beneficiaries. This can be a useful tool in preserving and managing commons outside the realm of government.

Ubuntu. "I am because you are." A traditional African expression, reflecting a philosophy of sharing, community, and generosity. The word is from the Bantu languages of southern Africa, but the idea is expressed in many languages throughout the continent.

water commons. An ethic that water is no one's private property and that it rightfully belongs to all of humanity and the earth itself—and needs to be managed accordingly.

wiki. A type of Web-based software that enables any number of people to contribute to and edit a shared body of information, collaborating in its evolution. Although Wikipedia is the most visible wiki project on the Internet, there are a wide variety of wikis on various subjects. The term *wiki* is a Hawaiian word for "quick."

—*David Bollier & Jay Walljasper*

Appendix C: Resource Guide

Commons 101

A quick resource guide to what we share

Commons in General

Commons Rising, an On the Commons report. Download at www
.OnTheCommons.org/content.php?id=1547

Digital Library of the Commons, dlc.dlib.indiana.edu/dlc/

International Association for the Study of the Commons, www.indiana
.edu/~iascp/

Kim Klein and the Commons, KimKleinandtheCommons.blogspot.com

Manifesto to Reclaim the Commons, a report by the World Social Forum.
Download at bienscommuns.org/signature/appel/index.php?a=appel

On the Commons, www.OnTheCommons.org

Shareable, www.shareable.net

State of the Commons, an On the Commons report. Download at www
.OnTheCommons.org/content.php?id=1548

Who Owns the World: The Rediscovery of the Commons, a book edited by
Silke Helfrich (Heinrich Böll Foundation). Download at www.boell.org/
commons/

Community Life

City Repair, www.cityrepair.org

Community Wealth, www.Community-Wealth.org

E.F. Schumacher Society, www.smallisbeautiful.org

Forum Organizing, www.forumorganizing.org

Ogallala Commons. www.ogallalacommons.org

Project for Public Spaces, www.pps.org

Rebar, www.rebargroup.org

West Marin Commons, www.westmarincommons.org

Economics and Politics

In the Public Interest, www.inthepublicinterest.org

New Economics Institute, www.newecomicsinstitute.org

New Rules Project, www.newrules.org

Privatization Watch, www.privatizationwatch.org

Wealth for the Common Good, www.wealthforthecommongood.org

Environment and Health

Blue Planet Project, www.blueplanetproject.net

Cap and Dividend, www.capanddividend.org

ETC Group, www.etcgroup.org

Food and Water Watch, www.foodandwaterwatch.org

International Center for Technology Assessment, www.icta.org

Our Water Commons, www.ourwatercommons.org

Our Water Commons, a report by Maude Barlow. Download at www
.onthecommons.org/content.php?id=2328

New Mexico Acequia Association, www.lasacequias.org

Trust for Public Land, www.tpl.org

Waterkeeper Alliance, www.waterkeeper.org

Information, Creativity, and Culture

Creative Commons, www.creativecommons.org

iCommons, www.icommons.org

P2P Foundation, p2pfoundation.net

Public Knowledge, www.publicknowledge.org

About the Contributors

Marcellus Andrews is a professor of economics at Barnard College and a commentator on National Public Radio's business affairs program *Marketplace*. He is the author of *The Political Economy of Hope and Fear: Capitalism and the Black Condition in America*. www.econ.barnard.columbia.edu/faculty/andrews/andrews.html.

Ken Avidor is a cartoonist and illustrator specializing in sustainable urbanism. He is creator of the *Roadkill Bill* comic strip. www.roadkillbill.com

Harriet Barlow, a veteran activist in many social causes, is co-founder of On the Commons and founding director of the Blue Mountain Center.

Maude Barlow, former UN senior water adviser, is national chairperson of the Council of Canadians and founder of the Blue Planet Project, working internationally to secure people's right to water. She is the bestselling author or co-author of sixteen books, including *Blue Gold: The Fight to Stop the Corporate Theft of the World's Water* and *Blue Covenant: The Global Water Crisis and the Coming Battle for the Right to Water*. www.blueplenetproject.net

Peter Barnes—an entrepreneur who co-founded Working Assets and a solar energy company—is co-founder of On the Commons. He is the author of *Capitalism 3.0: A Guide to Reclaiming the Commons* and *Climate Solutions: A Citizens Guide*. His 2001 book *Who Owns the Sky?* presented the cap-and-dividend solution for climate change.

David Bollier is the author of *Silent Theft: The Private Plunder of Our Commons Wealth* and *Viral Spiral: How the Commoners Built a Digital Republic of Their Own*. A fellow of On the Commons since 2004, he writes and speaks internationally about the promise of reclaiming the commons. He edits the OnTheCommon.org Web site with Jay Walljasper. www.bollier.com

James Boyle is the William Neale Reynolds professor of law and co-founder of the Center for the Study of the Public Domain

at Duke Law School. www.james-boyle
.com

Alexa Bradley, an organizer, popular educator, and activist for more than twenty years, is an On the Commons fellow. She co-directed the Minnesota Alliance for Progressive Action, a labor community coalition, and was a senior partner at the Grassroots Policy Project.

Rachel Breen, an artist and a fellow of On the Commons, is on the fine arts faculty of Anoka-Ramsey Community College in the Twin Cities.

Chuck Collins is a senior scholar at the Institute for Policy Studies, where he directs the Program on Inequality and the Common Good, and a fellow of On the Commons. He is the author of *I Didn't Do It Alone: Society's Contribution to Individual Wealth and Success* and the co-author (with Mary Wright) of *The Moral Measure of the Economy*. www.extremeinequality.org

Phillip Cryan—an organizer, policy analyst, and writer—serves as assistant organizing director of SEIU Healthcare Minnesota. His writing has appeared in the *Los Angeles Times*, the *Minneapolis Star Tribune*, *Foreign Policy in Focus*, and *Turning Wheel*.

Adam Davidson-Harden—assistant professor of global studies at Wilfrid Laurier University in Waterloo, Ontario—is the author of *Local Control and Management of Our Water Commons: Stories of*

the Rising to the Challenge, which can be downloaded at www.onthecommons.org/media/pdf/original/WaterCommons08.pdf.

Mark Dowie, an investigative historian living in Willow Point, California, and a former publisher and editor of *Mother Jones* magazine, is the author of *Losing Ground: American Environmentalism at the Close of the Twentieth Century*, nominated for a Pulitzer Prize.

Ben Fried is deputy editor of Streetsblog, a New York–based Web site covering transportation and community issues. www.streetsblog.com

Paula Garcia, a political activist and aspiring farmer, is executive director of the New Mexico Acequia Association. www.lasacequias.org

Larry Gonick, a cartoonist specializing in science and history, is author of *The Cartoon History of the Universe, Book III*, which won the 2002 Harvey Award for best graphic album of original material. www.larrygonick.com

Wenonah Hauter, executive director of Food and Water Watch, has worked extensively on water, food, energy, and environmental issues. www.foodandwaterwatch.org

D. Megan Healey, former resident assistant at Blue Mountain Center in upstate New York, is a bookseller at Modern Times Books in San Francisco.

Lewis Hyde—a poet, essayist, translator, and cultural critic—is the author of *The Gift*, a seminal 1983 work on the creative commons. He teaches creative writing at Kenyon College and is a fellow at Harvard's Berkman Center for Internet and Society. His newest book is *Common as Air: Revolution, Art, and Ownership.* www.lewis hyde.com

Ivan Illich, an Austrian philosopher and Catholic priest who lived in Mexico for many years, offered an astute critique of modern Western institutions in books such as *Tools for Conviviality*, *Deschooling Society*, and *Energy and Equity.* He died in 2002.

Josh S. Jackson studies landscape architecture at the University of California–Berkeley. He has written articles for *Good* magazine, *Lost* magazine, and *The Next American City.*

Robert F. Kennedy Jr. is president of the Waterkeeper Alliance, chief prosecuting attorney for the Hudson Riverkeeper, and senior attorney for the Natural Resources Defense Council. www.waterkeeper.org

Kim Klein, author of *Fundraising for Social Change* and co-founder of the *Grassroots Fundraising Journal*, consults for mission-driven organizations with Klein & Roth Consulting, and helps nonprofit organizations become more effective in promoting social change with the Building Movement Project. She also writes the influential blog

Kim Klein and the Commons. www.kim kleinandthecommons.blogspot.com

Winona LaDuke lives on the White Earth Reservation in Minnesota, where she founded the White Earth Land Recovery Project to regain the Anishinaabeg people's original lands. Recipient of the International Reebok Human Rights Award, LaDuke serves as co-chair of the Indigenous Women's Network. http://nativeharvest .com/winona_laduke

Brad Lichtenstein is a filmmaker whose works include *Frontline*'s Peabody Award–winning election year special, *Choice '96*, and *Almost Home*, a PBS Independent Lens documentary about people who live and work in a elder-care community. He is at work with DJ Spooky on a hybrid documentary-fiction film about the over-privatization of what belongs to the public. bradlichtenstein.wordpress.com

Peter Linebaugh, professor of history at the University of Toledo, is the author of *The Magna Carta Manifesto: Liberties and Commons for All.* His previous books are *The London Hanged: Crime and Civil Society in the Eighteenth Century* and *The Many-Headed Hydra: The Hidden History of the Revolutionary Atlantic* (with Marcus Rediker). www.utoledo.edu/as/ history/faculty/plinebaugh.html

Bill McKibben is one of America's preeminent environmental authors and philosophers. His bestselling 1989 book, *The End*

of Nature, drew wide public attention to the threat of global warming. His most recent book is *Eaarth: Making a Life on a Tough New Planet*. He is scholar-in-residence at Middlebury College and one of the founders of the international 350 campaign to curb climate change. www.BillMcKibben.com

David Morris—vice president of the Institute for Local Self-Reliance and founder of the New Rules Project—writes, speaks, and consults widely about community, energy, and environmental issues. His writing has appeared in the *New York Times*, the *Washington Post*, the *Wall Street Journal*, and *Japan Times*, and he is the author of *The New City States* and co-author of *Neighborhood Power*. www.newrules.org and www.ilsr.org

Dedrick Muhammad is senior organizer and research associate at the Institute for Policy Studies and co-author of "State of the Dream 2009." www.ips-dc.org

Cynthia Nikitin is vice president for public buildings and downtowns at Project for Public Spaces, a New York–based nonprofit, educational, and technical assistance organization with an international reputation for success in helping citizens create more livable communities. www.pps.org

Elinor Ostrom, a winner of the 2009 Nobel Prize in economics, is co-director of the Workshop in Political Theory and Policy Analysis at Indiana University as well as the founding director of the Center for the Study of Institutional Diversity at Arizona State University. Her 1990 book *Governing the Commons* was a breakthrough in modern thinking about the commons.

Robert B. Reich, U.S. secretary of labor from 1993 to 1997, is the author of numerous books on economics, business, and politics. He is a professor at the Goldman School of Public Policy at the University of California–Berkeley and a high-profile political commentator. robertreich.org and robertreich.blogspot.com

Jeremy Rifkin, president of the Foundation on Economic Trends, is an economist and bestselling author. He is a senior lecturer at the Wharton School of Business at the University of Pennsylvania, founder of the Third Industrial Revolution Global CEO Business Roundtable, and an adviser to the European Union. www.foet.org

Julie Ristau, a community organizer, popular educator, and organizational animateur, is co-director of On the Commons. She has been a farmer, publisher of *Utne Reader* magazine, executive director of the League of Rural Voters, holder of an endowed chair at the University of Minnesota Institute of Sustainable Agriculture, and co-founder of the Regeneration Partnership. She is currently co-chair of Homegrown Minneapolis, a municipal local foods initiative. www.onthecommons.org

Jonathan Rowe, co-director of West Marin Commons in Point Reyes, California, is a contributing editor at the *Washington Monthly* and *YES!* magazine. Co-author of *Time Dollars*, he is an On the Commons fellow. www.westmarincommons.org

Andy Singer is the creator of the *No Exit* cartoon. His work appears internationally in publications such as *Funny Times*, *Utne Reader*, *Carbusters*, the *Eugene Weekly*, and many others. www.andysinger.com

Korir Sing'Oei, a human rights lawyer in Kenya, is a co-founder of CEMIRIDE (Centre for Minority Rights Development).

Sean Thomas-Breitfeld is deputy director for idea generation and dissemination at the Center for Community Change and is involved with the Building Movement Project at Demos. www.communitychange.org

Jay Walljasper, an On the Commons fellow, is also a senior fellow at Project for Public Spaces, an associate of the Citistates Group, and a contributing editor to *National Geographic Traveler*. In addition to *All That We Share*, he is the author of *The Great Neighborhood Book* and co-author of *Visionaries: People and Ideas to Change Your Life*. He edits OnTheCommons.org with David Bollier. www.JayWalljasper.com

Susan Witt has been executive director of the E.F. Schumacher Society since 1980. The organization is now partnering with London's New Economic Foundation to create the New Economics Institute, where Witt will serve as education director. www.smallisbeautiful.org and www.neweconomicsinstitute.org

Credits

Many of the articles here appeared in a different form in OnTheCommons.org and in two On the Commons publications: *Commons Rising* and *The State of the Commons*. Other articles not cited below are adapted from material first appearing in *The Great Neighborhood Book* (New Society Publishers, 2007); *Ode* magazine; *Notre Dame* magazine; the *San Francisco Chronicle*; the *Minneapolis Star Tribune*; the *Boston Review*; *Utne Reader* magazine; and *Making Places*, the newsletter of Project for Public Spaces. The author and On the Commons wish to thank all the contributors and publications, which, in the spirit of the commons, graciously allowed us to use their material.

Chapter 1

"Do I Need Livestock to Join This Movement?," by Kim Klein, is adapted from the blog Kim Klein and the Commons. kimklein andthecommons.blogspot.com.

Chapter 2

"From Asian Villages to Main Street USA" is adapted from *YES!* magazine. www.yesmag azine.org

"The View from Africa," by Korir Sing'Oei, is adapted from *Pambazuka News*, an electronic publication focusing on social justice in Africa that reaches half a million readers in English, French, and Portuguese editions. www.pam bazuka.org.

"What's the Commons Worth?," by Peter Barnes, is adapted from the book *Capitalism 3.0: A Guide to Reclaiming the Commons* © 2006 by Peter Barnes, Berrett-Koehler Publishers, Inc. All rights reserved. www.bkconnec tion.com

Chapter 3

"A Garden Grows in North Philadelphia," by Jay Walljasper, is adapted from the Web site of Project for Public Spaces, a New York–based nonprofit that helps citizens improve communities. www.pps.org

Chapter 4

"A Brief History of Commons Destruction," by Peter Barnes, is adapted from *Capitalism 3.0: A Guide to Reclaiming the Commons* © 2006 by Peter Barnes, Berrett-Koehler Publishers, Inc. All rights reserved. www.bkconnection.com

"A Revolution of the Rich Against the Poor," by Jeremy Rifkin, is excerpted from the book *Biosphere Politics: A New Consciousness for a New Century* (Crown Publishers, 1991).

"Origins of Our Economic Powerlessness," by Ivan Illich, is from a 1982 speech delivered in Tokyo and collected in a book of his speeches, *In the Mirror of the Past* (Marian Boyars, 1992).

"Liberty and Commons for All," by Peter Linebaugh, is adapted from the book *The Magna Carta Manifesto: Liberties and Commons for All* © 2008 by Peter Linebaugh, published by the University of California Press.

"An Ancient Legal Principle Is More Important than Ever," by Mark Dowie, is excerpted from *Orion Nature Quarterly*. www.orionmagazine.org

"¡Viva la Acequia!," by Paula Garcia, is adapted from the publication *Sustainable Santa Fe: A Resource Guide*, edited by Seth Roffman. www.sustainablesantafeguide.com

"Our Home on Earth," by Winona LaDuke, is excerpted and updated from "Voices from White Earth: Gaa-waabaabiganikaag," the Thirteenth Annual E.F. Schumacher Lecture, given at Yale University, October 1993. The lecture is sponsored by the E.F. Schumacher Society. www.smallisbeautiful.org

Chapter 5

"The Economy Won't Prosper Until We Invest in the Commons," by Robert B. Reich, is reprinted with permission from Robert Reich, "From Consumers to Commons," *American Prospect* 20, no. 1 (December 15, 2008). www.prospect.org. The American Prospect, 1710 Rhode Island Avenue, N.W., 12th Floor, Washington, DC 20036. All rights reserved.

"Capitalism 3.0," by Peter Barnes, is excerpted from the book *Capitalism 3.0: A Guide to Reclaiming the Commons* © 2006 by Peter Barnes, Berrett-Koehler Publishers, Inc. All rights reserved. www.bkconnection.com

Chapter 6

"New Hope for Bridging America's Economic Divide," by Dedrick Muhammad and Chuck Collins, is an excerpt from the newsletter *Poverty and Race*, published by the Poverty & Race Research Action Council. www.prrac.org

"Citizenship 2.0," by David Bollier, was adapted from the speech "Commoners as an Emerging

Political Force," delivered at the iCommons Summit in Sapporo, Japan, in July 2008.

Chapter 7

"Roses Grow in Spanish Harlem," by David Bollier, is adapted from the book *Silent Theft: The Private Plunder of Our Common Wealth* (Routledge, 2002).

"The Little Library That Could," by Cynthia Nikitin and Josh Jackson, is adapted from *Making Places*, the online newsletter of Project for Public Spaces. www.pps.org

Chapter 8

"Commonskeepers," by Robert F. Kennedy Jr., is excerpted from *Waterkeeper* magazine, Fall 2006.

"Water for All," by Maude Barlow, is adapted from the book *Blue Covenant: The Global Water Crisis and the Coming Battle for the Right to Water* (The New Press, 2007).

"A Commons Solution to Climate Change," by Peter Barnes, is adapted from the book *Climate Solutions: A Citizens Guide* (Chelsea Green, 2008).

"In Trusts We Trust," by Peter Barnes, is adapted from *Capitalism 3.0: A Guide to Reclaiming the Commons* © 2006 by Peter Barnes, Berrett-Koehler Publishers, Inc. All rights reserved. www.bkconnection.com

Chapter 9

"The Alchemy of Creativity," by Brad Lichtenstein, was adapted from a presentation given to the National Alliance for Media, Art and Culture. www.namac.org

"When Knowledge Becomes Private Property," by David Bollier, is updated from the speech "Controlling Intellectual Property: The Academic Community and the Future of Knowledge," presented in 2003 to the Canadian Association of University Teachers in Ottawa, Canada.

Illustration Credits

Page 3: Photo by twoblueday/Flickr.com

Page 11: By Roberto Rizzato/Flickr.com

Page 14: Photo by Robert Pernell/Dreamstime.com

Page 18: Cartoon by Larry Gonick (www.LarryGonick.com)

Page 28: Photo by Jeannell Norvell/© iStockphoto.com

Page 33: Photo by Marcel Pelletier/© iStockphoto.com

Page 39: Photo by Image Golf/© iStockphoto.com

Page 45: Photo by Economists for Peace and Security

Page 58: Cartoon by Ken Avidor from the book *Roadkill Bill* (www.RoadkillBill.com)

Page 64: Photo by Kevin Edge Photography/© iStockphoto.com

Page 68: Cartoon by Ken Avidor from the book *Roadkill Bill* (www.RoadkillBill.com)

Page 77: Photo by Jay Walljasper

Page 83: Photo by Amazon Watch

Page 90: Photo by Ed Yourdon

Page 101: Photo by Stefan Powell/Flickr.com

Page 105: Photo courtesy of Northfield.org

Page 109: Cartoon by Andy Singer from the book *Attitude* (www.AndySinger.com)

Page 114: Photo by Marion Post Wolcott/Flickr.com

Page 119: Photo by Mark Saperstein/Courtesy of the Hyde Square Task Force

Page 120: Photo by caracter design/© iStockphoto.com

Page 124: Photo illustration by Louise Docker/Flickr.com

Page 125: Photo by Joi Ito/Flickr.com

Page 129: Photo courtesy of Gehl Architects

Page 135: Photo by Andyrob/Flickr.com

About the Authors

Jay Walljasper, co-editor of OnTheCommons.org, is a leading writer and speaker on urban issues, sustainability, politics, travel, social trends, and community revitalization. He is a fellow at On the Commons, senior fellow at Project for Public Spaces, a contributing editor of *National Geographic Traveler*, and an associate of the Citistates Group. Formerly the editor and editorial director of *Utne Reader* magazine and executive editor of *Ode* magazine, his writing has appeared in the *San Francisco Chronicle*, the *New Statesman*, *The Nation*, the *Chicago Tribune, Mother Jones, Better Homes & Gardens*, and the *Huffington Post*. He is the author of *The Great Neighborhood Book* and the co-author (with Jon Spayde) of *Visionaries: People and Ideas to Change Your Life*. He lives with his wife and son in Minneapolis. www.JayWalljasper.com

On the Commons is a citizens' network that highlights the importance of the commons in our lives and promotes innovative commons-based solutions to create a brighter future. www.OnThe Commons.org

Index